May you be blessed
in reading my book.

John S. Power
March 9/11

A MESSAGE FOR THE SOUL OF MAN

LEARN ABOUT YOUR SOUL AND PURPOSE

JOHN D. POWERS

iUniverse, Inc.
New York   Bloomington

A Message for the Soul of Man
Learn about Your Soul and Purpose

iUniverse books may be ordered through booksellers or by contacting:

iUniverse
1663 Liberty Drive
Bloomington, IN 47403
www.iuniverse.com
1-800-Authors (1-800-288-4677)

Because of the dynamic nature of the Internet, any Web addresses or links contained in this book may have changed since publication and may no longer be valid. The views expressed in this work are solely those of the author and do not necessarily reflect the views of the publisher, and the publisher hereby disclaims any responsibility for them.

ISBN: 978-1-4502-3184-8 (pbk)
ISBN: 978-1-4502-3186-2 (cloth)
ISBN: 978-1-4502-3185-5 (ebook)

Printed in the United States of America

iUniverse rev. date: 7/28/10

Dedication

A Message for the Soul of Man is dedicated to all those souls who believe there is a purpose for every life on earth!

This book is also dedicated to the memory of all the members of my family who have passed away in recent years. May their souls rest in peace.

John D. Powers
Grande Prairie, Alberta
2010

Quotations of Interest

St Thomas Aquinas
An Italian Dominican priest of the Roman Catholic Church
(1225–1274)

"As long as a thing has being, God must be present to it …
If the divine action should cease, all thingswould drop into
nothingness instantly."

St. Francis of Assisi
A Catholic priest and founder of the Franciscan Monks (1181–1226)

"Keep a clear eye toward life's end. Do not forget your purpose and
destiny as God's creature. What you are in his sight is what you are
and nothing more. Remember that when you leave this earth, you
can take with you nothing you have received—fading symbols of
honor, trappings of power—but only what you have given: a full
heart, enriched by honest service, love, sacrifice and courage."

Contents

Acknowledgments

A Message for the Soul of Man was put together with a revelation, papers on various related topics, sermons, bible studies, and devotionals.

The sermons, bible studies, and devotionals were designed to help the listener (now the reader) understand various aspects of the overall message concerning the soul and later, find God's purpose for man during his or her life on earth.

As such, the sermons, bible studies, and devotionals delivered to groups of people in Christian surroundings, helped me focus on the different ingredients of the message conveyed to me. That focus and the feedback of many people have been very helpful in bringing about the production of this book.

I am especially indebted to the pastors of the Salvation Army Church in Grande Prairie, Alberta, during the period of 1992–2008. Pastors Dave and Lynn Grice and Dale and Jo Sobool allowed me the privilege of speaking to the congregation on Sundays, conducting devotionals in seniors housing complexes, and conducting bible studies under the umbrella of the church—both in and outside the church.

Without their understanding and support, I don't believe *A Message for the Soul of Man* would have reached the level of publicity it has or have the chance of reaching a great part of the world that God desires.

I feel that God's hand has been—and continues to be—at work in furthering His message to all mankind. For this I can truthfully say "Thank God!"

Your humble servant in the Lord,

John D. Powers

Preface

Why is *A Message for the Soul of Man* so necessary now?

While "there is nothing new under the sun," I cannot help but be troubled by the level of crime and addiction in the world today—especially among young people. It is particularly upsetting when a good number of my own children and grandchildren were drawn into a lifestyle that can only be described as life destroying. The damage done to their bodies and brains is mostly irreversible. Their future as young people is lost forever.

Some, by overcoming their previous lifestyle, can return to a near normal existence, but what have they lost? The most valuable commodity of their existence is gone forever—*time*—measured in days, months, and years! Time lost during their most formative years is not even recognized as a *real* loss. It should be!

You can see that I agonize over all the young people who face the temptations of this world (or will) without the knowledge of who they really are and their intrinsic value as a human being placed on this planet by God.

The message in this book is intended for everyone in the world—especially the very young who need to be educated in the value of their body, the importance of their soul, and the purpose of the gifts and talents that God has blessed them with—including their time on earth.

Finally, they are the product of God's creation and they will ultimately answer to Him for what they accomplish (or don't) during their lifetime. They have the choice about how they live their lives—they need to know it!

They need the knowledge to work with. The reward of right living on earth can be eternal happiness for the soul in heaven. There is no greater goal in life!

John D. Powers
Grande Prairie, Alberta

PART 1

Preparing to Receive the Message

Stepping into a New World

As you open *A Message for the Soul of Man*, you will find yourself entering a new world. The challenge is to do so with a totally open mind.

I am going to share with you the experience I had quite late in life that could open your mind and heart to a totally new way of looking on your life—who you are, your purpose for being on earth, and your destiny.

I have a question for you that I would like you to consider carefully.

Do you believe there is an almighty God? Do you really believe?

Now that you have decided in your mind the answer to the question, it is time to learn the message that God placed in my heart to share with all mankind.

Most of what you will read, I put together as a practicing Christian and therefore it will be heavily weighted toward Christian beliefs. However, I learned as I studied and composed sermons and devotionals that there was something I was missing in God's Message to the souls of mankind.

What I had missed was simply, *God's Message was intended for all mankind*—not just Christians as you will learn as you read.

This book is not intended to influence the reader to accept Christianity as their religion. Non-Christians should treat any Christian-based material as information.

This book is intended to emphasize and explain who you are in relation to God.

My hope is that you will be as moved as I was when God revealed to me His message for all mankind and be further moved by the content of the message and the subsequent information that came to me.

God's intent seems to be very clear. He wants you to have a much better understanding of who you are, why you're here on earth, and what your ultimate destiny will be—given that you have the choice of living your life in whatever manner you wish.

It is my belief that God has an exciting new future planned for all mankind. In 2010, it is approximately two thousand years since the birth of Jesus Christ, four thousand since the birth of Abraham (Abram), and six thousand years since Adam and Eve. Is it time for a new revelation? You decide.

Before getting to the message, I should recount how the message came to me. I need to tell you my personal story—my journey into spirituality, if you will.

John D. Powers

My Journey into Spirituality

My journey into a new spiritual life began without any realization on my part as to what was happening. Looking back, I now see how events came about and why. Early in this book, I provide you with *A Message for the Soul of Man*. God placed this message in my heart and mind back in 1992. It struck me so forcibly that I was totally dumbstruck. The expression, I believe, is now blown away—an apt expression.

I believe I had to go through a special period of preparation before receiving the message to prepare me for what one might call a traumatic spiritual awakening. I had to be humbled, which I realize now in looking back was necessary, since I was so confident about my own control over my life. Up until this time, I had always succeeded at the many challenges presented to me over my varied careers and life situations. God and church were the furthest things from my mind.

I feel that it is necessary to provide you with this information about my preparation for receiving the message as it emphasizes the impact of God's message on me and how it has changed my life. I believe that the change in my life is as profound as the message itself.

I would like to share my testimony at this time for a couple of other reasons. First, there may be some within my church congregation and among my friends and family who wonder why I have been so heavily involved in the Church. If they had known me before, they would have wondered what had happened to me.

Secondly, I would like to reveal the reason for all of my past and continuing involvement with the Salvation Army—a church committed to the saving of souls.

My Preparation for Receiving the Message

In 1990, after a period of internal unrest, I lost my job with a local nonprofit business organization after being with them for fourteen years as general manager. I subsequently went through a period of two years where my family lost almost everything. Because of my age and previous position, I was either overqualified or too old to fit into any of the available positions. I couldn't buy a job! Soon after all my unemployment benefits were used up, I had to use the savings that we had put aside for retirement.

Needless to say, I was emotionally and mentally very low. My self-esteem—usually very high—was virtually nonexistent. On top of that, my wife was going through a tortuous time with her job and wanted to pack it in, which we couldn't afford.

I was despondent and melancholy. I listened to a lot of moving mood and religious music. I wondered what my life was all about—what was the purpose of it all? I had no control over my life. I was lost. I know that there are many who can relate to that feeling. I didn't know it at the time, but I was being prepared.

During that time, probably because of what was going on in the Church, I found myself thinking about God a lot. One Sunday during our difficulties, our grandson came home from church and said enthusiastically, "Gramp, God loves *you!*"

At the time, it struck me as strange that he should say that to me. I think that, since I was not much of a churchgoer, he believed that I could use this rather important information. It added to the realization that God exists and we are on this world for a purpose. The burning question was *what*. What was *my* purpose—especially at that point where we were virtually on the edge of bankruptcy? Life on earth did not hold much hope.

In 1992, I don't think I, or my family, had ever been in such dire straits—the stress, the uncertainty of the future, the danger of losing everything we had worked for, the church situation which was also very stressful—why was this happening? I couldn't even remortgage the house since I had no job! The outlook was very bleak!

Receiving God's Special Message

Then it happened. Eighteen years ago, over a period of nights—although I am not conscious of dreaming—I became aware of thoughts in my head that related to every soul on earth—not my problems, not our personal situation, not our church situation.

I had many things in my mind and I was excited. As I thought about the special message, I became overwhelmed by what was in my mind. I even became afraid because the feeling I had was so awesome—it is very difficult to explain. I knew that somehow God had placed a very special message in my mind and heart. I was His servant and I was to do something about this message.

Why Me? Why Now?

Now you have to appreciate that I was an "unchurched" person and had only gone to the odd Sunday service because my wife, Lavonne, was going and taking our grandson, Mike. Strangely enough, I hadn't thought about it until now. Some time before, she had felt a strong urge to start attending church again after a long time away.

When I was very young, I was raised and educated as a Roman Catholic and ultimately even received a degree in religious instruction. I was asked to become a teaching brother, but turned it down for a career and marriage. The point I want to make is that, other than reading the Bible through once, I had no training in Bible studies—only in Catholicism based on the teachings in the Bible.

Over many years, I had become one of the unchurched—totally caught up in the challenges of everyday life—never giving God a thought.

I knew that the content of the message in my head was powerful, but I had no idea whether it was based, in any way, on the Bible or, for that matter, that is was from God. Two questions assailed me: Why me and why now?

Before I knew it, I was compelled to write everything down. I recorded the message on cassette tape and made copies. Believe it or not, I feared that I might die suddenly and all record of the message would somehow disappear. In my mind, I felt that the devil was a threat and he would do terrible things to stop me from ever telling the message I had received.

It is strange, but in my heart, I knew that the message taken at its face value could change how people view their relationship with God—possibly strong enough to do something about it. I think this is what God really wants!

Considering that I was a Johnny-come lately to the Church, I knew very little about the actual contents of the Bible and I had a message to deliver! Who in their right mind would pay any attention to me? I knew that a message could also come from the devil and, in my own mind, I questioned the validity of the information I had received. I needed to check it out! I had learned that any revelation purporting to come from God should be supported by God's words in the Bible. I was a complete novice with respect to the Bible. Obviously, I had a task to perform at a time when I was completely destitute!

My Research about the Message

For a period of four or five years, I researched the subject—and I still do—trying to establish authenticity for the message from within the Bible—God's word. I found that the message was supported by the Bible! To me, the message was very clear and was centered in the soul. In my research, I found more profound emphasis on the "soul" in the Salvation Army hymnbook.

Then I discovered something that blew my mind. Back in the 1800s, revisions of the Bible (both KJV and NIV) took place where modern versions have replaced more than 498 direct references to the soul with about 136 references to the soul. I believe the changes have a tendency to de-emphasize the soul in favor of placing greater emphasis on the mortal person— *you*! The effect, I believe, has been to reduce the conscious awareness of the soul and to change the emphasis of what is subject to salvation—you or your soul!

Sharing the Message and More

For some of the reasons mentioned and because I was fearful of ridicule, the message was not made public until 1996. I have, however, shared it with five other people.

One was Pastor Dave Grice of the Salvation Army. I was concerned that it would contradict Salvation Army doctrine, but it does not appear to. In fact, Salvation Army doctrine places a great deal of emphasis on saving the soul. This is part of the reason that Dave will tell you that I have a passion for saving souls. Folks, believe it—until the message came to me, I had no such passion.

I shared the message with my wife and my grandson. The latter stated very simply that I had finally become a Christian. My wife, on the other hand, did not feel that the message made strong enough reference to Jesus and how a soul could be saved.

That bothered me until I realized that the Bible—both the Old Testament and the New Testament—set out very clearly God's wishes and the role that Jesus Christ has in bringing salvation to the soul. The message places the emphasis on helping the individual person understand how he is made and the opportunity he has for a personal relationship with God. Because of His great love for each one of us, God wants every soul to be saved.

Some may remember two sermons I gave in 1996 on the soul, which are reproduced later in this book, where I used the example of a marble given out at the door as representing each soul. Many still have that marble in their possession. With those two sermons, you have the essence of the message—so I have done part of the job. God has laid on me the task of making the total message public.

Since then, I have continued to provide sermons—all based directly or indirectly on (1) the soul, (2) God and God's presence, and more recently, (3) man's purpose on earth.

I've always been a strong player in anything I set out to do. Some may not see me fitting the role of a "soldier fighting to save souls." Who am I? Where does he think he gets off? Am I looking for power, position, and personal aggrandizement?

No, I can honestly say I am not looking for anything except to humbly serve God in a way that will help save souls. I think my enthusiastic involvement in the Church can be tied directly to the powerful impact of the message on me.

Seeking Confirmation, Encouragement, and Understanding

As a result, I have a burning desire to learn and know as much as possible about all matters relating to how to bring people to know the Lord. Remember that I was among the unchurched at the time. I have had a lot of catching up to do! Part of this endeavor has included many hours reading and researching the Bible—both printed and on the computer. Understanding the doctrine and mission of the Salvation Army has also been very important. I find the Army's mandate compatible with the message.

Over the years, at every step of my new existence, I have found encouragement and direction. Sometimes it came from a Bible study, a sermon, or an article, but the last one that really hit me came from my brother Bob in Toronto. I have shared with him, over time, some of the passion I have for saving souls. As a result, he faxed some information to me.

"When are we going to learn to do what God wants?"

"It is hard to be a Christian in this world today."

"If we love God with our heart, mind, and soul, we will survive, God willing."

"Did you know God has been talking to people in and through history for ages?"

He was referring to "The Dialogue of Saint Catherine of Siena" from 1347. She was told to write down everything while she was in ecstasy—reportedly when she dialogued with God the Father.

The book says, "The damned do not lose their being through any torment which they receive. Wherefore, I say to thee, that they ask for death and cannot have it, for they cannot lose their being; the existence of grace they lose, through their fault, but not their natural existence."

There is more, but the message was clear—the being, or the soul, being immortal, cannot die, and if condemned to eternal suffering, that suffering will not be relieved by death as occurs to mortals suffering on earth.

Isn't it strange that the past should reach out through my brother to bring a reaffirming message to me so that I might be encouraged to go forth with the message I received?

For me, that quote is a vivid description of *why* each of us must be conscious of our souls. Each of us has the opportunity to determine, through our choice, just what is going to happen to our immortal soul after death!

God's Purpose for Me and the Message

The main purpose of *A Message for the Soul of Man* is to get each one thinking about their soul! Another purpose is to get everyone to not only think about his or her soul, but also to understand that each person can decide where his or her immortal soul will reside throughout eternity! I think God wants each of us to be reminded to take responsibility for his or her own soul!

There is so much more I can tell you, but looking back to 1990, I can now see that God was working to bring me to a point where I would recognize that I have no control over my life and what has been given can be taken away. Only through being humbled was I prepared to receive His message.

A Wondrous New Beginning—Serving God

Just as quickly as my life had become a virtual disaster, it turned around just as dramatically. It was truly wondrous. One month after writing the message, I had a job and things started to turn around for us economically. In just two months, my income was equal or better than when I was with the nonprofit. In other words, through God's blessed mercy, I was able to return to as high a level of income as before. Thus, our family was able to maintain our standard of living while we again put money aside for our retirement.

However, there was a profound difference—I've told Pastor Dave this—I am very conscious that my real boss is God. I serve God—a God who loves us all with an intensity that no one could ever measure. In Matthew 4:10, Jesus said; "Worship the Lord your God, and serve him only," and "Anyone who does not take his cross and follow me is not worthy of me."

In Matthew 10:38, Jesus gave his all for mankind and calls us to "take up the cross." In many ways, that sums up where I have been ever since I received the message. "Take up Thy Cross" in the Salvation Army hymnbook really says it all.

Why Me?

I've still got one question: Why me? There are so many others who have had a longer and stronger association with God. I can't answer it, but maybe time will!

For the last several years, I have worked for the Salvation Army in Grande Prairie, Alberta, as the administrative assistant to the church officers in charge of the operations in Grande Prairie. This has allowed me to work for the Lord both at the practical level as well as at the spiritual level.

The latter has allowed me to continue my research and studies and to provide a ministry through devotionals, men's ministry, Bible studies, and even the odd Sunday sermon. Many of those sermons are reproduced in this book, but God has other plans for me.

God's Plan for Me

Circumstances have conspired to bring my employment with the Salvation Army to an end, thus freeing up my time to fulfill my commitment to the Lord. I am sure that God has arranged all this so that I might place all my effort on making His message public. Along the way, He has placed on my heart an expanded message that is aimed at the whole world. I am both scared and excited!

Sharing this document with you is a little like stepping into the River Jordan at flood—I am over my head and I am committed. The rest is in God's hands.

My Hope in Presenting the Message

With God's help, I want to convey a special personalized message that each reader can take from this book. This message will impact his or her life on earth and, ultimately, their soul in eternity.

It is my sincere wish that all will come to know God in a way that will encourage them to use whatever skills and talents they have to bring peace and happiness to the people they touch. I hope that their soul will know the happiness and joy of residing in heaven with God as a wholesome and holy person.

May the Lord be with you and yours and may you all know the glory and peace that come from a special relationship with God, your creator, envisioned in God's message to every soul!

PART 2

God's Message and Implications

A Review of Man's Biblical Beginnings

As mentioned earlier, I was a non-practicing Christian when I received the message. I had no real grounding in the contents of the Bible, although I believed in God, knew about Jesus, and generally had a working knowledge of the Old and New Testaments.

In fact, one of my big hang ups about religion was that having been brought up within the Catholic Church and no longer an attendee, I had great difficulty in picking out another church that I would comfortably attend if I was moved to do so. You can see, therefore, why I was completely surprised by both the message and its content. I felt that I had to return to basics and study the Bible in order to grasp the full significance of what God had revealed to me.

A Review of Man's Beginnings in Scripture

To help you to understand the significance of *A Message for the Soul of Man*, it would be worthwhile to review man's beginnings as set out in Old Testament scripture. Scripture, by the way, that is common to all three major Abrahamic religions—Judaism, Islam, and Christianity.

The important parts of the message relate to God, angels, souls, man, man's habitat, the universe, and God's Word in the Bible.

In the Beginning

Before anything existed, God existed. Outside of God, nothing existed—no measurement of time, distance, or depth. No material things.

Creation of Angels

God, in his great wisdom, created billions of angels to join with him in a beautiful heavenly abode where the angels coexisted with God. The angels enjoyed and basked in God's love, did his bidding, and learned that they would play a major role in what was to come. The angels were obedient to God—loving him and praising him. A full chapter is devoted to angels later in the book.

It came to pass, however, that one of the more prominent angels rebelled against God and caused the breakaway of many angels who became followers of Lucifer seeking to take over the power of God and have the adoration of angels. As a result, God banned Lucifer and his follower angels from the heavenly abode where they had once lived, casting them into the nether regions. Lucifer (also known as the devil) vowed vengeance against God and promised to thwart God's plans whenever and wherever he could. (See box on how the devil came to be. Ezekiel 28:12–18, Revelation 12:7–12)

Creation of Souls

God created another large group of beings, but with a different intent. He created billions of souls that also resided in the nether region, but with a different calling. God decided to give those souls the ability to make a choice whether they would love, obey, and serve God much as the good angels do. The foregoing is dealt in more detail within the message. However, before God could put souls in a place where they would come to exhibit the qualities he sought and would profess their love and obedience to him, he needed to create a habitat for all of this to happen.

Creation of the Habitat for Man

Over a short period of time (His time) he designed and created the earth, the universe, and all the things in it. While all of the angels observed this, God designed this world and universe to become the living and working place for man on earth, which was yet to be created. God made all living things in such a way as to be continually reproducing their species. This applied to plants, insects, animals, and ultimately humans.

Thus, all living creatures would have the ability to reproduce. He also introduced the ability and incentive to survive, providing them with internal desires—whether they are insects, birds, animals, or humans. Each has a thirst for water and hunger for food to nourish the body and keep them alive.

It is noteworthy that the right temperatures and conditions for reproduction from the very soil of the planet were set in place by God through the placement of the sun and other celestial bodies, which in turn has also influenced weather and exterior forces of weather on climate and growing conditions. The fluid state of the internal earth and movement of magma within also provide heat and exterior changes in the earth's crust.

The result before the advent of mankind is that God created fully functional living conditions for all human beings—much the same as preparing an aquarium to receive fish.

What we have just described is the first part of Genesis 1 in the Old Testament and the reason behind it.

Let us turn to the second part of Genesis 1, the creation of mankind.

The Creation of Man—Genesis 1:26–30, Old Testament

> Then God said, "Let us make man in our image, in our likeness, and let them rule over the fish of the sea and the birds of the air, over the livestock, over all the earth, and over all the creatures that move along the ground." So God created man in his own image, in the image of God he created him; male and female he created them.
>
> God blessed them and said to them, "Be fruitful and increase in number; fill the earth and subdue it. Rule over the fish of the sea and the birds of the air and over every living creature that moves on the ground." Then God said, "I give you every seed-bearing plant on the face of the whole earth and every tree that has fruit with seed in it. They will be yours for food. And to all the beasts of the earth and all the birds of the air and all the creatures that move on the ground—everything

that has the breath of life in it—I give every green plant for food."

The Creation of Man and Woman—Genesis 2:4, 7, 15–23, Old Testament

"This is the account of man and woman, when they were created.—the Lord God formed the man from the dust of the ground and breathed into his nostrils the breath of life, and the man became a living being.

The Lord God took the man and put him in the Garden of Eden to work it and take care of it. And the Lord God commanded the man, "You are free to eat from any tree in the garden; but you must not eat from the tree of the knowledge of good and evil, for when you eat of it you will surely die." The Lord God said, "It is not good for the man to be alone. I will make a helper suitable for him." Now the Lord God had formed out of the ground all the beasts of the field and all the birds of the air. He brought them to the man to see what he would name them; and whatever the man called each living creature, that was its name. So the man gave names to all the livestock, the birds of the air and all the beasts of the field. But for Adam no suitable helper was found. So the Lord God caused the man to fall into a deep sleep; and while he was sleeping, he took one of the man's ribs and closed up the place with flesh. Then the Lord God made a woman from the rib he had taken out of the man, and he brought her to the man. The man said, "This is now bone of my bones and flesh of my flesh; she shall be called 'woman,' for she was taken out of man."

This account of the creation of man and woman by God is shared by all Abrahamic religions—Judaism, Islam, and Christianity.

Importance of Reviewing Creation

To appreciate the significance of *A Message for the Soul of Man*, it is very important to know that everything God created was done to prepare a place where man would reside for a finite period of time. In other words, everything that you behold here on earth was put here for you—and the millions of persons who preceded you and those that will come after you.

The story of creation calls on you to believe in an all-powerful and all-knowing God! A God who is ever present and, has a plan and purpose for every soul as they journey on earth.

It has been two thousand years since Jesus lived and taught about God. It seems appropriate that God should, once again, send a message to all mankind.

Relationship between God, Man, and Soul

As you are about to find out, there is a very clear relationship between God's creations and God Himself. He created your soul, your body, and the world. He set in motion the joining of body and soul and you can be sure that God has a purpose for all He did.

The message you are about to read clearly describes the makeup of the body of each person on earth—past, present, and future. It also describes the relationship of the eternal soul to the mortal body. Central to the message is the importance of the soul and God's plan for mankind.

How the Devil Came to be

Ezekiel 28:12–18

Son of man, take up a lament concerning the king of Tyre and say to him: This is what the Sovereign Lord says: You were the model of perfection, full of wisdom and perfect in beauty. You were in Eden, the garden of God; every precious stone adorned you: ruby, topaz and emerald, chrysolite, onyx and jasper, sapphire, turquoise and beryl. Your settings and mountings were made of gold; on the day you were created they were prepared.

You were anointed as a guardian cherub, for so I ordained you. You were on the holy mount of God; you walked among the fiery stones. You were blameless in your ways from the day you were created till wickedness was found in you.

Through your widespread trade you were filled with violence, and you sinned. So I drove you in disgrace from the mount of God, and I expelled you, O guardian cherub, from among the fiery stones.

Your heart became proud on account of your beauty, and you corrupted your wisdom because of your splendor. So I threw you to the earth; I made a spectacle of you before kings. By your many sins and dishonest trade you have desecrated your sanctuaries. So I made a fire come out from you, and it consumed you, and I reduced you to ashes on the ground in the sight of all who were watching.

Revelation 12:7-12 And there was war in heaven. Michael and his angels fought against the dragon, and the dragon and his angels fought back. But he was not strong enough, and they lost their place in heaven. The great dragon was hurled down—that ancient serpent called the devil, or Satan, who leads the whole world astray. He was hurled to the earth, and his angels with him.

Then I heard a loud voice in heaven say: "Now have come the salvation and the power and the kingdom of our God, and the authority of his Christ. For the accuser of our brothers, who accuses them before our God day and night, has been hurled down. They overcame him by the blood of the Lamb and by the word of their testimony; they did not love their lives so much as to shrink from death. Therefore rejoice, you heavens and you who dwell in them! But woe to the earth and the sea, because the devil has gone down to you! He is filled with fury, because he knows that his time is short."

THE MESSAGE FOR THE SOUL OF MAN

By John D. Powers

FOREWORD

It is almost 2000 years since Jesus Christ was born, raised, died on the cross and was resurrected from the dead and ascended into heaven.

It is almost 4000 years since God chose Abraham to father a nation to whom He gave the designation of His 'chosen' people. In the intervening years between Abraham and Christ, many prophets brought forth God's laws and commandments. The purposes of these laws were twofold. The first was to admonish the descendants of Abraham to know, love and serve God in the purest form. The second was to create a state of justice for all men by following God's rules and laws respecting all members of the human race. The combination of these commandments would bring about righteousness in man and the 'salvation' of man's soul.

The teachings of Jesus Christ, which were based on God's laws amply described throughout the records of the Old Testament, reaffirmed once and for all the importance of following God's laws in addition to loving, not only God and oneself, but neighbors and enemies. Only by believing in God and following God's laws could man be saved.

It is marvelous that mankind, generally, believes in God. It is a miracle that the best read book in recorded history is the Bible and the record of the Jewish nation in the Old Testament. What is not impressive is that there appears to be fewer and fewer following the teachings of Christ and God's commandments in this world today.

At the same time, man's creativity has brought the human species closer to the brink of total self-destruction than ever before in history. Through the proliferation of expertise in nuclear energy; through the destruction of our human environment; through experiments in gene reproduction; through the spread of immorality, mind-altering chemical use and violence, mankind is coming closer to the potential for worldwide eradication - much like the dinosaurs.

The writer has always been aware of the importance of God in our lives and has been part of, and witness to, the conditions that prevail and assail our every step as human beings. Believing that priests, ministers and rabbis and the clergy and church, in general, have a special and sacred role in espousing God's word and saving souls, it is horrifying and shocking to experience the tremendous harm done to God-fearing people by persons professing to be God's spokesmen on earth (pastors) but are evil. The practice of religion has been dealt a number of setbacks in recent years by convictions for corruption and immorality among the clergy of many churches. Ungodly behaviors by those who represent God on earth undermine God's purpose, His teachings and His plan for mankind. Their behavior will bring severe punishment.

With a sense of time running out and with a concern that the human race is faced with extinction, I have been moved to write the following text. I do not feel worthy or even qualified in this task but the urge is too strong to resist.

Much of the information you are about to read is found in the Bible and has been there since it was first written. What has been needed for some time is some clarification.

Before going on, I invite you to close your eyes in a dark room with no sound of any kind and meditate. If you can transport yourself to a huge underground cavern with no light or sound you might achieve the effect I am suggesting.

Now use your God-given imagination and picture your mind outside of your body. Disconnect all the senses - nothing to taste, no hearing, no touching, no seeing and no smell. You are, at this point, disembodied, you are only a mind and free to roam. Take a few moments - relax - drift.

Now picture yourself in your mind's eye - much like looking in the mirror. Examine who and what you are. Can you sense peace and contentment or do you feel anxious or frustrated? Could you know happiness or sorrow in this state? Can you dream, plan, articulate words in your mind? Can you feel love and hate? Can you remember your wrongdoing and the things you have done right in your life? Can you remember specific instances where you hurt someone or did them harm physically, mentally or emotionally? Can you say honestly that you are good or bad at this moment?

Dear reader - if you have found this exercise difficult, do not be discouraged - if you have been able to do just a small, imperfect portion of the exercise know this - you have been attempting to examine your very own soul! If you can do that - what do you think God can do? I hope these few minutes will have prepared you for the thoughts that follow.

John D. Powers
Grande Prairie, Alberta
May 21, 1992

Questions to ponder - - What is man's purpose on Earth?
Why does man exist?
Why does the Bible exist?
Why did God choose certain people to be his "chosen" people?
Is there life after death?
Does the mind age?

THE MESSAGE FOR THE SOUL OF MAN

GOD

Know that God is eternal and is the Creator (of everything). He is God the Father, God the Son (Jesus Christ who took human shape) and the Holy Spirit. Most important, know this - God loves you!

Everything He has created is either inert or living. If it is living, it is designed to reproduce itself continuously unless destroyed by a catastrophe either of nature (God) or man-made. If it is inert, it is subject to physical laws that can alter or disturb its condition.

Everything that is visible or knowable was created by God - for a purpose.

God is perfect in every way and His perfection is mirrored in his creations.

THE SOUL

Among God's earliest creations or offspring were souls. A soul is a minute reflection of God. The soul has no shape and is not visible to the human eye. God is the source of all energy. The soul is but a particle of special energy that becomes the receptacle of all thought, emotion, feelings, understanding, knowledge and wisdom. In other words, the soul has an intellect and is capable of conceptualizing, planning and forecasting. It is creative, thus capable of recognizing God the Creator and His wondrous works. The soul, at the time of its creation, was neither good nor evil. It will assume one of these characteristics as it continues to exist. Further, it will cast a reflection of itself in the form of character and personality that will be readily discernable by virtually every life form.

God created souls as the offspring of Himself so as to provide them the opportunity to come to know, love and serve Him as *individual* entities. In doing so, He promised them (souls) that they would share with

Him (inherit) the glory and beauty of everlasting love in the Kingdom of Heaven. By multiplying Himself, He created the opportunity of an even greater Kingdom that could be shared with kindred souls - souls who have come to understand, love and acknowledge God as the Creator and infinite Being.

He created the soul as an image of Himself with the ability to reason, learn and acquire knowledge and understanding. He gave the soul the ability to feel and store emotion, joy, sadness, hurt, kindness and happiness. He made the soul the receptacle of all its own thoughts, experiences, mistakes and errors, and achievements both good and bad. The ultimate state of the soul is to reach a level of pure thought (enlightenment) and love directed to oneness with God Almighty. But God did more. He blurred, even removed the memory of Himself and gave the soul a free will; the will to choose right from wrong. The will to seek knowledge and understanding, thereby, coming to know, love and serve the Creator, God Almighty.

The soul exists as an entity unto itself seeking and thirsting for knowledge and purpose. It, like God, is eternal and will reach a point, within God's time clock, that dictates when each individual soul will have either succeeded or failed in its quest. At that point, the day of judgment, the soul will either be joined with God or suffer everlasting damnation.

Note that the soul does not have any of the attributes of man - no body or limbs, no sex, no skin pigment, no nervous system, no sense of smell, taste or touch. The soul cannot reproduce itself and does not form any special relationships with other souls. Communication between souls can only be achieved through a thought (energy) process which is free flowing. I.e. no words are spoken - no language is necessary.

The soul, at any one time, is the accumulated sum total of all the good and evil accomplished through the use of its talent, ability and free will. It cannot disguise itself and is exactly what it has become. This will range from the worst - evil - to the best - Godlike and holy. Salvation of the soul is achieved through God's forgiveness and remission of the effects of sin on the soul together with the soul's absolute belief in God and obedience to His will.

Finally, it should be recognized the soul exists independently. In keeping with God's plan, the soul, in its original form, must obey God or suffer damnation on the Day of Judgment.

The foregoing description of the soul and what follows may give rise to great debate. The Book of Genesis clearly indicates that God created the universe, the world, the components of the world and all living things. The creation of souls and angels are not described but are readily referred to many times throughout the Bible. Logic would, therefore, dictate that souls and angels existed before creation.

Man-made definitions of the 'soul' agree on one aspect. That after death of the body, the soul continues to exist. Unfortunately, some references to spirit and soul can be interchanged in the Bible, contemporary writings and definitions. This does serve to confuse the intellect.

MAN

God, in His wisdom, then devised His testing ground for the billions of souls He had created. He created man.

God's first creation, Adam, was very special. He placed Adam in the Garden of Eden under ideal conditions for human existence and with no apparent time limit on how long he would exist. God, in creating the universe and world, had brought about the continuous rebirth of each individual species. When God created man, he did the same thing - He also created sex and the desire to procreate or self produce. For this purpose, He created Eve. Thus came into existence the first man and woman biologically equipped to give birth to thousands of offspring over an indeterminate life-span.

But let us look closer at the man God created. We know Adam was created from the materials of earth to which all mankind's human form returns. God breathed into Adam and gave him life. **Genesis 2:7, Job 32:8**. To understand the real significance of this act on the part of God, we must remember who God is.

All Christians believe that God is made up of God the Father, God the Son and God the Holy Ghost or Holy Spirit. Adam was formed into the image of God - more importantly - he was formed into the image of God the Son who would take on the same human form as Adam, later, as Jesus Christ.

The creature known as man was given 'life' by God or the spark of life was created within man by the Spirit of God which set in motion all of man's intricate biological machinery - much like electricity lights up the light bulb or runs a computer when the 'power' is turned on.

The 'power' necessary to run the human form can be turned off at will by man himself (suicide), or by being killed through accident, disease or design or by simply dying at a point of deterioration of body parts where the body can no longer sustain itself, or finally, when God wills it. As we know, the interference of God in the life-force of any human being has been minimal since the birth of Christ. Some would even say since man's life span was restricted to about 100 years. **Genesis 6:3**.

Man's 'life-force' or spirit is a continuous flow of God's Spirit or His Holy Spirit, which acts as a two-way energy conduit between the human form and God Himself. **This 'life-force' is not the soul! This spirit in man is not the Holy Spirit,** but, simply the spirit *or* life energy *or* the power source of the body. It can be said that God is, indeed, present in every human's life and has a direct link with man's inner self. The Holy Spirit has special powers which are manifested in a variety of ways.

Through the spirit provided by God to man, the human body functions - the heart beats and pumps blood, the brain operates, the nervous system is active, the stomach digests and all the billions of cells and molecules that make up the human form do their work, die and are born again.

Many functions of different organs can be taken over by artificial, mechanical devices. The common denominator in all such devices is there must be a source of power - without it - the organ stops working.

Man is, indeed, a most wonderful creation of the Lord and was designed by God for a very special purpose.

MAN - A FORCE FOR GOOD AND EVIL

The reality is that everything that man is aware of was created for man's use. Man has dominion over his total environment with the exception of the forces of nature inherent in the very make-up of the planets and the universe.

Mankind is a force for good and bad - wars, pollution, consumption of resources, procreation leading to overpopulating in areas of limited food supply. Weigh that against man's ability to create great works that serve man - dams, buildings and cities, great ships and aircraft. Include great works of art and music.

Man, as we know him, has conquered diseases, pestilence, air, space and sea travel. He has harnessed huge forces of nature, physics and science.

But the greatest force of all is man himself as a creature (mammal). He must have air, water and food to exist. The body dictates, as self-preservation, the need to obtain these basic ingredients of life. The body is designed to function with other artifacts as tools of attack, defense and protection. Man is designed to utilize items that come into his possession to further the dictates of the body. This can be as simple as taking a club to kill an animal for food or making a battery-powered pacemaker assist the heart to beat.

The body has been given the use of many sensing receptors. The five major senses - taste, smell, hearing, vision and touch are best known. As such the body can know cold, heat, pain and suffering; it can be injured, become sick, feel hunger. The body also is equipped with a gratification process. - Fullness after eating quenched thirst after drinking, and warmth after being clothed properly, emotional gratification after sex. Of all the desires implanted in the human body, the desire for gratification does not distinguish between good and evil. When used for evil purposes, this is personified by greed, sloth and selfishness.

The body, independent of any direction from any external entity has, inherent in its very make-up, all the ingredients necessary to drive the survival instinct thus making bodily needs and desires a dominant force. The environment into which every new body is introduced also presents immediate obstacles that must be overcome or conditions that must be managed so as to assure continuing beneficial living conditions for the body.

The forces driving mankind from within and without are formidable and God has prepared all of this as a habitat for each and every soul!

"Don't you know that you yourself are God's temple and that God's Spirit lives in you? If anyone destroys God's temple, God will destroy him; for God's temple is sacred, and you are that temple." - **1 Corinthians 3:16-17**"

"But he who unites himself with the Lord is one with Him in spirit. Do you not know that your body is a temple of the Holy Spirit, who is in you, whom you have received from God?" - **1 Corinthians 6:17-19**

ABOUT THE MIND AND HEART

If the soul and spirit are as described, what about the role of the heart and mind?

As human beings, we have come to associate feelings, emotions and quality of the person with the heart and intelligence, memory, conceptualizing and awareness with the brain. We know what the functions of these organs are in the body. When we are joyful or scared our heart reacts to a stimulant triggered by the brain. We are not aware of the message from the brain, but we certainly are aware of the increased palpitations of the heart. Reference to the heart in the Bible is really reference to the quality of the person or emotion and character of the soul.

In respect to the mind, the thinking process can be traced to energy within the brain. Intelligence, awareness, memories, dreaming, learning were designed to be integrated with the work of the brain within the body. Hunger, for instance, is sensed and decisions made as to how to appease that hunger. The brain functions bringing attention to the problem, the soul, interpreted as the mind, decides on a course of action leaving a record of the proceedings and resulting gratification as a memory. References to the mind in the Bible assign qualities to the mind which can be applied equally to the soul. The soul benefits or suffers by directing the function of the brain controlling the actions of the body through the exercise of a free will.

"Those who live according to the sinful nature have their minds set on what that nature desires; but those who live in accordance with the Spirit have their minds set on what the Spirit desires. The mind of the sinful man (or mind set on the flesh) is death, but the mind controlled by the Spirit is life and peace, the sinful mind is hostile to God. It does not submit to God's law; nor can it do so." - **Romans 8:5-8**

Note how the word soul could be substituted for mind in the last quotation and Holy Spirit or God for Spirit.

A driving force within 'man' is the great need to love and be loved and to acquire knowledge. Pure love and pure knowledge, centered on the heart and mind, in our concept, is the ultimate goal being sought by the soul. The soul will find its goal if it uses the body as a means to achieve this. The perception of the degree of purity of heart and mind is a means of measurement for the soul.

Because of the veil between the soul and the soul's past, man had to have a way of describing what was 'felt by the heart and 'perceived' by the mind. Until God walked with Enoch (**Genesis 5:24**) and walked and talked with Noah (**Genesis 6:9**) many years after Adam and Eve, man was not aware of the existence of God or of his own soul within.

Man has a soul. Every person has a soul. Every person ever born has had a soul. It's a fact stated emphatically in the Bible. How did the soul get there?

THE JOINING OF BODY AND SOUL

At a very special moment, an individual soul enters and ultimately leaves a human body prepared for its user. At the moment the soul takes up residence in a human it is attached to the life-force already in place and takes over the controls.

This occurs after the external life-force of the mother is separated from the new born. At that same moment of entry into the body a veil descends to mask the soul's original point of departure. The soul has no recollection of its past.

At the death of the body, the process is reversed and is simultaneous with the leaving of the life-force. Once in a while, the life-force may slip away prematurely but return to continue the body functions. The soul moves in tandem with the spirit and may have a glimpse of kindred souls waiting for its arrival. This can be mirrored on the face of the human form in its final moment.

The stage has been set. Every soul is given the opportunity to come to know, love and serve God through the simple process of reason and understanding while bearing the responsibility of steering a human body through the difficulties brought about by being in the human form. The test is very hard and provides countless opportunities to commit sin. The soul that passes this test has earned God's salvation and reward.

GOD'S LAWS AND THE IMPORTANCE OF THE BIBLE

From this point on, reference to man must mean the soul included within the human form called man and synonymous with heart and mind.

Because of the veil between God and our selves, it is difficult for man to comprehend God's purpose.

God foresaw this and devised a very special plan. The plan was simple. God stated clearly some rules that He wanted mankind to follow. These rules were directed at 'man' who existed with God's spirit and housed a soul whose very salvation depended on the right choices being made despite the desires or 'weaknesses' of the body to which the soul was attached.

The 'rules', therefore, had to deal with how the soul within the body must conduct itself in its present form. Is there any wonder that God directed 'man' to know, love and serve God and to love his neighbor as himself? - **Matthew 22:37-40**

Review the Ten Commandments (**Exodus 20:1-17**) and see how they are directed at controlling the body's base desires but the first 3 commandments are directed explicitly to the soul.

God knew from the example of Adam & Eve (Genesis 3) that the challenges He had designed for the soul were monumental. He had to teach and remind every soul of its destiny. He had to teach by word and example and finally by demonstration to prove the existence of God in a way not easily forgotten.

God decided that He would select a people to bear witness to His power. To do this He had to chose someone to beget the people He had in mind, and then, they, through time and experience, must faithfully record the happenings of the chosen nation.

It came to pass that the Jewish nation became God's chosen people and they recorded their failures and successes in following God's direction. Thus, we have the record of the Old Testament in which God teaches, admonishes, punishes and reveals Himself. The primary lesson the Old Testament teaches is that failure to follow God's wishes will result in punishment if not total destruction. This lesson is demonstrated over and over again.

The soul of man has the teachings, the laws, the intellect, the will - all that is lacking is the belief!

God had to take the next step; a powerful demonstration, again faithfully recorded, to prove the existence of God. He brought to earth His Son who assumed human form and lived as one with all humanity.

Having demonstrated His human form in Jesus Christ, He then provided His teachings and laws once again for everyone to learn - **Matthew 22:37-40** - this time accompanied by miracles. Finally, to demonstrate that He was God, He arose from the dead to show that *life can exist after death!*

What were Jesus' last words? Just before He died on the cross, Jesus called out, "Father, into your hands I commit my spirit. When He had said this, He breathed His last." - **Luke 23:46**

Jesus had returned to God and the Holy Spirit, His body's spirit or 'life force'. Jesus, as the Son of God, was a pure and perfect soul and *One with God* as part of the Holy Trinity.

THE MESSAGE FOR THE SOUL IN MAN

At some time in the future, each body will die and give up its soul. Up to this time, each person thought the soul was some other entity. After all, how could it be us? We are going to die and cease to exist.

The person you know - IS your soul!

The soul, referred to in the scriptures, is **YOU** - the person and character you know to be you! **YOUR SOUL** will continue to exist after your body is gone - and you will know it, as you will have passed through the veil.

If you have not come to know, love and serve God, you will not be judged fit to enter the Kingdom of Heaven. You will suffer eternal damnation!

You can only be saved if you believe. If you believe, you will not sin, but, seek repentance and God's love.

EPILOGUE

Scholars and scientists will readily admit that the happenings in the Bible are true. While everyone acknowledges that the Old Testament is a history of the Jewish people, it is hard to imagine that it was ordained by God to occur and to remain in existence long after one would expect it. History exists for other civilizations but they do not receive the tremendous following of so many people. Both the Old Testament and the New Testament are unique in their content as well as the importance attached to them by so many millions of people

With so many having studied the Bible, why would not the foregoing Message have occurred to them? Attribute this to the veil that has been in place to cloud men's minds (souls) and realize that as mankind has become more creative in creating its own self-destruction, many must learn soon that there **IS** a purpose in life. What they did not realize is the greatest truth of all. ***Each* person *is a living soul and will go to their judgment day with a full record of good and evil stamped directly on their soul!*** That judgment day could arrive at any time. Choosing who will be with God in the Kingdom of Heaven will not be difficult. Every thought and deed has been and continues to be recorded so long as the soul shall live.

The only true salvation for those souls who have sinned is an acknowledgment of their sins, a sincere and contrite request for God's forgiveness and daily demonstration of following God's laws and walking in **HIS WAY.**

For the rest of your days, know that God loves you dearly and wants you to be with Him in heaven. Jesus said. **"Love the Lord your God with all your heart and all your soul and with all your strength and with all your mind; and love your neighbor as yourself." - Deuteronomy 6:5; Luke 10:27; Mark 12:30; Matthew 22:37-40**

Dear souls - the Message is clear - walk with God!

John D. Powers   May 21, 1992

THE BODY - A LIVING CELL
THE TEMPLE OF GOD

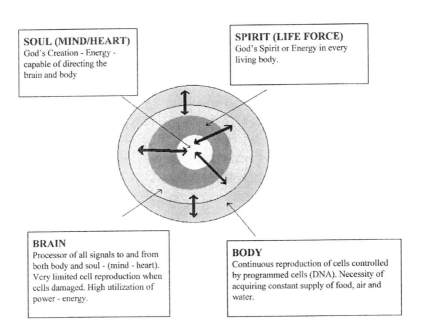

SOUL (MIND/HEART)
God's Creation - Energy - capable of directing the brain and body

SPIRIT (LIFE FORCE)
God's Spirit or Energy in every living body.

BRAIN
Processor of all signals to and from both body and soul - (mind - heart). Very limited cell reproduction when cells damaged. High utilization of power - energy.

BODY
Continuous reproduction of cells controlled by programmed cells (DNA). Necessity of acquiring constant supply of food, air and water.

Components of the body and soul as described in
A Message For The Soul Of Man

John D. Powers   May 21, 1992

What is God's Message really saying and what are the Implications?

Body and Soul

As I read and reread the message I had written down, I asked myself about the main thought that God wanted mankind to know and understand.

I realized that the message was for the soul of man. There is a distinction between *you* or the total person and their soul. Now why was this important?

I began to realize that I always thought of myself as *me*—I never gave any thought to my soul by itself. When the pastor referred to a new life or eternal life, I thought of it as a continuation of myself with a resurrected body. Do most people do the same?

The message goes into detail as to the make-up of the human body. It defines three separate parts—the body, the soul, and the spirit or life force. We first must acknowledge the power of God with the understanding that *everything* is possible. Only after we have accepted that can we come to grips with the tri-part human being. We know we have a body—we can see it and feel it. The soul or the spirit—how do you explain this concept without getting very confused?

You are asked to understand the fantastic beauty of the body and its workings. It is truly a universe in itself and, most importantly, virtually every cell is capable of reproducing itself many times over. In its simplest terms, that is how a wound heals. However, brain cells and the eggs in a woman's ovaries do not reproduce themselves. Only the aging process causes the body's cell reproduction capability to fade slowly.

Understanding That We Have a Soul

God's message is an attempt to get all mankind to understand the entire make-up of each human being so that each one can clearly understand that they are a soul! Each soul has been created by God!

The best analogy I can give you is the act of a person getting into a car, turning on the ignition, and driving off. The car is a tremendous example of man's ability to engineer a product that has the capability of doing exactly what it was designed to do and to do it very well over many years.

In that example, the car is the body and you, the driver, are the soul. This example has been used before, but now apparently God feels that it is very important to get everyone to understand this concept very clearly. Why?

God's Message and Man until Now

Let me leave that for a moment and turn to another part of the message that stood out in my mind. He made it very clear that He had placed into the hands of mankind a book containing his relationship with a "chosen people." Within the Old Testament is a very clear indication of what God wants man to do. It also records man's inability to comply. The New Testament also contains a very clear message given to mankind through the teachings, examples, and sacrifice of Jesus Christ, His Son. That was two thousand years ago. Is mankind responding or again messing up?

Change and Man's Evolvement

Think about the most dramatic change in our world in the last hundred years. While we have had major wars and obstacles—from a major economic depression to political turmoil to great battles for world power—the greatest and most dramatic change in this world has been man's ability to acquire knowledge and use it in greater and greater amounts.

The harnessing of the atom through to the rapid growth of the science of computerization, miniaturization and the development of advanced power sources has allowed man to become more creative in the development of a wide range of products. Our present-day society, as a result, is in a constant whirl of change!

This ability to acquire knowledge, to seek it avidly and relentlessly, and to use it is a gift that God has given man. Why?

Body, Free Will, and Purpose

Another part of God's message dealt with knowing our purpose for being here—on earth—with the body we received, the place and environment we were born into, the gifts and/or talents we have and that wonderful gift God gave us: free will! But all is not rosy because the challenges of life and the exercise of our free will combine to place us in danger of losing our direction and soon we all fight evil in many forms— most often not very successfully. Why?

> So what is the purpose of our life on earth? In Matthew 16:26, Jesus said:
>
> What good will it be for a man if he gains the whole world, yet forfeits his soul? Or what can a man give in exchange for his soul?" Everybody knows that they will not take any material things with them when they die. Everything remains behind. So what do they take with them when they die? The soul that departs from the body has, in its lifetime, gathered unto itself a full life of words, thoughts, feelings, emotions, memories, deeds, and beliefs, which taken together render that soul eligible for salvation or eternal damnation!

Your Soul and Judgment

A point that came through loud and clear is that judgment is immediate and you have no say in what happens. You had your chance and you had the opportunity, over your lifetime, to learn what was important in your life. There is that free will again—you always had the choice!

That is exactly the way God wants it. He created your soul and the mechanism that allows the placement of your soul in the body. He placed it all in an environment where you exercise your ability to learn God's purpose for you!

Research, Question, and the Soul

After I had received *A Message for the Soul of Man*, I did a great deal of research—especially in the Bible. I searched for confirmation of the things that the message contained. While I was doing that, I asked a question of many people and got a variety of answers. Some may have thought I was a little nutty. The question was, "Does the mind age?"

A good number thought that it did. They did not understand the functioning of the brain versus the mind. The same could be said of the heart. Some attribute character qualities with the heart—courage, love, kindness, etc. The heart, we all know, is an important body part, but does not *feel* emotions—even broken hearts. A heart can be affected by our emotions—as can the entire body. The qualities we give to the heart and the mind are qualities of the soul.

God's Message for Each Soul

God's message is for all of mankind. With all of man's knowledge now accumulated, man has the capability of understanding who he is and how he is made. This should bring him to a new understanding of God and man's relationship with God. As we begin a new century, a new era is dawning for mankind, but the success of this new age will be measured by how many souls actually learn to acknowledge God in their lives and the role of Jesus Christ in helping them with their spiritual journey through this world.

The message very clearly states man's purpose on earth: "To know, love, and serve God."

Is that too simple? My gut reaction to that as a non-Christian would be utter disbelief surrounded by a string of strong caustic words. The typical non-Christian—and even some so-called Christians—given their great knowledge, ability, pride, and self-control, would react with

"Who does He think He is? I have my own life to lead and I will live it as I see fit!"

God's Message was given in the New Testament when Jesus gave us His great commandment in Mark 12:30–31:

> "Love the Lord your God with all your heart and with all your soul and with your entire mind and with all your strength. The second is this: 'Love your neighbor as yourself.' There is no commandment greater than these."

His message is a reminder to all mankind that the soul of man must learn and understand this commandment—and follow it! If you don't, how can you be a Christian?

Soul-searching Questions

For a person to understand and accept God's message, he or she must do some very heavy soul searching. One could start off with some basic questions such as:

Do you believe that there is a God and that He is all-powerful and the creator of heaven and the universe, including your soul and your body?

Do you believe that you have a soul, which is eternal and cannot be destroyed except by God, the creator?

Do you believe that your soul is *you*—the conscious you who feels, knows, remembers, thinks, and plans—and that your soul will exist after your body has died?

Do you believe that your soul could be joined with God in heaven?

Do you know what real joy and happiness is? Can you imagine it existing forever?

Finally, do you want your soul to enjoy eternal happiness with God in heaven?

God's Love and Knowing Him

The key to understanding God's message and all the forgoing is simply love! You cannot remotely imagine the love that God has for every soul, but you can get inkling from a mother's love for her children.

What makes complying with God's wishes for us possible is a complete understanding and knowledge of God and your relationship with Him. That is the knowing part. The love part is easier when you know God and have entered into a special relationship with Him through His Son, Jesus Christ. By the way, personal prayer is the major path by which this communication and relationship is accomplished. The serving comes easier when you understand God's purpose for mankind and share in that purpose because of your love for God and all of mankind.

The tough part is visualizing yourself doing what was just described. Depending on where you are in your spiritual journey, you will find your place by examining your personal relationship with God.

Long-term Implications

There are long-term implications from *A Message for the Soul of Man* that may be upsetting to those who hold very strong beliefs they feel are not to be questioned.

The first implication is that to accept this message as valid, one must accept that God can work through people, even sinners, to convey His message. The Bible is full of examples. I believe that those who compose music, lyrics, poems, and prose or exercise an artistic talent in praise of the Lord are His messengers as well. God uses many tools to bring His word and presence to each person's attention. A good example is the celebration of Christmas and Easter.

A second implication is that the relationship with God is a God-soul relationship, which is direct and not routed through any church. The church is a body of believers who come together to worship and to fellowship with each other in praise of the Lord. Each soul is on an individual and sometimes-lonely journey where the soul will go through crisis after crisis until the individual leans on Jesus and God to help them with their journey. No one can do it for you, but it is nice to have lots of support!

The third implication is that acceptance of the message could become universal and adopted by every form of religion on earth. If you find that hard to accept, think that most religions believe in an almighty power and most religions adopt a code of conduct that is very similar in content to each other. Some countries even place God as the highest person in their belief system, whereas many so-called industrialized nations are putting God aside. Acceptance of God's message could reverse this process.

The fourth implication is that the question of abortion becomes very clear. If one accepts that the soul does not enter the body until the brain is functioning, this means that the body is not a complete human until the ninth week of embryo growth. Aborting or blocking the development of a child up to that time would not be any different than changing the course of a river or constructing a dam to control water—one of God's creations. However, conversely, aborting after that time would be murder or a sin.

The fifth implication is that God is always present and knows exactly what is transpiring in a person's life. Those who would circumvent God's wishes where there is a great deal of personal suffering by committing suicide and assisting in any way are committing a sin against God. It has been demonstrated that those who have a strong belief in God and are at peace with Him are able to handle their suffering a great deal better than those who do not have that relationship.

The sixth implication relates to the ultimate conditions on earth if God's message was universally accepted. Our present world is experiencing tremendous social problems, mostly associated with the seeking of pleasure, gratification, greed, and more. An understanding of what is meant by loving one's neighbor and following the wishes of Jesus in how we love our neighbor could bring about a change in conditions that would have a tremendous impact on our existence on earth. To achieve this, every person must learn and understand who they are and the importance of their soul. This implication virtually calls for a worldwide revival of faith in God and Jesus Christ. Now wouldn't that be a glorious and wonderful happening!

Making the Message Public

God wants his message to be made public. The reasons why I feel that it is important include:

- God wants to raise the awareness of who you really are and, in turn, the awareness of who God is.
- A clear understanding of yourself and your relationship with God will bring about a huge change in how the people of the world interrelate with each other and their living environment on earth.
- God wants you to have the big picture!

It will help individuals find worth in their own lives and the knowledge that everything they do impacts on the total world as well as all their relations, friends, and those dependent on them.

This Book Is for Everyone!

This book's purpose is to teach and tell each human being who they really are and to answer such questions as "Why am I here on earth? What is my purpose for living? Why was such an intricate and elaborate mechanism (the body) put together—to ultimately end in dust?

In explaining the answers, a whole range of questions come up such as:

- Who made us and the world around us? Why?
- Do we have a soul?

- Are there angels?
- Is there, in fact, a creator of all things who we call God?
- What is our role as mankind vis-à-vis world stewardship?

In putting forth the message, one must dwell on who God is and what is His purpose for all creation? Can anyone really know God? Many know about God, but don't really know Him! This book is about the relationship of God, creation, and each individual soul or person.

Knowing your individual relationship with God is the most important question in your short existence on earth. You will be fulfilled and you will know happiness and peace when you, as an individual, learn and fulfill your purpose in life.

One major difficulty that many will experience in reading this book will be setting aside for the time being strongly held views associated with a religious belief system that you were born or adopted into. Do not despair—it all fits into God's purpose for you and is within each belief system.

The purpose of the message is to raise your awareness of yourself—who you really are—and understand how you came to be who you are while remembering that you are unique!

Hundreds of books exist that talk about the subject matter of this particular book—all are worthy and informative and provide within their scope great truths and information that all bear on the main subject: you! This book seeks to provide even greater understanding of that same material.

If you truly understand God's purpose for your life and seek to fulfill it, you will live your life in a way that may bring you great happiness on earth.

God's message can affect many parts of life in different ways.

Religion:

An appreciation of the common thread that joins nearly all religions—belief in an almighty and powerful God! This is the first tier of all religions based on a single God. Everything that follows—whether Christian, Muslim, or Jewish—is the outcome of God's wishes. Acceptance of our common belief in God should help bring peace, understanding, and harmony to our relationships with those of other different faiths.

Children and Youth:

One of the greatest problems of youth is coming to know who they are—their strengths and weaknesses, talents and shortcomings, and their future. Creating a sense of purpose—sufficient to instill a desire to improve on all individual assets and talents would be a worthwhile goal. Setting goals early in life could start a young person on the path of accomplishment and worth. Understand that God has a purpose for everyone—the great adventure of life—to find your God-given purpose in life.

Addiction and Addicts:

Realize that God created you—your higher power—and provided you with all of the necessary abilities to live in this world. Realize that you are not only wasting your life on self-indulgence, but you are also not fulfilling the purpose of your life on earth by becoming more of a liability to your fellow man than an asset. Coming to know what a unique and wonderfully made person you are and how valuable you are in God's sight should be an encouragement to throw off the shackles of addiction and become the person you truly are and were meant to be.

Terrorists and Suicide Bombers:

If God created every soul and placed that soul in a body for a purpose known to Him, why should you take it upon yourself to thwart God's plan and wishes by killing any person? To do so sets you against God and guarantees the destruction of your own soul—no matter what kind of manmade excuse you can offer.

Mankind:

What is my purpose in life? Why am I on earth? How does an insignificant life become meaningful? Understanding or even having a glimpse of God's purpose for mankind can provide a sense of well-being with self and life. One's individual purpose may become known in one fell swoop or over a long period of time. Stopping a runaway horse from hitting or killing a future prime minister or working as a dedicated and caring nurse over many years - both have an impact. Knowing that while serving mankind you are also serving God can place your life and existence on earth on a very special level. Right now, most people don't have any idea what their purpose in life is.

World:

God's first place for Adam and Eve was the Garden of Eden. Heaven on earth? A place of abundance, beauty, and peace. A place we would all like to have. Beauty, peace, tranquility—no cares or wants. Heaven?

The diversity of man, his differences brought about over time, geography, language, custom, beliefs, commerce, and history have brought us to where we are now. As a people, we would like to remove all war, poverty, and misunderstandings. We would seek world peace, global understanding, and the ability to come together for the purpose of the common good. This means removal of greed, selfishness, self-aggrandizement, and coveting from world affairs. At Christmas, we hear that the challenge in life and the ultimate goal is to find peace on earth and good will to all men. We would all like our world to be a Garden of Eden.

You:

In the final analysis, everything that happens to you affects you in a special way. You become either the person you were supposed to be or something else. When your life is over, your soul lives on. Your soul embodies everything you have become and this you will find is where you really determine whether you reside in heaven or not. Simply put, your life on earth and the choices you make in life determine the ultimate destiny of your soul. It is your choice every step of the way. Your soul's future is in your hands—here and now!

Questions We Often Raise

God wants everyone to find the answers for themselves while they live on earth. I hope that His word (the Bible) and messages will help provide the answers we all seek. Questions that each of us asks include the following:

- Does the mind age?
- Is there life after death?
- What is my purpose on earth?
- Why was man born?
- Why does man exist?
- Who is God?
- Do you know God or do you know about God?
- Do we know why God created the universe, man, and everything around us?
- Why did God select certain people as his chosen people?
- Why does the Bible exist?
- What is the soul?
- What is the spirit?
- What is the Holy Spirit?
- Why do other religions exist?
- What is the significance of man's existence on earth?
- What is death?
- What is eternity? Will we—and can we—know it?

The purpose of this book is to convey to all mankind a message from God clearly outlining His purpose for mankind while stressing the necessity of men coming to understand who they really are and the importance of recognizing their own soul and that the soul will exist for eternity. Many of the questions are answered within *A Message for the Soul of Man*. Certainly many of the questions are explored through the sermons developed around specific topics.

God is assuming that each person, knowing who they are and understanding God's dual purpose, will respond by dedicating their lives to the service of mankind while seeking the salvation of their own soul through achieving a closer relationship with God with the help that has been provided by God's servants throughout the years, along with his messages provided through the prophets and His Word.

Background to the Book

The concept of this book has come about over a long period of time—approximately eighteen years.

It started with a revelation that bothered me from day one. I didn't believe one could have a revelation. The story of this book is really my education over many years—the emphasis being on God leading me through the path of understanding that He also wants others to come to realize. As such, I don't feel so much an author has I do a teacher of God's message for man. A great deal of the book includes excerpts of writings, sermons, and devotions that seem to bring one to a clear conclusion. They also mirror the progression I have made in coming to the point of writing this book. This includes matters that have occurred in my secular life, which have worked to advance what I think is God's plan for me, including my health at my advanced age.

With a humble sense of God's will and love, I write the thoughts and images that God has given me over the years. The primary purpose is to create a better understanding of God's plan and purpose for the life of every soul on earth—now and until the end of time.

The Future

God wants man to have stewardship of this world, bringing about peace, harmony, belief in God, and working through our earthly trials and tribulations to develop and create strong believers and commitments to do God's will with our God-given talents .

May God bless this endeavor and uplift the soul of the reader and grant each a glorious and wonderful awakening!

PART 3

Importance of the Soul of Man and the Soul's Journey

The Sermons and More

A Message for the Soul of Man has never before been fully revealed in a sermon, devotional, or Bible Study. Only a few people have been made aware of the total message. The message is too long and complex to discuss in any format other than in an extended Bible study, seminar, or book.

Do Something with the Message—Don't Disobey God

God gave me *A Message for the Soul of Man* with an expectation that I would do something with it. Strangely, through the intervening years after receiving the "Message," I could never forget it. It was with me during every waking moment—no matter how busy I was. In fact, there were many times, through a word or a sermon, I was reminded that when God asks us to do something, he does not like being disobeyed. The Old Testament teaches us about disobeying God.

Even while I was researching the Bible and becoming more involved in the church, I knew that I would have to do something with God's word: his message to me. I knew that each part of the message required special emphasis in order for all parts to be fully understood. For instance, if you didn't believe in God, how could you understand the concept of creation and what it means?

Sermons

The opportunity to talk about the message came about through my involvement in the church. I could present the odd Sunday service and sermon to the church congregation. This did not occur too often, but often enough that it allowed me to put together sermons that related to the message such as the soul, man, the Bible and God's love and presence in our lives.

As a result, over the years, I presented more than twenty sermons to the congregation. I was able to provide a fair amount of detail that I hoped would expand everyone's understanding of the message I had received back in 1992. Everyone (at least in my church) knew that when I spoke, it would invariably touch on the soul of man.

Sermons—A Medium for Teaching

With each sermon, I have been preparing those who listened to ultimately receive the full content of "The Message for the Soul of Man." I took pieces of the message and made them the subject of sermons on the odd Sunday I preached. The sermons, usually about twenty minutes in length, were used to focus on one portion of *A Message for the Soul of Man* with emphasis being placed on support from the Bible—both Old and New Testaments. The sermons can be treated as chapters since they are self-contained and short. Please note that all sermons were preached before the *A Message for the Soul of Man* was released in this book.

Listeners (and now readers) are asked to open their minds to concepts that they may not be familiar with or would normally disregard as not fitting within their concept of what the Bible speaks about. With each sermon, I found myself teaching about a topic important to the full understanding and appreciation of what I thought God's message was saying.

The Message Calls on Us to Reexamine Who We Are

While *A Message for the Soul of Man* seems simplistic, it is not. First of all, we have to accept the reality of our soul and secondly, acknowledge a God who is all-powerful and all knowing—the Creator of everything—and what that means.

Second, we have to accept God's presence and that of angels in order to deal with our God-given bodies, our free will, our power of choice, our responsibility, our limited lifespan, and our purpose in life as part of the overall development of mankind through the ages. In other words, we must accept that God exists!

Finally, we must accept that the soul exists forever and is subject to judgment—much of it based upon our thoughts, deeds, and activities as a soul guiding our body. The salvation of each soul determines the eternal future of each soul. That is the bottom line and the purpose of the whole message is for you to come to know it!

The Sermons are Important

As you learn about your gifts, talents, likes, and dislikes that God has placed in your soul, you will learn about God's love for you and that you are never alone. The sermons are an important part of the overall message as they try to impart an understanding of each segment of the message, which, ideally, you will accept.

I trust that the presentation of the sermons, devotionals, and Bible study material here will be informative and entertaining as you come to the section relating to the revelation of your purpose on earth as part of God's overall plan for mankind.

God's Hand in It

I know God's hand was in all of this as I was prompted to keep copies of my sermons. Many of my sermons have been reproduced in this book as a way of giving deeper meaning to the main topics within the message.

As mentioned earlier, I must remind non-Christian readers that the material in this book, along with the sermons, is very clearly pro-Christian since I am a Christian talking to a Christian congregation. God's message, like the word of God in the Old Testament, was generated for the people of that world regardless of their ancestry and spiritual leanings. In a similar manner, *A Message for the Soul of Man* focuses on who you are now—much as it would have been if you were born in the distant past before Christ or Mohammed. The universal message is not only directed at Christians, but at all mankind.

These sermons are not necessarily placed in chronological order, but most often relate to specific subject matter, expanding on different aspects of the message in an attempt to create a better understanding of each part.

In all cases, the purpose of each sermon is to teach about the soul, God, man, and God's purpose in bringing about the existence of mankind.

Why now? Why me? Preparing Me for the Rest of the Message

Over time, through all of my research and reflection, God planted or directed me to consider other facets of the message that I had not really considered. Why did God want his message released now? Why me?

Life Experiences

I think I began to realize that my whole life had been directed by God. I was brought to a place in my existence that embodied my whole life—spiritual and worldly education, work experience, marriage and children, and all of the problems and strife of life. I had received firsthand experience with tragedy and death, illness, disease, alcohol and drug abuse, financial stress, and the struggles of relationships with family and the outside world. In that respect, I know that I am not unique.

I remember in my younger days going to a movie theater and looking at the mass of heads sitting in front of me and thinking, *Who in this theater doesn't have a painful problem at this moment in their life?* I suspected none.

We Are All a Work in Progress

At any given time in our lives, we are all a work in progress. I used to think that I had control of my life, but I learned how quickly that can be turned around. It is hard to believe that God is always present in our lives and he does guide us. Just read your Bible.

God Has a Purpose for Each of Us

God has a purpose for each of us. Interestingly, most people who are asked what their purpose in life is can't tell you!

It came to me over several months that God had another message for me, which I was to gather from the many thoughts that had found their way into my mind. This more recent message or revelation spoke to God's purpose with respect to all mankind.

An Additional Message Revealed Later

You will find that additional message revealed in the sermons later in the book along with some interesting observations for you to consider from Bible Study material and preparation.

Just knowing who you are—your soul—was only the first part of *A Message for the Soul of Man.* God wanted you to know why you are here and to live your life accordingly as part of His overall plan for mankind.

My instincts tell me that we, as a people, are to prepare for wonderful and marvelous manifestations of God's power in the future.

The Sermons Play a Special Role

In the sermons, you will find that in addition to exploring the subject material, the opportunity is taken to draw heavily from Bible scripture to authenticate the information conveyed within the sermon. The actual message does not do this. We are told that without the support of God's word in the Bible, any message conveyed outside of the Bible may not be considered true. You can see, therefore, that the sermons play a special role in conveying the truth of the words and thoughts contained in *A Message for the Soul of Man.*

A Reminder about the Sermons

Please keep in mind that every sermon was preached with a particular focus on a part of the original message received, but was never revealed to the congregation in its entirety. I felt that it was necessary for my listeners to understand the importance of each component of the message. For instance, if one did not agree that God exists, then it is going to be difficult for them to believe about God's creation of their soul and more. Each sermon is an attempt to sway each person to accept the point and message of each sermon. Judge for yourself as you tie each sermon to the pertinent part of *A Message for the Soul of Man.*

Sermon Title: **The Soul - Sermon 1** Sermon given on July 26, 1996
This Sermon is the first sermon I gave after I had researched biblical
sources for the support of the "Message." The sermon introduces
the congregation to an explanation of what the **soul** is, as set forth
in the **"Message for the Soul of Man."** The analogy of a marble
is used.

THE SOUL – Sermon 1

Today, I would like to talk to you for a few moments about the "soul"
and touch on a little bit of my own personal spiritual journey. I've
chosen a rather heavy topic for my message today but one that has been
burning to get out for some time.

Dave's style of sermons has been to provide messages aimed at
teaching the practical side of living a Christian life, based on the
teachings found in the Bible.

In the old days, the preachers used to scare people, stressing that
they were sinners and their souls were damned forever unless they
were saved. To-day's church messages are based on teaching about
God's great love and mercy and how we can lead good Christian lives,
accepting Jesus as our Lord and Savior.

The two scenarios follow very closely the thrust of the Old and
New Testaments - The Old Testament stated God's laws and recorded
the harsh punishment for not obeying God's laws. The New Testament
teaches of God's great love and through belief in God, acceptance of

Jesus Christ, as Savior, and confessing our sins, we (our souls) will be saved!

As a young lad, I was raised in the Catholic faith and went through all of the ritualistic steps that assured me I was a Christian and that I was going to heaven. Mind you, there was always purgatory and if I really was a terrible sinner - there was hell. Quite frankly, it is so long ago now, I cannot remember how my soul was referred to other than I knew it was my soul that was going to go to heaven, hell or purgatory. My body was remaining behind as dust.

Being of an inquiring mind, the question, as I continued in life was two-fold - what was the purpose of life and where is my soul? How do I know it exists? Has anyone here had the same thoughts? Why are we on this earth? Who or what is the soul?

For the first - what is the purpose of life, I read many of the works of the philosophers - some were adamant that man was it - the end-all and be-all. Many people have that belief today. Much of my own life was spent trying to prove that man is in complete control of his own material destiny and if he does good and not bad, he will not have much to worry about spiritually.

Look at the quote from Matthew 16:26, 27 - are we here to amass a fortune or, for us boys, to have the most toys? Do you know that saying - "he who dies with the most toys - wins?"

The second question, who, what, where is the soul? - Everyone agrees that the soul exists and is a part of the human being and continues to exist when the body dies. The dictionary states that some religions believe this to be true.

The Doctrines of the Salvation Army found under Articles 7, 10 & 11 state the position of The Salvation Army on the subject of the soul and salvation.

Article 7: "We believe repentance toward God, faith in Our Lord Jesus Christ and regeneration by the Holy Spirit are necessary for salvation."

Article 10: "We believe that it is the privilege of all believers to be "wholly sanctified", and that their "whole spirit and soul and body" may be preserved blameless unto the coming of our Lord Jesus Christ". (1 Thess. 5:23)

Article **11:** "We believe in the immortality of the soul; the resurrection of the body; in the general judgment at the end of the world; in the eternal happiness of the righteous; and in the endless punishment of the wicked."

The important fact is the whole emphasis in the Bible and the ministry of Jesus Christ is to save souls!

In my studies, I found an interesting fact. The old King James version of the Bible, written in 1611 + has 498 references to the soul. The new King James Version (revised 1881 & 1946) has 341 references whereas in the New International version (1978) of the Bible there are only 136 references to the soul and, of these, only 23 references are in the New Testament. (See Table of Bible Mentions of the Soul)

Table of Bible Mentions of the 'Soul' - Updated		
Number of times the word "soul" is mentioned.		
Bible Name	In the Total Bible	In the New Testament
New International Version	136	23
New American Standard	289	44
The Message	163	32
Amplified Bible	190	79
New Living Translation	73	29
King James Version	498	55
English Standard Version	269	43
Contemporary English Version	26	12
New King James Version	341	52
New Century Version	35	25
21st Century King James Version	501	56

American Standard Version	495	54
Young's Literal Translation	520	61
Darby Translation	536	58
New International Readers Version	41	20
Today's New International Version	96	23

Source: Internet - BibleGateway.com

Our own Salvation Army hymn book has 281 references to the soul. This could be explained by the fact that much of the words for the hymns were written in the mid and late 1800's before the full influences of the changes to the Bibles took hold.

My question is - why was there such a change in emphasis. As an example, I looked at Genesis 2.7 "-- the LORD God formed the man from the dust of the ground and breathed into his nostrils the breath of life, and the man became a living being. (NIV)" The KJV says <u>living soul</u>. In fact most of the references in later versions of the Bible were changed to a personal pronoun - us, you, they, and we. The result, I think, is to blur what is meant when we talk about the soul.

I believe, we as human beings, tend to view ourselves as total identities which is all-inclusive - body and soul together as a person. It is hard to divorce the soul from "me" or "us" when we are personally, vibrantly alive and active.

But it is important for us to focus on the soul as the message of "salvation" deals with each and every soul - that, which is left after death. Let's look at salvation for a moment through some quotes from the Bible.

"- to give his people the knowledge of salvation through the forgiveness of their sins." Luke 1:77

"For the wages of sin is death; but the gift of God is eternal life through Jesus Christ our Lord." Romans 6:23

"That if you confess with your mouth, "Jesus is Lord," and believe in your heart that God raised him from the dead, you will be saved. For it is with your heart that you believe and are justified, and it is with your mouth thatyou confess and are saved." **Romans 10:9-10**

"Just as man is destined to die once, and after that to face judgment, so Christ was sacrificed once to take away the sins of many people; and he will appear a second time, not to bear sin, but to bring salvation to those who are waiting for him." **Hebrews 9:27-28**

"The hour has come for you to wake up from your slumber, because our salvation is nearer now than when we first believed". **Romans 13:11**

"Though you have not seen Him, you love Him; and even though you do not see Him now, you believe in Him and are filled with an inexpressible and glorious joy, for you are receiving the goal of your faith, **the salvation of your** souls." **1 Peter 1:8-9**

All those quotes are from the New Testament of the NIV Bible and do not mention the soul until the last quote.

The Christian faith is based on the salvation of the soul or stated another way – the promise of eternal life (in heaven) for all those who believe in God, confess their sins and acknowledge Jesus Christ as their Lord and Savior. Upon making this commitment, we (or our soul) is filled with the Holy Spirit or as some say "re-born" and we become a part of the family of God.

When we talk about salvation, we are talking about saving the soul - my soul·· your soul - the souls of everyone in the world. As a matter of fact - think about that for a moment - there are 5.5 billion people alive in the world today and expanding. Each person has a soul! I wonder how many souls have lived on earth up to this time. How many billions? How many more will there be before the last days?

So the focus of salvation is the soul. Let's talk about the soul for a moment. What are the attributes of the soul - how is the soul described in

Scripture? Think of these attributes as a moment by moment description of any soul as it journey's through life. Maybe you have felt one of more of these examples.

Here are some examples from the old KJV - the soul lives; longs for; sins; knows anguish and affliction; the souls lusts; seeks; desires; knows bereavement, sorrow, bitterness, adversity; the soul is troubled, weary; mourns; hates; loves; knows deceit and violence, hunger and thirst; the soul can be redeemed, comforted and filled with goodness and wisdom; it knows right and wrong and can weep, feel empty, wearied and burdened and the soul knows tribulation and anguish for doing evil or sinning.

From our Hymn book, more attributes of the soul - the soul can be wayward, wounded, fainting, stray, oppressed, fearful, thirsty, sin bound, distressed, struggling, stained with sin, trembling, full of woe, guilty, ailing, weary, lost, haunted, grief-stricken, sin-sick, unclean, and the soul can die! The soul is aware, looks, hears, feels, trusts, doubts, sings, can be satisfied, desires, yearns --   and the soul has a special quality - it is the temple of the Lord in which the Holy Spirit can reside. The soul can be cleansed and healed, filled with tremendous love, perfect peace, swelling hope and flooding joy and know a sense of rapture, a freedom and liberty from sin.

In other words much of the attributes we give to the soul can easily be identified with the heart (feeling) and the mind (knowing). It could be said, then, that the evidence of the presence of the soul IS the existence of a heart and mind. We can consciously feel or know all those attributes I just mentioned

Question - do you know your own soul? Do you know the state of your soul?
Each one of us is on a personal journey - a journey of life on earth and a spiritual journey which, according to the Bible, will result in the eternal life or death of our souls. Each of us has choices to make on this journey - the result of those choices determines where we - individually - as a soul - will stand on judgment day.

I think you agree that God is the Creator of all things - including man and his soul. Can we also agree that because He created us, He loves us as His own - much like the love of a parent? - - - But, like a parent, He wants our love.

One of the reasons why the whole subject of the soul has so captivated me is my conviction that if more people knew and understood what the soul is, there might be less inclination to abuse our bodies and commit sin. Stated another way, armed with information about God's great love and plan for us (our souls), we might be better equipped to fight the temptations the devil continually places in our path particularly the temptations our young people experience in today's society.

So what is God's plan for us and how can we know our own soul?

If you believe in God and the authenticity of the Bible as God's word then God's plan for us (or each soul) is very straightforward. It is found in the teachings of Jesus.

Jesus said: "Love the Lord your God with all your heart and with all your soul and with all your mind.' This is the first and greatest commandment. And the second is like it: 'Love your neighbor as yourself." **Matthew 22:37-39**(NIV)

Too simple? Think about it - **your primary purpose in life** is to love God, yourself and love each other! If you truly love God, yourself and each other 'what room is there for the devil to work his temptations? **If you have a true and deep love, you will do everything in your power to protect and nourish the object of your love - <u>God</u> - <u>your soul</u> - and the <u>souls of others</u>.**

Today you received a stone, pebble, or marble - whatever you want to call it. When I was picking these up, I dropped a couple and was promptly told that I had lost my marbles. Thinking about today, they may have been right.

Hold the marble in your hand - squeeze it - examine it - you will find that all the marbles given out have a similarity but are not the same.

Each marble individually *has* its own characteristics - shape, feel, color, clarity. Isn't that a little like your soul? No soul - no person is exactly the same - each is unique - each was created by God and - each is loved by God.

We are now in the information age, the nuclear age, the age of the atom, the age of miniaturization, some might say the age of enlightenment - man is reaching new heights in technology and knowledge every day.

You are aware of the impact of computers, their speed and capacity to work with large amounts of data. You are also aware that it is possible to put *your* entire personal medical, statistical, financial data on a small computer chip embedded in a plastic card the size of a credit card.

You are aware that computers are capable of recording and storing everything you input.

Would you be surprised, then, if I told you that the little marble or pebble that you hold cannot be destroyed and will stay with you and record your every thought and deed - good or bad; your emotions - love or hate, like or dislike, your memory, knowledge, talent - everything you think, feel and do - good and bad. This little marble will continually assess your spiritual state and determine whether you are good or evil throughout your whole life? At the point your body dies, whenever that might be, the marble will be left as the complete and unalterable record of your whole life on earth. **Your soul, everyone's soul, is like that little marble I described- the difference is, you cannot feel it or see it!**

If man can create the computer chip I mentioned earlier, what do you think an all-powerful God is capable of? Is it possible your soul is exactly like the pebble - only God-made rather than man-made?

Of course, your soul is not a pebble or a marble - it is very special· your soul is you. Isn't that the 'why' for the revisions in the Bibles - you, me, we, and they - are all souls - in a living body?

In my own personal journey, I believe that God is in my heart (and soul) and in a world full of troubles, dangers and temptations; I must work hard at continuing to know, love and serve Him. I believe that is why I stand here now.

If the example of the marbles helps you understand your soul or helps someone, who doesn't know God, understand their relationship with God and His love for them, then this Message has done its job. God's will be done.

If your soul is stained with sin, downtrodden and heavy, - if your soul is burdened with pain and sorrow, you can know the joy of salvation or the joy of renewal that fills to overflowing your soul - just ask Jesus to come into your heart and ask the Holy Spirit to in-fill your soul. God's everlasting love and peace await those souls who will turn to God, confess their sins and acknowledge Jesus Christ as Lord and Savior.

If you have made that commitment today, fill in the blue card, pass it to me, and someone will contact you shortly to help you with your spiritual journey.

Please keep the marble as a reminder of this Message - maybe explain it to someone you love and you feel needs to know about their soul.

"May God Himself: the God of peace, sanctify you through and through. May your whole spirit, soul and body be kept blameless at the coming of our Lord Jesus Christ." **1 Thessalonians 5:23** (NIV)

Sermon Title: **The Soul - Sermon 2** Sermon given: October 6, 1996
The second Sermon about the soul goes into more detail as to how
the **soul**, spirit and life-force come together in the person of **man**.

THE SOUL - Sermon 2

On Sunday, July 28th, 1996, I had the privilege of bringing the Message
to you and the topic, for those who were not present at that time, was
the "Soul". For those who were present, bear with me while I once again
use the example of the marble to explain the concept of the soul before
going on.

Those who do not already have a marble, I hope you have one
now - it will help you understand what I will be telling you in a few
moments.

Two interesting observations about my last talk about the soul - one
was a question - "what is the spirit?" and the second was an observation.
This person felt that a person's conscience was, in fact, a window on their
soul. Today, I will talk about the spirit but I will leave the interpretation
of the 'conscience' to you.

In talking about the soul earlier, I pointed out the attributes of
the soul listed in both the King James Version of the Bible and The
Salvation Army Hymn book found in the pews. Some of you may have
taken the time to look up some of those references. I concluded that all
the attributes listed could be placed under characteristics quite often
given to the heart and the mind. What you feel and what you think is

70

thought to be qualities of the heart and mind but is really attributes of the soul. The actual heart, as you know, is a pump within our chest. The mind is a reference to our consciousness and we place it in the vicinity of the "brain" which is the "processor" of all the body's functions - many of which are automatic.

In another reference to the soul, it is described almost like a vessel that can be cleansed and be the dwelling place of the Holy Spirit just as your body is the dwelling place of your soul until death.

Some of you may ask - "why this tremendous emphasis on the soul?" The answer is very simple - it is the reason why God sent His only Son to live and die on earth - to bring salvation to mankind.

Jesus' life and death on earth served three purposes. The **first** was to demonstrate God's great love for each and every soul; the **second** was to atone for the sins of man with one great sacrifice and the **third** was to demonstrate, through deed and the word (teachings of Jesus), how man would find individual salvation for his soul.

God has only one agenda - His wish is that all souls (mankind) will come to know Him, love Him and serve Him. It is demonstrated clearly in the position given the first of the Ten Commandments.

From Exodus 20 - **And God spoke all these words: "I am the LORD your God"**, who brought you out of Egypt, out of the land of slavery. **"You shall have no other gods before me."** "You shall not make for yourself an idol in the form of anything in heaven above or on the earth beneath or in the waters below. You shall not bow down to them or worship them; for I, the LORD your God, am a jealous God, punishing the children for the sin of the fathers to the third and fourth generation of those who hate me, but showing love to a thousand generations of those who love me and keep my commandments." **"You shall not misuse the name of the LORD your God, for the LORD will not hold anyone guiltless who misuses his name."** "Remember the Sabbath day by keeping it holy." "Six days you shall labor and do all your work, but the seventh day is a Sabbath to the LORD your God. On it you shall not do any work, neither you, nor your son or daughter, nor your manservant or maidservant, nor your animals, nor the alien within your gates. For in six days the LORD made the heavens and the earth, the sea, and all that is in them, but he rested on the seventh day. Therefore the LORD blessed the Sabbath day and made it holy."

Question for you? If everyone was a committed Christian, would anyone work on the Sabbath?

Let us return to the soul. **It is important for you to know who or what is your soul.** Your soul is the object of your salvation as you leave your body behind after death. Let us then describe for you your soul using the marble as our example.

Hold the marble in your hand - squeeze it - examine it - you will find that all the marbles given out have a similarity but are not the same. Each marble individually has its own characteristics - shape, feel, color, clarity. Isn't that a little like your soul? No soul - no person is exactly the same - each is unique - each was created by God and - each is loved by God.

We are now in the information age, the nuclear age, the age of the atom. The age of miniaturization, some might say the age of enlightenment - man is reaching new heights in technology and knowledge every day.

You are aware of the impact of computers, their speed and capacity to work with large amounts of data. You are also aware that it is possible to put *your* entire personal medical, statistical, financial data on a small computer chip embedded in a plastic card the size of a credit card.

You are aware that computers are capable of recording and storing everything you input through the keyboard, voice or even the monitor through touch.

Would you then be surprised, then, if I told you that the little marble or pebble that you hold cannot be destroyed and will stay with you and record, like a computer, your every thought and deed - good or bad; your emotions - love or hate, like or dislike, your memory, knowledge, talent - everything you think, feel and do good and bad. This little marble will continually assess your spiritual state and determine whether you are good or evil throughout your whole life?

At the point your body dies, whenever that might be, the marble will be left as the complete and unalterable record of your whole life on earth. **Your soul, everyone's soul, is like that little marble I described - the difference is, you cannot feel it or see it!**

But now let us go further. The next statement is crucial. If you believe in God, you must also believe that He is all-knowing, all-powerful, always present - everywhere. Your soul was created by God just like He created the heavens, the earth, sun and moon. He created animals and humans, everything we see and He created much that we do not see. For instance, He created angels. He created mountains and He created atoms and molecules - all things large and small. He created fire, electricity, water and all manner of gases. Water is interesting - in school you learned, like I did, that water is created from two gases - oxygen and hydrogen - 1 part to 2 parts which is what the formula H2O means. That's a marvel in itself! Two elements that you cannot see, come together to make an element you not only can see, but touch, smell and even drink.

Does everyone know what is meant by energy? Energy is power or a force. Most objects have energy. Some of it is latent or stored energy, some is active like steam, fire or electricity.

Energy, to the economist, is a synonym for fuel; to the scientist, it is one of the fundamental modes of existence, equivalent to and inter-convertible with matter.

Now we are into how marvelous a creation man is.

A while ago, I asked Dr. Betty Robinson how does the body create heat and how does it maintain that heat at a constant temperature. The answer is the level of heat is controlled by sensors feeding the brain but the actual heat itself is created by the constant vibration of **every cell** in your body. Heat generated by movement - that is one form of energy.

If a person has a brain scan, electrical energy in the brain is detected and measured. The method of sending signals or data to the brain from sensors from any part of the body is by a combination of **both chemical and electrical impulses** between nerve cells.

To really blow your mind, think of this, and I have been present when it was proved - your body can store upwards of a million volts of static electricity without damage - now that is amazing. If God can create such wonderful mechanisms as the universe and the body, should anyone be surprised by any of the marvels of His creations?

Now let's talk about the soul. The soul is a creation of God, therefore, it is perfect. The soul is an invisible, energized entity that has the ability to think and store knowledge on every possible plane - emotional, mental, and physical. The soul is God-like in that it is capable of conceptualizing, rationalizing, reasoning, remembering, conceiving, extrapolating, - in other words - the soul is probably the most beautiful of God's creations beside the angels.

There are two schools of thought as to when each soul was created. Some believe souls are created at the time of human conception. Others believe that souls have existed since before creation and were created at the same time as the angels. I subscribe to the latter. There are also theories on what happens to the soul after the body dies while waiting for the final judgment.

I won't touch on these two areas today as I would like to keep your focus on the soul itself. A minute ago I described the soul as an invisible, energized entity that has the ability to think and store knowledge. The soul, therefore, can acquire information and knowledge on a continuing basis. It has the ability to work with that knowledge (or process it) and determines a course of thinking and/or action.

This, folks, is the most important point of all. **The soul can choose!** It has the power of choice! By virtue of the choices it makes, the character of the soul takes on the qualities that can be defined as good or bad - holy or evil. This can be shown as arrogance or humbleness, hateful or lovable, dishonest or honest. The soul (you) have the freedom of choice at all times - in any and all situations.

You will remember that some of the angels, led by Lucifer or the Devil, rebelled against God and were thrown out of the Kingdom of God. This very event tells us that the angels, too, had the power to choose. Lucifer wanted more than the exalted position he already had.

Does that not raise the question -"**Why did God create angels and souls?**" This goes to the heart of understanding God. God is God Almighty with power no person can truly visualize or understand. No one can possibly come close to understanding God's capacity for love and the wondrous joy of being loved by God. There is nothing on earth that can come close.

God created angels and souls so that He could share with each, His great love.

The condition placed on that love is acknowledgment of God as the loving creator. To know is to love, and to love is to serve. Knowing, loving and serving God was His condition. He gave both angels and souls the ability to choose freely so that each of their own free will would give their love to God.

On earth we have an expression to prove the existence of true love. It goes something like this "If you love someone, set them free. If it be true love they will return to thee." Isn't this what God did for you and for me? And then He sent His Son, Jesus Christ, to help us learn this great lesson of love!

Now let us turn to the spirit.

"... and the dust returns to the ground it came from, and the spirit returns to God who gave it." Ecclesiastes 12:7 (NIV)

A simple little quotation from God's word and it is absolutely accurate.

In that quotation it would be easy to say that the spirit referred to is the soul - it is not! The spirit referred to is, also, not the Holy Spirit.

We are, in fact, dealing with three separate things here. Unfortunately, both secular and biblical dictionaries do not help much.

So the question, **"what is the spirit?"** arising out of my last message, is very appropriate.

Often, the terms - spirit and soul, spirit and Holy Spirit become substituted one for the other, especially by those who have no knowledge of the Bible, which makes it difficult for them to comprehend what is meant in any particular passage.

Usage of the words spirit and soul, outside of the Bible, sometimes is not explicit enough in meaning - even in some dictionaries and encyclopedias.

Let us look at a couple of passages from Scripture that clearly separate spirit, soul and body.

1 Thessalonians 5:23 "May God himself, the God of peace, sanctify you through and through. May your whole spirit, soul and body be kept blameless at the coming of our Lord Jesus Christ."

Hebrews 4:12 "For the word of God is living and active. Sharper than any double-edged sword, it penetrates even to dividing soul and spirit, joints and marrow; it judges the thoughts and attitudes of the heart".

Luke 23:45 Jesus called out with a loud voice, "Father, into your hands I commit my spirit." When he had said this, he breathed his last.

In the first two there is a clear indication that the spirit, soul and body are three distinct entities.

The soul is not the spirit - although most think of it as spirit-like - i.e. present but invisible.

Spirit vs. Holy Spirit. Many times within the Bible the word spirit is used but the "s" is not capitalized. As a first indication of meaning, it would be reasonable to assume that when the "s" in the word Spirit is capitalized it mean that the reference is to the Holy Spirit or Holy Ghost which is the third member of the Trinity of God.

Should we assume that all references to the spirit are really references to the Holy Spirit or the manifestation of the Holy Spirit? I don't think so. The Holy Spirit becomes indwelling, in our soul, when we believe in God, accept Jesus Christ, His Son, as our Lord and Savior and repent of our sins.

A study of the role of the Holy Spirit in Scripture, in both the Old and New Testament will show that the Holy Spirit plays a special role in providing knowledge, conviction, understanding and direction to those with whom God has a relationship.

In the third biblical quote, Jesus is quoted as saying that His spirit is committed into the hands of God at which point His body expired. **Jesus, as the Son of God, and part of the Holy Trinity IS both God and the Holy Spirit** - none of which He would give up. Therefore, the spirit referred to in His words is something else.

When God created Adam (and all men) He breathed into his nostrils. Thus, man is alive because of God's spirit (breath) - the spirit in this case being the very life-force that inhabits man - that includes ALL MEN and WOMEN! Man can have this spirit - he must have it in order to live - but until man accepts the word of God acknowledges his sins and accepts Jesus as Savior - only then does the Holy Spirit enter into a man's soul. At that point, all three exist - soul, spirit and Holy Spirit.

Let me make very clear that the life-force or 'spirit' in each and every person, regardless of belief, sinner or saint, newly born or old, is the life-force that keeps their body alive - it is our mortal body's power source. By no stretch of the imagination does this make each individual God-like or a part of God as some New Age thinkers would have us believe. We may be created in His image but we are not God - we are God's creation! The source of all human life comes from God. **Do you wonder that God knows our every thought and deed?**

Here is the picture then. The new human is conceived by a man and a woman and at the moment of conception ... the joining of the sperm and egg - God's Life force is invoked, like turning on a light bulb. As the embryo develops the soul enters the body and is connected by the developing brain (much like a receiver is hooked up) to the body and the total nerve and sensory system.

Upon birth, the soul strives to assimilate every bit of information that comes to it through the brain - pushing back, on a daily basis, the shroud of the unknown. The baby's senses respond to the warmth of the love it is wrapped in, the cooing voices, the bright lights and bright colors that greet its eyes.

Can you remember your youth when you were continually discovering something new about life? Can you remember the first time you realized that big cities existed where millions of people dwelled or that milk came from cows and not cartons?

Was your soul present at creation? "Behold, I create new heavens and a new earth: and the former shall not be remembered, nor come into mind". **Isaiah 65: 17**

As the baby turns into an adult, it will have become aware of its total world. Remember your teens, when you thought you knew it all just to find out that you didn't. We go through life like that - ever learning through knowledge acquisition and experience - throwing back the veil of darkness to reveal more and more about ourselves and God's universe.

Eventually, we grow old and die. At that point, the mortal body turns to dust, God's life-force is returned to Him and our immortal soul is now faced with judgment. If the Holy Spirit has been with us, the journey is a certain one - our soul ascends into the Kingdom of God.

Using the marble analogy, if you are holding the marble in your hand (the hand is your body) - take your hand away and all that is left is the marble (our immortal soul) - remember - you cannot destroy your soul!

"For what hope has the godless when he is cut off, when God takes his life?"

This quote from Job 27:8lays it on the line. Take a look at your marble - if that is your soul and it no longer resides in your body, you can no longer do or say those things that will have an impact on your soul. This is the moment of truth - what happens to your soul now, you no longer have any control over. **Your soul is now in God's hands! If you have the Holy Spirit you have nothing to fear!**

I hope that the message conveyed today, along with the marble, will help you focus your heart and mind on the importance of your soul and your relationship with God.

I urge you to pick up your Bible and read - study God's word daily - determine for yourselve the truth of what I have told you. Ask the Holy Spirit to help you understand, ask Jesus to come into your soul and make you pure - ask God to forgive you your sins and accept you (your soul) into the Kingdom of Heaven.

Let us pray fervently together the prayer that Jesus told us to pray.
"Our Father, who art in heaven, hallowed be Thy Name,
Thy Kingdom come, Thy Will be done, on earth as it is in heaven.
Give us this day our daily bread and forgive us our debts as we
also have forgiven our debtors, and
lead us not into temptation but deliver us from evil,
for Thine is the Kingdom, the Power and the Glory,
forever and ever," Amen

If you want to know more about your spiritual journey, fill out the blue request form found in the pews and pass it to me after the service. We want to help you to have that special relationship with Jesus and God, the Father that so many souls crave for but cannot find.

1 Thessalonians 5:23 "May God himself, the God of peace, sanctify you through and through. May your whole spirit, soul and body be kept blameless at the coming of our Lord Jesus Christ."

May God bless and keep you and yours, as His, till the end of your days! Go in peace. Amen.

Sermon Title: **What is Life?** Sermon given on August 3, 1997
Having placed the different elements of man together, the nature
of **'life'** is discussed with special emphasis on life's components
especially the power of individual choice in life.

What is Life?
(The Soul's Journey)

Today is the first day of the rest of your mortal life!

What is life? There is no definition to be found in dictionaries or
encyclopedias that adequately explains what life is! You know what life
is as you are a living example of what life is? Now try to describe it.

In the past, I have described the soul, the life-giving Spirit and the
Holy Spirit. The soul is a like a huge memory bank. It holds all your
past and present thoughts, memories of all your words, deeds, hopes,
feelings, dreams and much more. Your soul becomes the sum total
of who you are based on all life experiences. At any given moment,
your soul is either good or bad. If death of the body occurs, the soul
is separated from the body which, then, can no longer be used to
determine the soul's life experiences. Those who have their marbles will
recall that the soul is indestructible or immortal. Life for your soul can
be described as eternal regardless of where it will spend eternity. So...
your soul comes into the world - and it is your soul that leaves it! Not
so your body - that is temporary.

"When you leave your body to go on to eternity - you take nothing
of this earth – so what is important?" Dwight D. Eisenhower

Life Components

Today I want to focus on certain aspects of mortal life that you may or may not think of. You will live your life or a good part of it before some of the things I'm going to tell you now start to be important.

The First component of life is Control: We all have the sense that we somehow manage our own destiny. To some extent it is true. We certainly play a major role. But, think of this!

Did you personally have control of when, where or how you were born or even who your parents were to be?

Do you have control of when, where or how you will die?

Do you have control over what diseases or natural disasters you will be subject to? Or what will happen as a result?

Do you have control over how people will interact with you?

Do you have control over the total course of your mortal life?

The Second component of life is Gifts: All of us have certain qualities - some we seem to be born with - others we seem to have the ability to acquire. Do you think of the special talents that you personally have? Are you musically inclined? Have a great intellect? Can carve exquisite objects? Were you born healthy without any deformity?

Do you have a brain that works - controls all your body functions and allows you to use your tongue, hands, eyes, hearing for the betterment of your earthly well-being?

What about the gifts that God gave you to maintain life - Air, water, food – the animals and plants of the world. The world is a giant environment designed for the well-being of mankind. Your body is a marvel of engineering.

What about the gift of emotion and feelings? What would life be like without being able to feel anything about it? Love, even hate, joy, sorrow, hurt, healing, a sense of fulfillment for a deed well done, failure and so much more. Are these not gifts?

Many of God's gifts we have without ever acknowledging them. We take a lot for granted.

The Third component of life is Time! A couple of poems are of interest.

When as a child I laughed and wept,
Time crept.
I was a youth I waxed more bold,
Time strolled.
When I became a full-grown man,
Time ran.
When older still I daily grew,
Time flew.
Soon I shall find, *in* passing on,
Time gone.
O Christ! Wilt Thou have saved me then?
Amen.   Author - Henry Twells

Just a tiny little minute
only sixty seconds in it
Forced upon me. Can't refuse it.
Didn't seek it, didn't choose it,
I must suffer if I lose it,
Give account if I abuse it.
Just a tiny little minute,
But eternity in it.   Author Unknown

"Everything requires time. It is the only true universal condition. All work takes place in time and uses up time. Yet most people take for granted this unique, irreplaceable and necessary resource. Nothing else, perhaps distinguishes effective executives as much as their tender care of time." Peter Drucker. "There is a time for everything ..."- good reading - **Ecclesiastes 3:1-15**

The fourth component of life is Sin: Everyone is prone to sin. Sin in mankind is as old as the Bible. When we sin we separate ourselves from God. It is the perennial battle of life. Sometimes we find ourselves tempting fate with the attitude that we can control our sinning - that we will not get 'caught' in the consequences of sinning. The Bible says "For the wages of sin is death, but the gift of God is eternal life in Christ Jesus our Lord." **Romans 6:23**. Death or eternal life is of the soul. The story of an eagle can possibly illustrate this point. An eagle was perched on a block of ice just above Niagara Falls. The swift current carried the ice and the majestic passenger closer to the edge of the great precipice.

The cries of the other birds and animals warning the eagle of danger that lay ahead were to no avail. "I have great and powerful wings," he boasted. "I can fly from my perch at any time. I can handle it." Suddenly the edge of the falls was only a few feet away. The torrent of water rushed the block of ice over the great falls.

The eagle spread his powerful wings to mount up over the impending doom only to discover too late that his claws had become frozen to the cake of ice."

None of us are immune to the consequences of sin.

A little wisdom from the past -
"One leak will sink a boat and one sin will destroy a sinner" John Bunyan 1684
(A little arrogance helps make the slope a lot slippier - author)

Did you know that you cannot sin without affecting someone? So what you do and say has an effect on others and can come back to complicate your soul's spiritual journey on earth in many unpredictable ways.

Reviewing:

Our mortal life is made up of situations and conditions that we can and cannot **control**; blessed with **gifts** that we can use or abuse; provided with **time** (a lifetime) we can fritter away or use wisely and, finally, we must contend with the temptation of **sin** throughout our whole life!
God's all-knowing Gift - The Power of the Soul to Choose:

Add to the mix of life's components, the one item that determines the final outcome for our soul. In His great wisdom, God gave each soul the power to choose – **the power of choice over our earthly destiny, use of our gifts, use of time and the temptations of sin and, in so doing, the choice of our ultimate spiritual destiny.**

In a dictatorship, your whole existence is determined for you by the central authority. If it all goes wrong, you blame the leaders. In a democracy, the people collectively choose their leaders, laws, freedoms and more. If things go wrong in a democracy, the people must accept responsibility and correct the problem. The first system does not allow choice. The second is based on the power of choice. Each soul has that power to handle the choices they make in life. Like the democracy, each soul must accept the responsibility for the wrongs committed.

As in a democracy, you choose your own destiny, the destiny of your soul, through the exercise of personal choice here on earth!

You can choose what college you will attend, you can choose your career, you can choose the person you marry and raise a family. You can choose to waste your time in meaningless activity and indulge in self-gratification in drink, drugs and other sinful pleasures. "There is a certain charm about the forbidden that makes it unspeakably desirable." Mark Twain

Unfortunately, the combination of the choices you make and the things that occur in your life over which you have no control often brings about a state of uncertainty and even chaos. Do you ever wonder whether you made the right decision or choice? Are you uncertain about the future?

So what is life? Life is the journey your soul has been given, using human form, to determine its eternal destiny.

The Age of Uncertainty:

Have you ever been lost? I mean really lost - not knowing where to turn! Are you a lost soul? Are you lost right now?

Are you happy? Are you content? Have you been searching for something in your life? If you have, could you describe exactly what you have been searching for?

Have you suffered pains and hurts, known disappointment, discouragement and even grief? Have you experienced utter, lonely, hopelessness while enjoying family and friends, a good job and even wealth?

Do you feel that your life has been for nothing? ... That your life has no worth?

Do you feel like a little bit of flotsam on the great sea of life - adrift, rudderless, tossed and turned or are you the captain of your ship and you have full control of your destiny?

A poem by Theodore W. Brennan might describe what happens to so many of us.

I looked upon a farm one day,
    That once I used to own;
The barn had fallen to the ground,
    The fields were overgrown.

The house in which my children grew,
    Where we had lived for years
I turned to see it broken down,
    And brushed aside the tears.

I looked upon my soul one day,
    To find it too had grown
With thorns and nettles everywhere,
    The seeds neglect had sown.
    The years had passed while I had cared
    For things of lesser worth;
The things of Heaven I let go
    When minding things of earth.

To Christ I turned with bitter tears,
    And cried, "0 Lord, forgive!
I haven't much time left for Thee,
    Not many years to live."

The wasted years forever gone,
   The days I can't recall;
If I could live those days again,
   I'd make Him Lord of all.

God's purpose for our soul is very simple. He wants us to know, love and serve Him with our whole heart and soul and strength - but, He wants it to be our choice. He has given us our journey on earth to sort it all out. Will we make Him Lord of all or wait until it's too late?

Jesus is calling us to be with Him:

Jesus is calling each one of us. Sometimes, I think he uses a 2x4 to get our attention, like it was for me. God uses the Bible and His ministers on earth to help lead you and guide you in His direction. Look again at the Bible passage read earlier - **John 14:1-17**.

His message is simple, direct and comforting if you make the choice...

Do not be troubled.
Trust in God - Trust in Jesus;
Know that a place in Heaven is being prepared for you (your soul);
Jesus is the Way - to Heaven, to the Father
Follow Jesus - do what He did - Love Him and obey His commands

- - - and you will receive the Spirit of Truth - the Holy Spirit who will be with you and IN you forever!

God loves each and every one of you. Will you put your trust in God?
Will you heed that soft and gentle call from Jesus, will you put your trust in Jesus,
Will you place all your cares at His feet?

If you feel that tugging at your heart, if you want help with life's burdens, if you want the strength of the Holy Spirit to enter and sustain you, just ask - just ask Jesus to come into your heart.

Scripture for the Sermon "What is Life?"
John 14:1-17

"Do not let your hearts be troubled. Trust in God; trust also in me. In my Father's house are many rooms; if it were not so, I would have told you. I am going there to prepare a place for you. And if I go and prepare a place for you, I will come back and take you to be with me that you also may be where I am.

You know the way to the place where I am going." Thomas said to him, "Lord, we don't know where you are going, so how can we know the way?" Jesus answered, "I am the way and the truth and the life. No one comes to the Father except through me. If you really knew me, you would know my Father as well. From now on, you do know him and have seen him."

Philip said, "Lord, show us the Father and that will be enough for us." Jesus answered: "Don't you know me, Philip, even after I have been among you such a long time? Anyone who has seen me has seen the Father. How can you say, 'Show us the Father'? Don't you believe that I am in the Father, and that the Father is in me? The words I say to you are not just my own. Rather, it is the Father, living in me, who is doing his work.

Believe me when I say that I am in the Father and the Father is in me; or at least believe on the evidence of the miracles themselves. I tell you the truth, anyone who has faith in me will do what I have been doing. He will do even greater things than these, because I am going to the Father. And I will do whatever you ask in my name, so that the Son may bring glory to the Father.

You may ask me for anything in my name, and I will do it. "If you love me, you will obey what I command. And I will ask the Father, and he will give you another Counselor to be with you forever -- the Spirit of truth. The world cannot accept him, because it neither sees him nor knows him. But you know him, for he lives with you and will be in you. (NIV)

Will you heed His call?

ADDITIONAL READING FOR "WHAT IS LIFE?"
About SIN: See Bible verses **Matthew 5:29-30; Numbers 32:23; Psalm 51:1-6; Proverbs 6:16-19; Ezekiel 18:4-32; Romans 6:23**
About TIME: See **Ecclesiastes 3:1-17**
About LIFE/DESTINY: See **Ecclesiastes 9:1-6; Job 14:1-2**

<u>**QUOTES OF INTEREST**</u>
BIRTH
Our birth is but a sleep and
   a forgetting;
The soul that rise with us,
   our life's star,
Hath had elsewhere its
   setting,
And cometh from afar,
Not in entire forgetfulness,
But trailing clouds of glory
   do we come
From God, who is our home.
   William Wordsworth

CHOICE
I shall be telling this with a sigh
Somewhere ages and ages hence:
Two roads diverged in a wood, And I –
I took the one less traveled by,
And that has made all the difference.
Robert Frost

Read God's Word (The Bible) daily if you would know how to live on earth and be assured of eternal life for your soul!

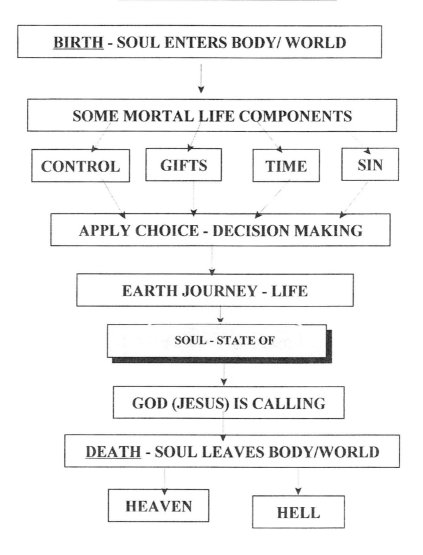

WHAT IS LIFE?

BIRTH - SOUL ENTERS BODY/ WORLD

SOME MORTAL LIFE COMPONENTS

CONTROL | GIFTS | TIME | SIN

APPLY CHOICE - DECISION MAKING

EARTH JOURNEY - LIFE

SOUL - STATE OF

GOD (JESUS) IS CALLING

DEATH - SOUL LEAVES BODY/WORLD

HEAVEN | HELL

PART 4

Relationship between God, Man, and Soul

Introduction

The sermons that follow in this section were designed and delivered to help each listener realize that they have a soul within them that is subject to judgment after leaving the body.

It seemed to me that knowing God, knowing who He is, and how powerful He is was important in order to understand that God is an all-powerful influence in how we live our lives.

A Message for the Soul of Man comes from God and by its very nature places before you concepts that you need to accept. The more you learn about God, the better you will understand God's reason for all of creation—including you.

Just realizing who God is should be very important to each of us. Without realizing God's presence and His place in our soul's existence, we would not understand the message that God has for each soul—and why.

May you be blessed by the reading of the sermons that follow and talk about the relationship between God, man, and the soul.

Salvation – Then and Now

In today's message, I would like to cover about 6,000 years of time;
touch on a few happenings in time; make a few observations and end up
with a perspective on the future. All in the interest of explaining to you
what salvation is all about - both in the past, now and in the future.

There are two parts to the message I have for you about Salvation.
The first is that the total Bible was written for the singular purpose of
bringing about each soul's salvation and secondly, as part of the first,
God's developing plan for mankind is revealed in His Word and is
evident as one comes to know and understand God.

This is The Salvation Army and those among us who are soldiers
are committed Salvationists - we are people who believe in Christ's
redeeming power to save souls from sinful ways and by following Him
be assured of life everlasting with God in heaven. The Mission Statement
of The Salvation Army is found in the back of the Hymn Book, where
it speaks of redemption.

William Booth, the founder of the 'Army' said in his book "In
Darkest England, and the Way Out" , "To get a man soundly saved it
is not enough to put on him a pair of new breeches, to give him regular
work, or even give him a University education. These things are all

outside a man, and if the inside remains unchanged you have wasted your labor. You must in some way or other graft upon the man's nature a new nature, which has in it the element of the Divine."

When you think about that - that is a real challenge! William Booth wrote that in 1890 - 100 years ago.

So **what is salvation?** - The World Book Dictionary definition of salvation is
(1) The act of saving or state of being saved: preservation from destruction, ruin, loss or calamity; (2) a person or thing that saves; (3) the act of saving the soul; deliverance from sin and from punishment for sin.

The definition of salvation can be temporal or physical or it can have a spiritual application. In the Vine Dictionary of Biblical Words, one meaning of Salvation in the New Testament is "spiritual and eternal deliverance granted immediately by God to those who accept His conditions of repentance and faith in the Lord Jesus Christ, in whom alone, it is to be obtained. (Acts 4:12), and upon confession of Him as Lord, (**Romans 10:10**); for this purpose the gospel is the saving instrument (**Romans 1:16; Ephesians 1:13**).

The Salvation Army Doctrine #6: We believe that the Lord Jesus Christ has by His suffering and death made atonement for the whole world so that whosoever will may be saved.

The Salvation Army Doctrine #7: We believe repentance towards God, faith in our Lord Jesus Christ, and regeneration by the Holy Spirit, are necessary for salvation.

The Doctrines, based on the Bible, describe what we, as Christians, understand "salvation" to be. **Note - the whole topic of "salvation", in the New Testament, is based on the birth of Jesus Christ and His atonement for our sins.**
What, then, does "salvation" mean in the Old Testament - before Christ? Salvation is mentioned 119 times in the KJV Bible. (78 times in the NIV)

Let us take a look at history for a moment and see what has been meant by salvation over many years.

In my research on this subject I came across an interesting fact. In the Old Testament the number of years of history contained in the Book of Genesis is 2,369 years. The rest of the Old Testament covered only 1,238 years for a total of 3,607 years (almost 4000 years). Another interesting fact is that Adam & Eve were created about 4004 BC, Abraham was called by God to be the leader of His chosen people about 2,000 BC and of course, Jesus Christ was born 2000 years ago. It sort of begs the question - what's next? What happens in or around the year 2000AD?

As I stated earlier, Adam & Eve were created about 4004BC. It isn't until 2446BC that God commands Noah to build an ark. The actual Flood occurred in 2348BC and the inhabitants of the Ark disembarked the following year. In this case, the salvation of Noah and his family and the animals came as a result of Noah building the Ark at God's command. The salvation was physical or temporal. God was known to the descendants of Adam & Eve but their sinning caused God to destroy them with the flood.

About 2000BC, Abraham was born and ultimately God called on him to take all his possessions from the land of Ur and go to a new land that God would give to him and all his descendants. Abraham obeyed God's call and, after many years, did enter the Promised Land. Abraham knew God. One could assume that while other people in the region worshiped idols, there were some who continued to be aware of the presence of an unseen God.

God's presence was felt by Abraham's family and his descendants - Isaac, Jacob & Esau, and Joseph. But there came a time when famine in the land forced the people to go to Egypt where they settled for almost 150 years.

During that time the Jewish people prospered and grew in numbers. So much so that Pharaoh became concerned and finally enslaved the Jews in hard bondage.

Moses then appeared on the scene to lead the Jewish nation out of Egypt. - To deliver them from under the yoke of slavery. Crossing the Red Sea through parted waters demonstrated God's power and they were 'Saved"! Thus their salvation from bondage took place through God's power. You can see how easy it is to make the transition from bondage in Egypt to bondage in sin. This salvation was physical but as we learn later, it turned into a spiritual salvation as well.

God's plan was to make the Jews a holy nation - His people would follow His laws and live their lives as He directed. God started with the 10 commandments and demonstrated his presence daily with manna from heaven. God scolded His people for wrongdoing and punished them for disobedience. This relationship was to continue for many years.

God educated the Jewish nation to become a nation devoted to God and His commands. This is called a theocracy. Theocracy is probably the oldest form of government in which power and authority are seen as derived directly from God, and rulers are considered either incarnations or representatives of divine power.

In ancient times theocracy was widespread, ranging from the Egyptians to the Inca empires, Persia to China and Japan. During the Middle Ages in Europe the pope claimed ultimate authority in governing based on his religious authority, and later kings used the "divine right of kings" to justify their absolutist rule.

Early Puritan colonies in New England like Massachusetts Bay and New Haven had leaders who claimed to derive their authority from God. While today secular and religious authority is for the most part separated in the Western democracies, their fusion in such political units as the Iranian Islamic Republic is still strong.

Through the time of the conquest of Canaan, through to the setting up of the Kingdom of Israel, God, through his leaders - prophets and judges taught the Jewish people - mostly through trial and error - that sinning against God has serious consequences and honoring and worshiping God provided redemption for sins. The underlying sense of the people was that the ultimate states was complete trust in and love of God in return for a peaceful and prosperous kingdom of God on earth. Salvation was being redeemed from sinful ways in order to be with God in a wonderful earthly kingdom. Many, many times the Jewish people suffered defeat at the hands of their enemies because they had sinned. Many, many times - right up to the last recorded writings of the old Testament, the Jewish people were given new opportunities to serve God - from defeats, bondage and destruction they were saved or allowed to start over again. This was the salvation of the Jewish people in that age. Again it was a physical salvation brought about by God's intervention.

How could anyone doubt the supremacy of God?

David's Prayer in Psalm 35 is typical of the relationship to personal salvation from the dangers presented by the enemy.
"Contend, O LORD, with those who contend with me;
Fight against those who fight against me.
Take up shield and buckler; arise and come to my aid.
Brandish spear and javelin against those who pursue me.
Say to my soul, "I am your salvation.""

The sinning never stopped and finally, we enter the dark years preceding the birth of Jesus Christ. From 500-600BC on, the Jewish people were hearing about a Messiah who would come from the house of David and would create a new kingdom. The salvation of the Jewish nation was in the hands of a savior to be born in the future. The Messiah would be a God/King/Leader who would conquer all and restore the Jewish nation to the glory of the Kingdom of Saul, David & Solomon.

That was the hope of Salvation of the different communities of Jews throughout the Middle Eastern world at the time Israel was dominated in turn by Babylon, Persia, Egypt, Syria and finally Rome.

Then we come to the birth of Jesus Christ - entering a world full of domination (by Rome), sin, uncertainty - the Jews sought a savior - someone who would take them out of their worldly woes and make them supreme again. They sought salvation of an earthly/god-like quality.

But this was not to be - in fact by 70AD the Jews were literally run out of Jerusalem not to return until the state of Israel was created in 1948 - almost 2000 years later.

In summary, the term "salvation" for the people of the Old Testament has predominantly been physical, brought about by God. In the later years, the salvation sought after has been for a kingdom of God on earth. There is the belief that this earthly kingdom is still to come.

So we know what salvation is in the Old Testament. We all know the story of Jesus and his atonement for our sins by dying on the cross -- He became the sacrificial lamb of atonement to God for all mankind. So I think we all understand what "salvation" means in the New Testament.

I wonder how many can empathize with the plight of Clarence?

Little Clarence climbing a tree began to fall swiftly toward the ground....

O Lord! He said: - Save me! Save me!

Never mind, Lord, my pants got caught on a branch!

In the New Testament, God clearly established that His message is directed at the soul of man.

Can you see God's plan? In the Old Testament He taught man how they should live and He established the awareness of His awesome power in the sight of man.

He demonstrated His fury at disobedience and sin while supporting those who demonstrated to Him, in turn, their adoration of their God. They turned to Him in time of need as the only source of salvation from the ills and evils of life.

Ultimately, the Jews looked for a savior to redeem them to a wonderful place in God's Kingdom on earth where all their enemies would no longer threaten them and they would know peace and prosperity. We can identify with that.

The stage was set for God's next lesson. The lesson was three-fold - God showed His great love for each of us by the sacrifice of His Son on the cross; the second was to emphasis that the Kingdom of God was attainable for all souls who cared to make a decision ... and third, He told each of us that we need to love God with our whole heart and soul and strength and love our neighbor as ourselves.

Romans 10:9-10 "That if you confess with your mouth, "Jesus is Lord," and believe in your heart that God raised him from the dead, you will be saved. 10 For it is with your heart that you believe and are justified, and it is with your mouth that you confess and are saved. "(NIV)

Hebrews 9:27-28 "Just as man is destined to die once, and after that to face judgment, 28 so Christ was sacrificed once to take away the sins of many people; and he will appear a second time, not to bear sin, but to bring salvation to those who are waiting for him. "(NIV)

1 John 1:9 "If we confess our sins, he is faithful and just and will forgive us our sins and purify us from all unrighteousness." (NIV)

It has often been pointed out that if everyone followed that simple rule of loving our neighbor - life on earth could be very pleasant. Unfortunately, we have a tendency to sin and the devil, relentlessly, places temptations in front of each of us every day.

With the message of salvation so clear, why isn't everyone a Christian? Why has church attendance dropped so low despite the majority of people believing in God?

A MacLean poll a few years ago indicated that 90-95% believe in God. The recent poll done by The Ottawa Citizen found that 75% said religion and spirituality are important to them; only 25% said they attend church. Why?

The reason, I believe, for such low attendance in church is the lack of proper focus. For the last 500 - 600 years there has been a splintering of the original religious hold on people held by the Catholic Church. We now have a multiplicity of churches - a true smorgasbord of religious entities. The last splintering occurred just recently when a whole church congregation split with the established church to support a gay minister - they've started a new church - and they are not gays! This kind of situation along with the taints of church leaders through financial and sexual misdeeds helps create a lack of confidence in churches as a whole. That is why the majority of people can believe in God and not attend church.

We need our ministers, pastors and priests as the truly dedicated ones help us with our spiritual growth - and it doesn't occur overnight. Even when we experience that special moment when we ask Jesus to come into our heart, we need the help of our pastor and fellow Christians to uplift us and support us in a new life.

So what is God's plan for the next 1000 years? As we speak more and more information is being placed in men's hands. So much so, that our ability to create new products is accelerating at a fantastic rate. The products we create, with the help of the computer, have so many components that have to work together; we are getting close to emulating the very nature of creation itself. Think about God's creations all around you including yourself. It is just possible that man may think of himself as godlike, but, in truth, if He cares to look, man will understand the true power of God through understanding the process of creation itself. Keep in mind that the devil is not idle in all of this - he continues to work on our sinful nature and more situations are created where man can sin - VLT's for instance.

With such understanding and the intelligence that goes with it, man will come face to face with the question - why?

No man-made creation exists without a reason - whether it is the computer itself, a telephone, a car, a bridge, a space station, etc. In each there is a purpose.

What than is man's purpose - God's Creation? What is that vacuum in man that need's filling despite all of his achievements? Who is richer Mother Teresa in her lifetime or Bill Gates, owner of Microsoft?

Jesus said; "What good will it be for a man if he gains the whole world, yet forfeits his soul? Or what can a man give in exchange for his soul?" (**Matthew 16:26 NIV**)

Years ago, I was part of Queen's Park Government Think Tank studying the effects of computerization. At that time, we did not have a concept of how powerful computers would become. We certainly knew that, as a new tool for man, it would revolutionize labor and the economy and our whole lifestyle. What has amazed me is that much of what has happened in the last 5 - 10 years I thought would have occurred earlier. I certainly did not anticipate the magnitude of change that is being wrought. The bottom-line of this issue was that the acceleration of knowledge would create a "have" and a "have-not" society which is actually taking place now.

There are those who have difficulty in living in this new society because of inability to learn, understand or even cope. There are those among the "haves" who have difficulty in living in this society because of the pressures of competition, the need to succeed, the responsibilities of power and decision-making and more.

So pressures come with the new information age and the new millennium that create challenges for us all. Where does one turn for peace? - Of mind and body and soul? - Regardless of whether you are among the "haves" or the "have-nots"?

God's plan is to have **each soul** come to **know** - (know God and His attributes and that fact that He made each soul and loves each of us with a passion you could not begin to understand)

To **love** Him - (when you know Him in the manner I have just described it will not be hard to love Him), and finally

To **serve** Him (a natural result of loving, easy in the desire but, difficult in the doing)! **Matthew 12:30** NIV

That is why William Booth said "You must graft upon the man's nature a new nature, which has in it the element of the Divine." God can do that but, man must be receptive - he must surrender all to God.

The relationship between God and each soul is a unique, personal relationship which supersedes everything else. All the things of this earth are there to serve the ultimate communion of God and soul.

Sermon Title: **Devotion on Music** Sermon given on January 17, 1999
This is a discussion on the value of music for the **soul**. It acknowledges
the talent of composing and playing of music as a **gift of God** to
the soul. Music is another form of worshiping God.

Devotion on Music
Layman's Sunday

This morning, we have come together, as a congregation, to praise the
Lord with prayer and music. What a great opportunity to join together
in a special way, in the house of the Lord, knowing that God, who loves
us all dearly, is with us at this very moment. I hope you can sense His
presence.

`Personal prayer is the individual acknowledgment that God exists
(else why pray?). It is the single most important act that a Christian can
perform as a believer and it creates a special bond between God and
each soul. Through this bond, God can enter your heart and soul - but
this bond must start with each of us, individually - we must be willing.
This is where music takes on great importance.

Music can act as a catalyst to set up that special communication
between ourselves and God.

God tells us, through His *word*, to "sing and make music in your
heart to the Lord" - taken from a phrase read this morning from
Ephesians 5: 19. "Speak to one another with psalms, hymns and spiritual
songs. Sing and make music in your heart to the Lord,"

What a wonderful way to communicate with our God. And it IS a very special and personal communication between God and each soul.

I came across a little poem by an Unknown Author printed in the June 6th 1998 issue of "The War Cry." It reads

> "How many of us ever stop to think
> Of music as a wondrous **magic link**
> With God; taking sometimes the place of prayer,
> When words have failed us 'neath the weight of care?
> Music, that knows no country, race or creed;
> But gives to each according to his need."

Indeed, it IS a wondrous magic link with God. Music is like a conduit between our soul and God - a way God communicates with us and a way we can, through our consciousness and emotions, experience a special relationship with Him.

Music is a powerful language that touches us all - sometimes as an expression of sorrow, of love, of hope and hopelessness - sometimes it is an expression of joy and happiness, of thanksgiving and adoration. And sometimes music can console us in our darkest hours of grief and despair. How many of us can attest to this power of music? Have you ever been moved to tears by music? I think we all have.

I believe that God reaches out and touches souls (ordinary people) and asks them to serve Him in special ways. Many of those He has inspired had no idea, at the time, that their particular work would be so powerful or have such an affect.

If they knew that they were to be the servant of the Lord and have an impact on many souls, they would have been overwhelmed. God does, indeed, work in mysterious ways. There are many examples of how God works in music and touches souls as a result. You may even know of a few, including yourselves. I know I have been.

As an example of how God works in just ordinary people to accomplish magnificent things, let me tell you about a Canadian, Irish-Immigrant who lived from 1819 to 1886. His name was Joseph Scriven.

He was born in Dublin and educated at Trinity College there. At age 25, he immigrated to Canada in 1844 and, for a while, taught school. Finally, he became a tutor to the Pengelly family who lived at Rice Lake near Port Hope, Ontario.

Joseph did not possess much and devoted a lot of his spare time to helping those who were handicapped or financially destitute. He was always helping someone in need.

Twice he experienced great personal tragedy. In England, his bride-to-be drowned the evening before their wedding. It was to get away from this painful experience that he came to Canada.

Then in Canada, a romance developed, but before he and Eliza Roche could be married, she died suddenly after a brief illness in 1855.

Scriven wrote his mother in Ireland of the tragic death of Eliza and sent the poem "What a Friend We Have in Jesus" written in the time of his own grief, yet meant to comfort her.

Turn in your Salvation Army hymn book to Song 645. Look at the words in the 1st verse –(*see box)* - what a powerful message - God is telling you how to deal with the difficulties of life. He is doing it through a very ordinary person who has suffered great loss.

Music can be traced back to man's earliest days - it has always been with us. What would life be like without music? Do you know that virtually every advertisement you see on TV and hear on radio includes music? I think you would agree that music is used as a means of "warming us up" to the message contained in the advertisement.

The ability to create and appreciate music is one of God's greatest gifts to mankind. It is one of the means that God gives us to acknowledge

Him – through praise and petition, in music, over above the spoken word, in prayer.

God works with the gift of music, within each soul, in two special ways.

First, He gives us the ability to relate to music - it can reach very deep into your individual being - you can experience joy and happiness, sorrow and melancholy - you can be uplifted and consoled by music both in a personal way and spiritually. This gift can help you find your spiritual path as you will see in a moment.

The second way God works within a soul is to provide the gift of creating music, playing music and inspiring the artist with words and vision. If you read about the great composers, you will find that much of their work was done quickly and very intensely - as if to stop they would lose the moment. Handel's Messiah, written in August 1741, took 24 days to complete. Handel's desire to compose was inspired by prose written by a friend about Christian redemption. I believe God inspired that total scenario. Handel's Messiah has become one of the greatest masterpieces of music of all time.

In fact, look at your hymn books. Look at the hymns and the words. The stories behind each hymn and how they came about are fascinating. You cannot help but feel God was working with each author and composer to help them bring a special spiritual message to each person who would hear and sing these hymns. Some of the messages are very profound and combined with music - are powerful.

Think, also, of those who have been given the gift or talent to play an instrument with beauty and eloquence. Think, too, of those who have a talent for singing and for poetry - so many of God's gifts are associated with music and when used to praise the Lord can be overpowering. For all of this, we should thank God for His blessings. We are particularly blessed in our congregation.

In the story of Joseph Scriven, no mention is made of his relationship with the Lord. There is no record of early religious training - on the contrary, he attended a military academy with the intention of following in his father's footsteps.

How does one account for such a beautiful message and music coming from this man?

Just listen to the words and music and you will know why it has become one of the world's most popular hymns - sung in many languages.

Feel the impact of the words and music and know that it was inspired by God!

What is the message here? It is simple - God wants you to pray. He wants you to take time to communicate with Him - both in prayer and music. He may call on you to serve him. Even though you might not feel worthy, will you answer that call?

Let this music be our prayer as a reminder for us - please join in singing verse two and three and then all of verse 1.

This devotion (sermon) was given with 4 pieces of background music.
1. Serenity (Giovanni Marradi) - 3:26 minutes
2. Reggy's Theme (Giovanni Marradi) - 3:23 minutes
3. Is it you? (Giovanni Marradi) - 3:11 minutes
4. What a Friend -- (Carman) - 3:02 minutes Total 13 minutes

Hymn
What a Friend We Have In Jesus

What a friend we have in Jesus,
All our sins and grief's to bear!
What a privilege to carry
Everything to God in prayer!
O what peace we often forfeit,
O what needless pain we bear,
All because we do not carry
Everything to God in prayer!

2   Have we trials and temptations?
Is there trouble anywhere?
We should never be discouraged:
Take it to the Lord in prayer.
Can we find a friend so faithful
Who will all our sorrows share?
Jesus knows our every weakness:
Take it to the Lord in prayer.

3   Are we weak and heavy laden,
Cumbered with a load of care?
Precious Savior, still our refuge:
Take it to the Lord in prayer.
Do thy friends despise, forsake thee?
Take it to the Lord in prayer;
In his arms he'll take and shield thee,
Thou wilt find a solace there.

Joseph Scriven (1819-86)

Sermon Title: **Time & Eternity**   Sermon given on July 25, 1999
This Sermon is about knowing **God**. What is time? What is eternity?
Destined for birth and death, soul's allotted time on earth then
heaven or hell!

Time and Eternity

Today, I would like to talk about God, Creation, Time, Immortality,
Eternity or Eternal Life. Each of the topics mentioned could take hours
to discuss - which we don't have. I'm going to cover a lot of ground in
a short time. Let's talk about God.

There is an ancient tale from India about a young man who was
seeking God. He went to a wise old sage for help. "How can I find
God?" he asked the old man. The old man took him to a nearby river.
Out they waded into the deep water. Soon the water was up just under
their chins. Suddenly the old man seized the young man by the neck
and pushed him under the water. He held the young man down until
the young man was flailing the water in desperation. Another minute
and he may well have drowned. Up out of the water the two of them
came. The young man was coughing water from his lungs and still
gasping for air. Reaching the bank he asked the man indignantly,
"What did that have to do with my finding God?" The old man asked
him quietly, while you were under the water what did you want more
than anything else?" The young man thought for a minute and then
answered, "I wanted air. I wanted air more than anything else?" The
old man replied, "When you want God as much as you wanted air, you
will find him..."

How many of us actively seek God? Do we really know God? If we do, is He a part of your life? As Christians, we believe in God, we know He is all powerful, all knowing, He is everywhere. Just think of God for a moment.

The Webster Dictionary describes God as "the Supreme Being, creator and master of all." God has a special attribute that is best described in this story of a mother and her son.

A mother was approached by her young son, who asked, "Mommy did God make Himself?" Realizing that such questions by children are very important and must be answered, she dropped what she was doing and sat down with her youngster for a little talk. Pointing to her wedding band, she said, "This is a 'love ring, which your daddy gave me when we were married. Look at it closely and tell me where it begins and where it ends."

The youngster examined it carefully arid then said, "There's no starting place and stopping place to a ring." The mother replied, '"That's the way it is with God.

He had no beginning and has no end, yet He encircles our lives with His presence. He is too wonderful - too great, for our minds to understand. Nobody ever made God. He always was!" Somehow the boy realized that for God to be God, He could not have been created. He had to be without beginning and without end.

God is the Alpha and Omega - the Beginning and the End. He existed before Creation and He created all from nothing! Revelation 21:6

God is the Creator of the Universe, the heavens and the earth. Let me remind you of the words from -
Genesis 1:1-5 "In the beginning God created the heavens and the earth. Now the earth was formless and empty, darkness was over the surface of the deep, and the Spirit of God was hovering over the waters. And God said, "Let there be light," and there was light. God saw that the light was good, and he separated the light from the darkness. God

called the light "day," and the darkness he called "night." And there was evening, and there was morning -- the first day." (NIV))

Keep this passage in mind as I am going refer to it two or three times....

God also created Adam & Eve and placed them in the Garden of Eden.

Eden, that's the Biblical name of a place in the Euphrates Valley, where, according to the Old Testament, God planted a garden which He made the habitat of Adam and Eve. When Adam and Eve disobeyed God's command and ate of the fruit of the tree of knowledge, they were banished from the Garden of Eden. The Hebrew word Eden means "delight." In post-Biblical literature, the Garden of Eden became identified with Paradise, in which the sons of the righteous abide in eternal life.

Question: How long did Adam & Eve live in the Garden of Eden? Did they know about the passing of the days - was it important to them? In other words, was the measurement of time important? I think the answer to the last question is no - time was not important. When Adam & Eve sinned and were banished from the Garden of Eden, they were condemned, as were all their descendants, to lives of toil and hardship - like us - **from dawn to dusk - every day!**

It is at this point in man's existence, that the measurement of time becomes very important - so much so that it was one of man's earliest concerns.

How do we describe time? What is time?

Dictionary definition: time n. 1, the relationship of any event to any other, as being before, simultaneous, or after; continuous duration. 2, the measurement of duration, as by a clock. 3, an epoch, era, period, season, etc. 4, an extent of duration, as an hour, day.

The sun provided man's earliest clock, the natural time interval being that between successive passages of the sun over the local meridian - the solar DAY. For many centuries the rotation of the earth provided a standard for time measurements. In everyday life, we can think of time in the way Newton did, ascribing **a single universal time - order to events.**

Whether for agricultural, legal, or religious purposes, the ability to measure time was of the utmost importance in ancient Egypt and Greece. Homer and Hesiod both suggest that men recognized some connection between the sun, stars, moon, earth, and time, but were unable to observe very effectively the cosmos for purposes of chronology.

Only with the advancement of astronomy, beginning with Thales in the early sixth century BC, could the Greeks begin to utilize the heavens for designing accurate calendars and sundials. Eventually, Plato, in his Timaeus, would declare,

"The sun, moon, and... planets were made for defining and preserving the numbers of time."

Now you can understand the significance of God's early act of Creation and the defining of a day and a night described in Genesis. It was all necessary for the measurement of time and the keeping of a record of historical events!

Casual observation over the course of one's life makes the cyclical nature of seasons self-explanatory. One need have no appreciation of the earth's orbit around the sun to discover that fall follows summer, preceded by spring, the successor of winter...

Knowledge of the advent or conclusion of seasons is critical to the success of civilization.

A farmer dependent exclusively on his own perceptions of season is at a grave disadvantage when he plants his crops. A premature warm front, for example, could cause him to plant too early. Conversely, belated warm temperatures might cause him to wait too long before planting, resulting in his crop's destruction by winter frost before harvest time.

Likewise, the success of civic calendars hinges on their ability to correlate with the solar reality. Accuracy demands that calendars be based on the earth's revolution around the sun. Compared to today's scientific method, calendars in ancient times were very flawed and needed many corrections over time.

The importance of time is addressed by Peter Drucker, relating it to the successful manager in business.

"Everything requires time. It is the only truly universal condition. All work takes place in time and uses time. Yet most people take for granted this unique, irreplaceable, and necessary resource. Nothing else, perhaps, distinguishes effective executives as much as their tender care of time."

Today we live in a fast paced world that is constantly changing at a breathtaking pace... We are reminded constantly about time - working hours, appointments, business luncheons, Sunday church services, birthdays, anniversaries, monthly mortgage payments, car payments and the list goes on and on.

Time is one of the many elements into which we emerge from the womb.
Each one of us is given an indefinite period of life time as a resource or a measurement.

According to life statistics, as a male, my life expectancy is 72 years. That translates into 26,280 days, or 630,720 hours or 37,843,200 seconds. I have 2,555 days left - God willing. Therefore, I have lived 90% of my allotted time.
And then, we die ----

Scripture tells us that man is destined to die - we all know it.

So, if you or I should die to-day, or tomorrow, where would we spend eternity?

Hebrews 9:27 "Just as man is destined to die once, and after that to face judgment,"

According to God's Word, you and I will spend eternity in one of two places, heaven or hell. -

Matthew 25:46 "Then they will go away to eternal punishment, but the righteous to eternal life." (NIV)

You have lived your whole life under the measurement of time - living second by second, day by day, year by year until you have a history, a present and a future (you hope). You have planned your existence around family, work, church and home - all related to time.

Time exists for each of us and we don't really realize its relationship to our world and our place in it.

There are many facets of our life on earth that we don't realize. For instance, do you know that you are on this planet earth which is traveling 66,000 miles an hour through space - it's the only way it covers its orbit around the sun to make our year.

Did you know that, if you are standing at the equator, you are spinning with the earth at a speed of 1,000 miles an hour? Can you sense the speed?

Do you know the source of the air you breathe?

We obtain our time by the movement of our earth, moon and sun - all set in motion by God - at Creation.

Can you imagine what 100 million light years is? Can you understand and fathom the total universe? Can you comprehend how you can have billions of individual cells at work in your body? Can eternity be measured in time?

How then, can <u>you</u> relate to eternity or eternal life?

There is a problem in the relationship between the terms 'time' and 'eternity'. The usual practice in discussing biblical topics is to use these terms as if everyone knew the precise meaning of each, when in fact no one seems able to define either, nor state the relationship in a way that is universally acceptable.

Still our common usage seems to imply that we do have some general ideas which arise from experience in respect to time, and regarding eternity but they are not well defined. Actually, we really don't spend a lot of time thinking about it, do we?

Awareness of time arises from a sequence of events. It is related to movement and change. If the whole universe stood still, time, or our perception of it, would cease!

It is possible that the biblical terms for time periods were not meant to extend beyond the ages covered by history and predictive prophecy, the writers describing events, processes, and purposes within these bounds. Eternity itself may not have been a topic or concept within the scope of their thinking.

Actually there is no scriptural example of eternity as such and no direct reference to the concept in the Bible but, there is reference to everlasting life.

Remember that time was set in place by God in the very beginning and time is related to the celestial bodies associated with our earth. Then, when we die and our souls are no longer of this earth - time ceases!

When we die, we (our souls) are no longer part of the world we now live on!

Our souls are now in God's realm or kingdom - **eternity!**

Eternity or Eternal "without beginning or end!" (Sound familiar?)

Eternity is described as perpetual, endless, everlasting, continual, ceaseless; timeless, **infinite,** unending; incessant, constant; immortal, imperishable, deathless.

I describe eternity as the place where measurable time does not exist or is absent.

Can you imagine eternity in your mind? Can you imagine existing where time is not present? Close your eyes for a moment and drift in space - maybe you can get a momentary sense of eternity?

There are a couple of indications from Scripture -

One is when the angel Gabriel announced to Mary that "You will be with child and give birth to a son, and you are to give him the name Jesus. He will be great and will be called the Son of the Most High. The Lord God will give him the throne of his father David, and he will reign over the house of Jacob forever; **his kingdom will never end**." **Luke 1:30-33** (NIV)

The other is from **1 Corinthians 15:50** "I declare to you, brothers, that flesh and blood cannot inherit the kingdom of God, nor does the perishable inherit the imperishable. "
This is another way of saying that mortals cannot enter the kingdom - only immortal souls.

We know that our soul's <u>eternal life</u> will be spent in heaven or hell!

Heaven - described as the abode of God; the place or state of existence of the blessed, after death; a state of bliss; supreme happiness or exaltation. Other terms include kingdom of heaven or God; eternal blessedness, eternity; Paradise, Eden, abode or isle of the blessed; celestial bliss, glory.

Both the Old & New Testament place God in Heaven. Jesus came from Heaven - sent the first time to die on the cross. His second coming (from heaven) will be in judgment of mankind.

In Matthew 6:19-20, Jesus, Himself provides advice for mankind and speaks of heaven.

"Do not store up for yourselves treasures on earth, where moth and rust destroy, and where thieves break in and steal. But store up for yourselves treasures in heaven, where moth and rust do not destroy, and where thieves do not break in and steal. For where your treasure is, there your heart will be also." (NIV)

Hell is described as the abode or state of the wicked after death. Other terms include Hades, place of torment; hellfire, everlasting fire, fire and brimstone; purgatory, limbo, abyss, bottomless pit; hell on earth.

Hell is the place of eternal punishment of unrepentant sinners condemned at the Last Judgment. The New Testament describes hell as a place of corruption and unquenchable fire and brimstone. Modern theology usually regards hell as ultimate separation from God, the confirmation of the sinner's own choice.

In summary, your soul does, has and will exist in two separate dimensions. In mortal life, your soul exists in the time frame established by God at Creation.

Man's soul, after the death of the body, is no longer subject to the measurement of earth time.

Outside of the mortal body, your soul exists in eternity. **This implies that the soul is immortal.**

IMMORTALITY is described as the life of the soul after death. This belief is found in both primitive and advanced cultures. It was important in Greek philosophy, notably that of PLATO. Immortality is a fundamental tenet of Christianity and of Islam and is generally accepted in Judaism.

The soul is immortal but, there is no proof of immortality!

The Bible does speak to us about immortality, the soul and eternal life.

Proverbs 12:28 "In the way of righteousness there is life; along that path is immortality." (NIV)

Matthew 10:28 "Do not be afraid of those who kill the body but cannot kill the soul. Rather, be afraid of the One who can destroy both soul and body in hell." (NIV)

Matthew 25:46 "Then they will go away to eternal punishment, but the righteous to eternal life." (NIV)

Romans 2:6-7 God "will give to each person according to what he has done." To those who by persistence in doing good seek glory, honor and immortality, he will give eternal life. (NIV)

If you agree that the soul is immortal and that eternity exists outside of this mortal and very important life, **what are you doing with the rest of your mortal life?** How much time remains in your mortal life?

Jesus came to earth so that you might be given the direction you need? God loves each and every soul! His greatest desire is that you (your soul) will spend eternity with Him in His Kingdom - Heaven - Paradise - and enjoy eternal happiness!

God has given you this **finite** time on earth to make your choice as to where you will spend eternity. God sent His only son to earth to atone for our sins and to help you open the door to heaven. **It must be your choice to do so!**

Right up to that last second of your mortal life - <u>you can choose</u> eternity in heaven or hell! The promise of everlasting life with God in heaven is found through Jesus - He tells us this.

John 3:16 "For God so loved the world that he gave his one and only Son, that whoever believes in him shall not perish but have eternal life." (NIV)

Listen to the words of Jesus -

"For I have come down from heaven not to do my will but to do the will of him who sent me. And this is the will of him who sent me, that I shall lose none of all that he has given me, but raise them up at the last day. For my Father's will is that everyone who looks to the Son and believes in him shall have eternal life, and I will raise him up at the last day." **John 6:38-40** (NIV)

"Do not let your hearts be troubled. Trust in God; trust also in me. In my Father's house are many rooms; if it were not so, I would have told you. I am going there to prepare a place for you. And if I go and prepare a place for you, I will come back and take you to be with me that you also may be where I am." **John 14:1-3** (NIV)

On one occasion an expert in the law stood up to test Jesus. "Teacher," he asked, "what must I do to inherit eternal life?" "What is written in the Law?" he replied. "How do you read it?" He answered: "'Love the Lord your God with all your heart and with all your soul and with all your strength and with all your mind'; and, 'Love your neighbor as yourself.'" **Luke 10:25-27** (NIV)

Jesus said to Martha, the brother of Lazarus, "I am the resurrection and the life. He who believes in me will live, even though he dies; and whoever lives and believes in me will never die. Do you believe this?" **John 11:25-26** (NIV)

You know about God; you know about mortal life and time; you know about eternity and the immortality of the soul; you know that your lifetime on earth is very short - and you know that you have the opportunity of enjoying everlasting happiness with God in Heaven. It is a decision you have to make while you have time!

Will you seek God; will you seek God like He is the very air you breathe? Will you seek the Kingdom of Heaven through Jesus Christ? You know that Jesus was sent to atone for the sins of man and to show each one of us how to enter the Kingdom of God. Jesus is the way to heaven and everlasting peace and happiness!

We need to spend some time with Jesus (God) - a time of quiet and solitude - as in the garden - just with Him - talking and listening - not only now but daily - just you and Jesus (God) -

In closing, Lets sing that song "I Come to the Garden Alone" *(see below)*

Prayer

Hymn - I Come To the Garden Alone

I come to the garden alone, while the dew is still on the roses, and the voice I hear, falling on my ear, The Son of God discloses.

He speaks, and the sound of his voice is so sweet the birds hush their singing, and the melody that he gave to me within my heart is ringing.

I'd stay in the garden with him though the night around me be falling, but he bids me go; through the voice of woe, His voice to me is calling.

Chorus

And he walks with me, and he talks with me, and he tells me I am his own; And the joy we share as we tarry there, none other has ever known.

Understanding

Before I begin, let me report on an "Interview with God", I found on
the Internet. I thought it was interesting.

Interview with God

Going to God's abode, I knocked on the door.

"Come in," God said, "So, you would like to interview Me?"

"If you have the time," I said. God smiled and said: "My time is
eternity and is enough to do everything. What questions do you have
in mind to ask me?"

"What surprises you most about mankind?"

God answered:
- "That they get bored of being children, are in a rush to grow
  up, and then long to be children again.
- That they lose their health to make money and then lose their
  money to restore their health.

- That by thinking anxiously about the future, they forget the present, such that they live neither for the present nor the future.
- That they live as if they will never die, and they die as if they had never lived..."

God's hands took mine and we were silent for awhile and then I asked ..."As a parent, what are some of life's lessons you want your children to learn?"

God replied with a smile:

- "To learn that they cannot make anyone love them. What they can do is to   let themselves be loved.
- To learn that what is most valuable is not what they have in their lives, but who they have in their lives.
- To learn that it is not good to compare themselves to others. All will be judged individually on their own merits, not as a group on a comparison basis!
- To learn that a rich person is not the one who has the most, but is one who   needs the least.
- To learn that it only takes a few seconds to open profound wounds in persons we love, and that it takes many years to heal them. To learn to forgive by practicing forgiveness.
- To learn that there are persons that love them dearly, but simply do not know how to express or show their feelings.
- To learn that money can buy everything but happiness.

- To learn that two people can look at the same thing and see it totally different.
- To learn that a true friend is someone who knows everything about them ... and likes them anyway.
- To learn that it is not always enough that they be forgiven by others, but that they have to forgive themselves."

I sat there for awhile enjoying the moment. I thanked Him for his time and for all that He has done for me and my family, and He replied,

"Anytime. I'm here 24 hours a day. All you have to do is ask for me, and I'll answer."

- People will forget what you said.
- People will forget what you did, but
- People will never forget how you made them feel

Do you understand the nature of your God and His great love for each and every soul? Do you understand what's happening to you and around you that provides means for the devil to re-direct your attention away from God and your relationship with Him?

Let's say a short prayer of adoration and to seek understanding.

Understanding

The word "understanding" is a noun meaning intelligence; mental apprehension and appreciation. You have this state when you 'understand'. The word "understand" is a verb (an action word) which means to grasp the meaning (of); comprehend, have full knowledge (of), be told (of), realize; believe.

Other ways of describing this state of understanding is to say you know, comprehend, grasp, catch, perceive, discern, construe, fathom, gather, assume, realize, and believe.

The burden - importance of man's soul

When God laid on me a very explicit task several years ago (1992) - to teach about the importance of man's soul and its destiny, I knew exactly what was described and even some of the impact. What I did not know then and still finding out was - why? Why this particular Message about the soul and why this appeal should be made on an intellectual level rather than rely on the Word contained in the Bible. The Bible is still the mainstay of God's word. What would we do without it?

The one understanding every person should be very clear on is - understanding what God wants - what His fervent wish is - to have each soul with Him in heaven.

That is the message of Jesus Christ recorded in the New Testament and that is still His message to-day. We find the knowledge of how to achieve His goal within the total Bible - if we care to look. God gave us the rules He wants us to live by regardless of the age in which we live.

To learn how important God's Laws are let's go back, for a couple of minutes, to Nehemiah's time about 2,500 years ago - about 500 B.C. This passage of Scripture - **Nehemiah 8:2-12** emphasizes the importance of understanding God's laws.

Nehemiah 8:2-12

"So on the first day of the seventh month Ezra the priest brought the Law before the assembly, which was made up of men and women and all who were able to understand. He read it aloud from daybreak till noon as he faced the square before the Water Gate in the presence of the men, women and others who could understand and all the people listened attentively to the Book of the Law.

Ezra the scribe stood on a high wooden platform built for the occasion. Beside him on his right stood (the elders) Mattithiah, Shema, Anaiah, Uriah, Hilkiah and Maaseiah; and on his left were Pedaiah, Mishael, Malkijah, Hashum, Hashbaddanah, Zechariah and Meshullam.

Ezra opened the book. All the people could see him because he was standing above them; and as he opened it, the people all stood up. Ezra praised the LORD, the great God; and all the people lifted their hands and responded, "Amen! Amen!" Then they bowed down and worshiped the LORD with their faces to the ground.   The Levites - (the priests) Jeshua, Bani, Sherebiah Jamin, Akkub, Shabbethai, Hodiah, Maaseiah, Kelita, Azariah, Jozabad, Hanan and Pelaiah - instructed the people in the Law while the people were standing there. They read from the Book of the Law of God, making it clear and giving the meaning so that the people could understand what was being read.

Then Nehemiah the governor, Ezra the priest and scribe, and the Levites who were instructing the people said to them all, "This day is sacred to the LORD your God. Do not mourn or weep." For all the people had been weeping as they listened to the words of the Law.

Nehemiah said, "Go and enjoy choice food and sweet drinks, and send some to those who have nothing prepared. This day is sacred to our Lord. Do not grieve, for the joy of the LORD is your strength."

The Levites calmed all the people, saying, "Be still, for this is a sacred day. Do not grieve."

Then all the people went away to eat and drink, to send portions of food and to celebrate with great joy, because they now understood the words that had been made known to them." (NIV)

The nature of man - made in God's image

The Bible tells us that man was made in God's image and would have domain over every living thing on earth. The history of mankind is the history of human evolution from ancient times to the present using man's greatest gift from God – his intelligence. Man has domain over much of this world and all its living creatures because of the tremendous accumulation of knowledge over the years.

Man's ability to create, to develop new things, to apply the continuing growth of knowledge to benefit mankind is phenomenal - almost God-like. There is a sense that man is in complete control of his present and future in a personal sense as well as a global perspective. The speed of change and the exhilarating advances in new technology are almost blinding in their brilliance.

Listen to this.

"Imagine machines so tiny they are imperceptible to the human eye. Microscopic circuits, sensors and pumps, they cost only a few pennies apiece because tens of thousands of them are fabricated at once. They can be tiled together to form vast, high-resolution video displays as thin as wallpaper. They can be implanted in the human body to analyze illnesses and dispense medicines as needed. They can be integrated into minuscule devices that can see, hear and even smell.

Science fiction? Not at all. Such technological feats may soon be commonplace thanks to the emerging science of micro-electro-mechanical systems (MEMS). Research into MEMS draws on many disciplines, including chemistry, physics, biology, material science and engineering. And it illustrates how basic and applied research can work together to produce benefits that multiply exponentially over time. In the case of MEMS, they may spark a micro-industrial revolution."

(Source - Article" Chasing the Future" - one of a series of articles by Microsoft on new technology)

"The Internet is changing our lives. Not only is it being used to access information and to share ideas, but people and businesses now use the Internet to research and purchase goods and services. E-commerce offers a new market to sell your products or services to local or distant markets, no matter what your business is.

(Source Alberta Agriculture, Food and Rural Development)

At some point in the not too distant future, we will rely on the computer and the Internet for virtually every transaction and communication in our lives. The paperless society is really not far away. I can't spend a lot of time on discussing the rapidly increasing amount of new technology that is constantly changing our future except to say this - the information explosion is and will impact every person's life to such a degree that we will have a hard time maintaining a grip on everyday life. (Reality)

What is important may become inundated with the sheer magnitude of the information around us and available to us 24 hours a day.

Let me give you an example of the sheer magnitude of information now available to you on the Internet. The numbers I am giving you relate only to sites of information and do not include the hundreds of off-shoots and pages of pictures and information that can accompany every site and sub-site.

You want to find out about a certain topic. You turn to the Internet through your computer or hand-held Internet phone. You type the subject title into what is called a "search" engine (and there are several). For this demonstration and for those who would like to know, I used a search engine called Web crawler

Here is what I found - **Epilepsy** has 2,310 sites to go to; **Diabetes** has 7,856; **Tornadoes** have 1,662; **love** - 123,107; **sex** - 49,536; **genes** has 5,969; **religion** has 41,763; **death** has 78,091; **heaven** - 23,643; **hell**-22,335; **angels** - 17,789; **Jesus** - 21,100; **the word "understanding"** - 73,772; **universe** - 25,027; **space** - 116,298; **Los Angeles** - 102,280; **Toronto** - 29,685; **Edmonton** - 6,722; **Grande Prairie** - 19,504

A total of over **3/4 million sites** with just these few topics and this was only one search program. Think of the thousands of other topics one could look up.

It does not take a genius to know that the sheer magnitude of the information at our fingertips is mind-boggling and at the same time - exciting. It is all fodder for the mind, our intelligence and our ability to use the new technologies for the betterment of mankind. What I am suggesting here is that it is very important to understand what the future holds for each one of us.

We must strive to understand what is happening to our world and lives brought about by the new age of technology and the swiftness of change and conditions of living. The value of intelligence and the natural desire to roll back every obstacle to learning is truly interesting and exciting!

But we must, also, realize that man is essentially the same as he was 2 - 3,000 years ago - he just has different tools.

The dangers of losing sight of God's wish for us (our souls).

With so much to occupy our minds and our energies, it can be very easy to be drawn into a state where we our caught up in the things of this world and forget that our souls will ultimately leave this worldly environment. God, in His wisdom, provided people with words of wisdom found in **Proverbs 2:1-22.** - compiled up to about 200 BC from the time of King Solomon.

Proverbs 2:1-22

"My son, if you accept my words and store up my commands within you,

2 turning your ear to wisdom and applying your heart to understanding,

3 and if you call out for insight and cry aloud for understanding,

4 and if you look for it as for silver and search for it as for hidden treasure,

5 then you will understand the fear of the LORD and find the knowledge of God.

6 For the LORD gives wisdom, and from his mouth come knowledge and understanding.

7 He holds victory in store for the upright; he is a shield to those, whose walk is blameless,

8 for he guards the course of the just and protects the way of his faithful ones.

9 Then you will understand what is right and just and fair -- every good path.

10 For wisdom will enter your heart, and knowledge will be pleasant to your soul.

11 Discretion will protect you, and understanding will guard you.

12 Wisdom will save you from the ways of wicked men, from men whose words are perverse,

13 who leave the straight paths to walk in dark ways,

14 who delight in doing wrong and rejoice in the perverseness of evil,

15 whose paths are crooked and who are devious in their ways.

16 It will save you also from the adulteress, from the wayward wife with her seductive words,

17 who has left the partner of her youth and ignored the covenant she made before God.

18 For her house leads down to death and her paths to the spirits of the dead.

19 None who go to her return or attain the paths of life.

20 Thus you will walk in the ways of good men and keep to the paths of the righteous.

21 For the upright will live in the land, and the blameless will remain in it;

22 but the wicked will be cut off from the land, and the unfaithful will be tom from it." (NIV)

We find another caution in the New Testament in **Ephesians 5: 15-20** which comes to us from about 60 AD. - almost 2000 years ago. Think of how well this applies today.

Ephesians 5:15-20

"Be very careful, then, how you live -- not as unwise but as wise, 16 making the most of every opportunity, because the days are evil. 17 Therefore do not be foolish, but understand what the Lord's will is. 18 Do not get drunk on wine, which leads to debauchery. Instead, be filled with the Spirit. 19 Speak to one another with psalms, hymns and spiritual songs. Sing and make music in your heart to the Lord, 20 always giving thanks to God the Father for everything, in the name of our Lord Jesus Christ."(NIV)

Summation

If there is a message to what I have told you to-day - it is to seek understanding not only of God's wish for each soul but, also, on how to live our lives amid the tumult and upheavals of present day living as each one of us tries to make sense of what is happening so rapidly around us.

We can be swept up in events so much so that we forget about our soul. Believe me; the devil is working hard to accomplish just that!

Therefore, it is important to always be aware of and keep God's Laws. Keeping your faith in Christ alive through prayer and joining with fellow Christians in worship is the minimum we should be doing. Living as Christians and guiding others to Christ is also a positive means of keeping our faith alive.

Let us make this prayer from King David's time - **Psalm 119:33-40** - our prayer today - in the midst of our own personal turmoil so that we can claim God's protection for ourselves and families in the days ahead.

Psalm 119:33-40

"Teach me, 0 LORD, to follow your decrees; then I will keep them to the end.

34 Give me understanding, and I will keep your law and obey it with all my heart.

35 Direct me in the path of your commands, for there I find delight.

36 Turn my heart toward your statutes and not toward selfish gain.

37 Turn my eyes away from worthless things; preserve my life according to your word.

38 Fulfill your promise to your servant, so that you may be feared.

39 Take away the disgrace I dread, for your laws are good.

40 How I long for your precepts! Preserve my life in your righteousness."(NIV)

Take a moment to reflect on your life. Where are you right now in your spiritual journey through life? Do you understand God's will for you? Do you understand that Jesus is there to help you? - Through every trial - just seek Him out!

Please understand. No matter what - God is there for you - any time, all the time - 24 hours a day. Would you like an interview? Just ask!

Let us pray.

Dear God. Do not let the speed and nature of technological change impair our ability to know, love and serve you. Dear God, preserve us from the intrigues of the devil and protect our souls that they may be kept holy and unblemished by sin.

Dear Lord, bless us and all our families. Bless the Grices and our new pastors - Capt's Dale & Jo Sobool as they assume the duties that You have destined for them. May you strengthen them and guide them. In Jesus name, we pray. Amen

Sermon Title: **"I Am" - Part 1** Sermon given on June 27, 2004
This Sermon is about learning about ourselves, our **body** and
our world. An exploration of how body is made up. Our body is
wonderfully made and is proof of **God**'s existence.

"I AM" - Part 1

Good morning! First let us pray -

Say after me - I AM! - Together and louder - I AM! ....

The words remind me of TV commercial for a vacation package
where the woman is scouting out options on the computer and says - or
is about to say - "I am..." when her husband intervenes and says " ... a
goddess!"

I thought that was so cute! It got me thinking about "I am" and who
or what we really are. I thought also of another famous quote.

"Cognito ergo sum" this is a Latin quote from the famous philosopher
Rene Descartes who just happened to coin one the most famous maxims
in the history of philosophy.

"Cognito ergo sum" - I think therefore --- **I am!**

Today I'm going to talk about the "I am". Just - who am I?

Today I want to share with you a few attributes of our bodies (my body, your body) to underline the words "fearfully and wonderfully made" - you heard those words in Psalm 139.

To assist me, I have used the book entitled "Fearfully and Wonderfully Made." by authors Dr. Paul Brand and Philip Yancey.

Bear with me as I read some excerpts from their very excellent book. I am going to talk about the human body - specifically, the eyes, creating a baby, cells, genetic code or DNA, bones, skin and touch, muscles and the brain and neurons.

I am going to cover a lot of territory in a few minutes but I hope these few minutes will be well spent in getting to the real "guts" of what we mean when we say "I am".

Do I have your attention? You're looking at me through your **eyes**. Did you know each of your eyes has one hundred and seven million cells? Seven million are cones, loaded to fire off a message to the brain when a few photons of light cross them.

Cones give us the full band of color awareness, and because of them we can easily distinguish a thousand shades of color. The other hundred million cells are rods, backup cells for use in low light. When only rods are operating, we do not see color (as on a moonlit night when everything looms in shades of gray), but we can distinguish a spectrum of light so broad that the brightest light you can perceive is a billion times brighter than the dimmest. One of the most wondrous of all human activities is **procreation.** This is the fertilization of the egg in a woman's womb with a single sperm to create a baby! .

Over nine months the cells in the egg divide up functions in exquisite ways. Billions of blood cells appear, millions of rods and cones-in all, up to one hundred million, million cells from a single fertilized ovum.

And finally a baby is born, glistening with liquid. Already his cells are cooperating. His muscles limber up in jerky, awkward movements; his face recoils from the harsh lights and dry air of the new environment; his lungs and vocal chords join in a first air-gulping yell.

Within that clay-colored, wrinkled package of cells lays the miracle of the ecstasy of community. His life will include the joy of seeing his mother's approval at his first clumsy words, the discovery of his own unique talents and gifts, the fulfillment of sharing with other humans.

He is many cells, but he is one organism. All of his <u>hundred trillion cells</u> know that. Truly a wonder!

Talking about **cells** - they work tirelessly in the body. Individually they seem puny and oddly designed, but I know these invisible parts cooperate to lavish me with the phenomenon of life. Every second my *ultra young* smooth muscle cells modulate the width of my blood vessels, gently push matter through my intestines, open and close the plumbing in my kidneys. When things are going well-my heart contracting rhythmically, my brain humming with knowledge, my lymph laving tired cells - I (probably like you) rarely give these cells a passing thought.

Cooperation, a curious phenomenon of cells outside the body, is the essential regimen of life inside. There, every heart cell obeys in tempo or the animal dies. Each cell is flooded with communication about the rest of the body.

How does the roaming white cell responding to an injury know which cells to attack as invaders and which to welcome as friends? No one knows, but the body's cells have a nearly infallible sense of ***belonging***.

All living matter is basically alike; a single atom differentiates animal blood from plant chlorophyll. Yet the body senses infinitesimal differences with an unfailing scent; it knows its hundred trillion cells by name. The first heart transplant recipients died, not because their new hearts failed, but because their bodies would not be fooled. Though the new heart cells looked in every respect like the old ones and beat at the correct rhythm, ***they did not belong***. Nature's code of membership had been broken. The body screams "Foreigner!" at imported cells and mobilizes to destroy them. This conundrum of the immune reaction kept organ *transplant* science in a kindergarten phase although there have been dramatic changes.

To complicate the process of identity, the composite of my body today - bone cells, fat cells, blood cells, muscle cells-differs entirely from my components ten years ago even more so thirty years ago. <u>All my cells have been replaced by new cells</u> (except for nerve cells and brain cells, which are never replaced). Thus, my body is more like a fountain than a sculpture: maintaining its shape, but constantly being renewed.

How does each cell know what to do? It is locked in the **genetic code** of each cell which individually carries the entire **DNA** strand produced at the time of conception.

Every cell possesses a genetic code so complete that the entire body could be reassembled from information in any one of the body's cells.

The DNA is so narrow and compacted that all the genes in all my body's cells would fit into an ice cube; yet if the DNA were unwound and joined together end to end, the strand could stretch from the earth to the sun and back more than four hundred times.

Can you imagine the extent and complexity of what I have been telling you?

But there is more to the body than cells. Let's talk about **bones** for a moment. Remember Ezekiel?

No Exxon researcher has yet discovered a material as well-suited for the body's needs as bone, which comprises only one-fifth of our body weight. In 1867 an engineer demonstrated that the arrangement of bone cells forms the lightest structure, made of least material, to support the body's weight.

No one has successfully challenged his findings. As the only hard material in the body, bone possesses incredible strength, enough to protect and support every other cell.

Sometimes we press our bones together like a steel spring, as when a pole-vaulter lands. Other times we nearly pull a bone apart, as when my arm lifts a heavy suitcase.

In comparison, wood can withstand even less pulling tension, and could not possibly bear the compression forces that bone can. A wooden pole for the vaulter would quickly snap. Steel, which can absorb both forces well, is three times the weight of bone and would burden us down.

The economical body takes this stress-bearing bone and hollows it out, using a weight-saving architectural principle it took people millennia to discover; it then fills the vacant space in the center with an efficient red blood cell factory that turns out *a trillion new cells per day.*

One finds bone's design most impressive in the tiny, jewel like chips of ivory in the foot. Twenty-six bones line up in each foot, about the same number as in each hand. Even when a soccer player subjects these small bones to a cumulative force of over one thousand tons per foot over the course of a match, his living bones endure the violent stress, maintaining their elasticity.

Not all of us leap and kick, but we do walk some sixty-five thousand miles, or more than two and one half times around the world, in a lifetime. Our body weight is evenly spread out through architecturally perfect arches, which serve as springs, and the bending of knees and ankles absorbs stress.

Although bone has come to symbolize death at Halloween and in museums, the surgeon knows that symbol lies, for the skeleton is a growing organ. When you cut bone, it bleeds. Most amazing of all, when it breaks, it heals itself. Perhaps an engineer will someday develop a substance as strong and light and efficient as bone, but what engineer could devise a substance that, like bone, can grow continuously, lubricate itself, require no shutdown time, and repair itself when damage occurs?

When bone breaks, an elaborate process begins. Excited repair cells invade in a swarm. Within two weeks a cartilage-like sheath called callus surrounds the region and cement-laying cells enter the jellied mass. These cells are the osteoblasts, the pothole-fillers of the bone. Gradually they break down the callus and replace it with fresh bone. In two or three months the fracture site is marked by a mass of new bone that bulges over both sides of the broken ends like a spliced garden hose. Later, surplus material is scavenged so the final result nearly matches the original bone.

Without a skeleton, we would collapse. Bone then is another wonder of our body.

There is no organ like the **skin**. *Averaging a mere nine pounds, it flexes and folds and crinkles around joints, facial crags, gnarled toes, and fleshy buttocks. It is smooth as a baby's stomach here, rough like a crocodile there. A bricklayer's hands may be horny, taut, and layered with sandpaper, but flaccid, pliable folds shroud his abdomen. Intricate spot-welds fasten a leg's wrap, holding it tautly to the muscle layer; an elbow droops loosely, like the skin of a cat that can be tossed by the scruff of its neck.*

Choose sections of the scalp, the lip, the nipple, the heel, the abdomen, and the fingertip to view through a laboratory microscope. They are as different as the skins of a host of species-a patchwork somehow growing in a continuous sheet over the body. Tiny ridges crisscross skin's surface to provide traction, much as a snow tire does. Amazingly, for no apparent reason, each of us is given a different pattern for the ridges, a flourish which the FBI capitalizes on in its fingerprint files. The ridges themselves give texture and the power to grasp a slippery object.

The skin does not exist merely to give the body an appearance. It is also a vital, humming source of ceaseless information about our environment. Most of our sense organs-the ears, the eyes, the nose-are confined to one spot. The skin is rolled thin like pie dough and studded with half a million tiny transmitters, like telephones jammed together waiting to inform the brain of important news.

Think of the variety of stimuli your skin monitors each day: wind, particles, parasites, changes in pressure, temperature, humidity, light, radiation. Skin is tough enough to withstand the rigorous pounding of jogging on asphalt, yet sensitive enough to have bare toes tickled by a light breeze.

The word **touch** swells with such a plethora of meanings and images that in many dictionaries, including the *Oxford English,* its definition runs the longest of any entry.

You can hardly think of a human activity - sports, music, art, cooking, mechanics, sex - that does not vitally rely on touch.

Those seemingly useless hairs blanketing our bodies act as levers to magnify the sensation of touch. We can discern a thousandth of an ounce of pressure on the tip of a half-inch hair.

Touch distribution was not handed down at a blackjack table. ("God does not play at dice," said Einstein): the sensitivity of each square inch of skin is programmed to fit the function of that body part. Our fingertips, tongues, and lips are the portions of the body used in activities that need the most sensitivity.

We should not leave the subject of skin without observing that without it we might have a hard time keeping everything in place!

Six hundred **muscles**, which comprise 40 percent of our weight (twice as much as bones), burns up much of the energy we ingest as food in order to produce all our movements. Tiny muscles govern the light permitted into the eye. Muscles, barely an inch long, allow for a spectrum of subtle expression in the face - a poker player or an international trade negotiator learns to read them as important signals.

Another, much larger muscle, the diaphragm, controls coughing, breathing, sneezing, laughing, and sighing. Massive muscles in the buttocks and thighs equip the body for a lifetime of walking. Without muscles, bones would collapse in a heap, joints would slip apart, and movement would cease.

Human muscles are divided into three types: smooth muscles control the automatic processes which rumble along without our conscious attention; striated muscles allow voluntary movements, such as piano playing; and cardiac muscles are specialized enough to merit their own category.

A hummingbird heart weights a fraction of an ounce but beats eight-hundred times a minute; a whale heart weighs one thousand pounds - in contrast to either, the human heart seems dully functional, but does its job well enough to get most of us through seventy years with no time off for rest.

Hmm . . . at my age, I should be worried - it would seem my time is about up!

We have hundreds of muscles that go undetected: we don't think about them. They are the automatic muscles that control our eyelids, breathing, heartbeat and digestion. We cannot voluntarily stop our heartbeat or breathing.

No one can commit suicide by holding his breath; accumulating carbon dioxide in the lungs will trigger a mechanism to override conscious desire and force the muscles of ribs, diaphragm, and lungs to move.

Consider the electrical network linking every home and building in metropolitan New York City. At any given second lights are turned on and off, toasters pop up, microwave ovens begin their digital countdowns, water pumps lunge into motion. Yet that enormous interlinking of decisions and activities is marked by randomness. A far more complex **switching system** is operating in your body at this second as you listen to me and it is perfectly controlled and orderly...

In the physical body as well as the spiritual, a muscle must be exercised to continue growing. If, through paralysis, we lose movement, atrophy will set in and muscles will shrink away until they are absorbed by the rest of the body.

A cell called the **neuron** is the most important unit in communication inside the body. Twelve billion neurons are poised for action at birth.

<u>Every other cell in the body dies away and is replaced every few years,</u> <u>but not the neuron.</u> How could we function if the reservoirs of memory and our information about the world were periodically sloughed away? <u>When the neuron dies, it does not grow back.</u>

Finally, highest of all in the hierarchy of neurons and the nervous system are the cerebral hemispheres of the **brain**, the holy of holies of the body - most protected by bone, most vulnerable to injury if the protection is ever breached. There, ten billion nerve cells and one hundred billion glia cells (which provide the biological batteries for brain activity) float in a jelled mass, sifting information, storing memories, creating consciousness.

It would take hours, even days to completely explain all the wonders of your body. But think of this - you are but one of billions of creatures and living things on this planet. If nothing else you are truly "fearfully and wonderfully made". I hope you agree.

There is a reason I have spent this time talking about the wonders of the body. The most fundamental reason is to emphasize the value of our bodies especially for those young people who are faced with decisions about what they do with their bodies. The temptation to abuse our bodies is rampant in today's society. But there is nothing new under the sun. The Bible speaks to this very situation as you will hear.

After hearing about the wonders of your body, what thoughts come to your mind?
Let me share a few of my thoughts and questions.

First: Can everyone see that the intricate make-up of our bodies - for that matter - all living and breathing things - is the work of an all-powerful being - God? Does anyone need more proof that God exists?

Second: The next question that pops into my head is this. Why did God make this world and all its living creatures - including man? Let's look at the Bible.

Genesis 2:7 the LORD God formed the man from the dust of the ground and breathed into his nostrils the breath of life, and the man became a living being. (NIV) *and God did something very special –*

Genesis 1:27-30 "So God created man in his own image, in the image of God he created him; male and female he created them.

28 God blessed them and said to them, "Be fruitful and increase in number; fill the earth and subdue it. Rule over the fish of the sea and the birds of the air and over every living creature that moves on the ground."

29 Then God said, "I give you every seed-bearing plant on the face of the whole earth and every tree that has fruit with seed in it. They will be yours for food. 30 And to all the beasts of the earth and all the birds of the air and all the creatures that move on the ground -- everything that has the breath of life in it -- I give every green plant for food." And it was so. "(NIV)

The Bible clearly sets out man's relationship to the rest of created things - He placed them there for our use (or misuse).

Hebrews 2:5-8 "It is not to angels that he has subjected the world to come, about which we are speaking. 6 But there is a place where someone has testified: "What is man that you are mindful of him, the son of man that you care for him? 7 You made him a little lower than the angels; you crowned him with glory and honor 8 and put everything under his feet." In putting everything under him, God left nothing that is not subject to him. Yet at present we do not see everything subject to him." (NIV)

Third: The next question that crosses my mind is, "Why do we so royally screw up our lives and the lives of others?" The Bible has interesting comment here as well.

Romans 1:18-32 "The wrath of God is being revealed from heaven against all the godlessness and wickedness of men who suppress the truth by their wickedness, since what may be known about God is plain to them, because God has made it plain to them. For since the creation of the world God's invisible qualities -- his eternal power and divine

<u>nature -- have been clearly seen, being understood from what has been</u> <u>made, so that men are without excuse.</u>
(The wonderful body I've talked about!)

For although they knew God, they neither glorified him as God nor gave thanks to him, but their thinking became futile and their foolish hearts were darkened. Although they claimed to be wise, they became fools and exchanged the glory of the immortal God for images made to look like mortal man and birds and animals and reptiles.

Therefore God gave them over in the sinful desires of their hearts to sexual impurity for the degrading of their bodies with one another. They exchanged the truth of God for a lie, and worshiped and served created things rather than the Creator -- who is forever praised. Amen.

Because of this, God gave them over to shameful lusts. Even their women exchanged natural relations for unnatural ones. In the same way the men also abandoned natural relations with women and were inflamed with lust for one another. Men committed indecent acts with other men, and received in themselves the due penalty for their perversion.

Furthermore, since they did not think it worthwhile to retain the knowledge of God, he gave them over to a depraved mind; to do what ought not to be done. They have become filled with every kind of wickedness, evil, greed and depravity. They are full of envy, murder, strife, deceit and malice. They are gossips, slanderers, God-haters, insolent, arrogant and boastful; they invent ways of doing evil; they disobey their parents; they are senseless, faithless, heartless, ruthless. Although they know God's righteous decree that those who do such things deserve death, they not only continue to do these very things but also approve of those who practice them." (NIV)

2 Timothy 3:2-7 "People will be lovers of themselves, lovers of money, boastful, proud, abusive, disobedient to their parents, ungrateful, unholy, 3 without love, unforgiving, slanderous, without self-control, brutal, not lovers of the good, 4 treacherous, rash, conceited, lovers of pleasure rather than lovers of God -- 5 having a form of godliness but denying its power. Have nothing to do with them. 6 They are the kind who worm their way into homes and gain control over weak-willed women, who are loaded down with sins and are swayed by all kinds of evil desires, 7 always learning but never able to acknowledge the truth." (NIV)

How many have fallen into sinful practices like those talked about in the Bible?

According to **2 Peter 2:19** "... <u>a man is a slave to whatever has mastered him.</u> " (NIV)

Fourth: Question - Why? Why? Why? Here we have this beautiful and wonderful body - a beautiful world - beautiful living plants and animals.

Suffering and natural or man-made calamities, by comparison, serve to emphasize the beauty of God's creations - of which we are a part. Why does man sin? When does he stop? How can he stop sinning?

Five: Maybe the answer comes when we face the question why did God make you in His image?

I'm banking on God's love of man to work within each of us to bring us to the truth as expressed in –

Ecclesiastes 3:11 *"He has made everything beautiful in its time. He has also set eternity in the hearts of men; yet they cannot fathom what God has done from beginning to end." (NIV)*

The Bible is our guide as it reminds us of God's desire for us.
1 Corinthians 6:19 *"Do you not know that your body is a temple of the Holy Spirit, who is in you, whom you have received from God?" You are not your own; "(NIV)*

In your body resides your soul. Cleansed of all sin it can become the dwelling place of the Holy Spirit. When the Holy Spirit is indwelling the Bible tells us -

Galatians 5:22-24 "...the fruit of the Spirit is love, joy, peace, patience, kindness, goodness, faithfulness, gentleness and self-control.

Against such things there is no law. <u>Those who belong to Christ Jesus have crucified the sinful nature with its passions and desires</u>. "(NIV)

Ephesians 5:15-20 "Be very careful, then, how you live -- not as unwise but as wise, making the most of every opportunity, because the days are evil. Therefore do not be foolish, but understand what the Lord's will is. Do not get drunk on wine, which leads to debauchery. Instead, be filled with the Spirit. Speak to one another with psalms, hymns and spiritual songs. Sing and make music in your heart to the Lord, always giving thanks to God the Father for everything, in the name of our Lord Jesus Christ." (NIV)

Each one of us - "fearfully and wonderfully made" have been given riches and opportunity beyond our wildest imagination. We can sink into sinful ways and loose our way or we can reach out and ask Jesus to cleanse our hearts and souls and accept Him as our Lord and Savior.

So how do you complete the phrase "I am" as a statement of your belief in yourself and the future of your eternal soul?

Can you stand up and say with conviction - "I AM - A CHRISTIAN!"
I am a believer in Jesus Christ and life everlasting for my soul in heaven.

If you can sincerely say that then I ask you to take the knowledge I have imparted to you today and <u>talk to at least one person</u> about your belief and why you are a Christian. That someone could be a very young person who needs to know what you know about the value of their body and mind. Share it with them.

Can you imagine what would happen if everyone did exactly that?

Let us close in prayer and song. – Prayer – Show us the way.

Turn to Song #487 Have Thine Own Way Lord

Benediction Chorus #53 - Spirit of the Living God 2x

Sermon Title: "**I Am**" - **Part 2**   Sermon given on August 1, 2004
This Sermon is a discussion about how **God** speaks to man; God's
special relationship with man; God's calling; The acceptance of **The
Bible** as God's revelation to man.

"I AM" – Part 2

In "I Am – Part 1" I talked about how wonderfully and fearfully each
of our bodies is made. The fundamental purpose of that discussion was
to establish proof of God's existence, and His mighty power, as found
within each of our own bodies. Each body is a small universe made up
of billions of parts that all come together to work in unison to provide
us with a life.

At the same time, each body houses an eternal soul - you, which
remains within your body so long as it lives. Latest longevity stats
indicate about 79 years for Albertans. In that time, we either mess up
or accomplish something with our lives!

Remember the quote "I breath therefore I am"? This simply denotes
that each of us is alive! We exist. The question for each of us, then, is
what do we do with this body of ours? How should we live? And, what
is the purpose of our lives?

Think for a minute. What would happen to each baby if its mother
and/or father were to walk away and leave it? How would it survive?
How would it learn? How would it grow up? What would become of
the child? Parents just don't do that! Thank God! There is a hands on
relationship between parent and child.

Today, in Part 2 of "I Am", I'm going to talk about God and His rather special relationship with mankind. Specifically - His relationship with each and every one of us. You are about to learn something about God that you may not have known or realized before.

Let me take you back to when God created man about 4000 BC

Genesis 1:27-30 "So God created man in his own image, in the image of God he created him; male and female he created them. God blessed them and **said** to them, "Be fruitful and increase in number; fill the earth and subdue it. Rule over the fish of the sea and the birds of the air and over every living creature that moves on the ground."

Then God **said**, "I give you every seed-bearing plant on the face of the whole earth and every tree that has fruit with seed in it. They will be yours for food.

And to all the beasts of the earth and all the birds of the air and all the creatures that move on the ground -- everything that has the breath of life in it -- I give every green plant for food." And it was so." (NIV)

Genesis 2:15-17 "The LORD God took the man and put him in the Garden of Eden to work it and take care of it. And the LORD God **commanded** the man, "You are free to eat from any tree in the garden; but you must not eat from the tree of the knowledge of good and evil, for when you eat of it you will surely die." (NIV)

We don't know how long Adam & Eve lived in the garden but we do know that God conversed directly with Adam. After a time Eve was tempted by the evil serpent to eat of the fruit of the tree of knowledge of good and evil. She, in turn, tempted Adam and after eating the fruit, they realized that they were naked and attempted to hide from God. God **called** to the man, "Where are you?"

You know the rest of the story. Adam and Eve were driven from the Garden of Eden never to return.

Soon after, Cain and Abel were born to Adam and Eve. Later, God **spoke directly** to Cain after he had attacked and killed his brother Abel.

Genesis 4:9-12 Then the LORD **said** to Cain, "Where is your brother Abel?" Cain replied, "I don't know - Am I my brother's keeper?"

The LORD **said**, "What have you done? Listen! Your brother's blood cries out to me from the ground. Now you are under a curse and driven from the ground, which opened its mouth to receive your brother's blood from your hand. When you work the ground, it will no longer yield its crops for you. You will be a restless wanderer on the earth." (NIV)

Now about 1500 years later – around 2350 BC, God again **spoke directly** to a man – in this case Noah.

Genesis 6:11-21 "Now the earth was corrupt in God's sight and was full of violence. God saw how corrupt the earth had become, for all the people on earth had corrupted their ways. So God **said** to Noah, "I am going to put an end to all people, for the earth is filled with violence because of them. I am surely going to destroy both them and the earth.

I am going to bring floodwaters on the earth to destroy all life under the heavens, every creature that has the breath of life in it. Everything on earth will perish. But I will establish my covenant with you, and you will enter the ark -- you and your sons and your wife and your sons' wives with you. "(NIV)

So Noah built the ark as God commanded and took the animals in. Then the flood came and went and the inhabitants returned to dry earth.

Genesis 9:1 After the flood had subsided, then God blessed Noah and his sons, **saying** to them, "Be fruitful and increase in number and fill the earth." (NIV)

You will notice from the excerpts of the Bible I have mentioned that God spoke or conversed ***directly with man***, and God's actions had a direct and immediate impact on the descendants of Adam and Eve. i.e. banishment from the garden and annihilation by flood. Such, we learn, was God's wrath against sinful man.

The post-flood era was the second beginning for mankind. It also brought about a shorter life span for man and a new covenant never to repeat the devastation of man with a flood again.

Around 2000 BC – about 300 years later, God again intervened directly into the affairs of man -

Genesis 12:1-3 The LORD had <u>said</u> to Abram, "Leave your country, your people and your father's household and go to the land I will show you. "I will make you into a great nation and I will bless you; I will make your name great, and you will be a blessing. I will bless those who bless you, and whoever curses you I will curse; and all peoples on earth will be blessed through you." (NIV)

God selected a particular man and his family as the recipients of his special revelation and **spoke to him directly**.

Genesis 12:7 The LORD appeared to Abram and <u>said</u>, "To your offspring I will give this land." So he built an altar there to the LORD, who had appeared to him. (NIV)

A short time later when Abraham and his son Lot disagreed – they parted.

Genesis 13:14-17 "The LORD <u>said</u> to Abram after Lot had parted from him, "Lift up your eyes from where you are and look north and south, east and west. All the land that you see I will give to you and your offspring forever.

I will make your offspring like the dust of the earth, so that if anyone could count the dust, then your offspring could be counted. Go, walk through the length and breadth of the land, for I am giving it to you." (NIV)

Later, God spoke to Abraham to test him.

Genesis 22:2 "Then God <u>said</u>, "Take your son, your only son, Isaac, whom you love, and go to the region of Moriah. Sacrifice him there as a burnt offering on one of the mountains I will tell you about." (NIV)

Genesis 22:10-12 "Then he reached out his hand and took the knife to slay his son. But *the angel of the LORD* **called out** to him from heaven, "Abraham! Abraham! "Here I am," he replied.

"Do not lay a hand on the boy," he **said**. "Do not do anything to him. Now I know that you fear God, because you have not withheld from me your son, your only son." (NIV)

Genesis 22:15-18 The *angel of the LORD* called to Abraham from heaven a second time and **said**, "I swear by myself, declares the LORD, that because you have done this and have not withheld your son, your only son, I will surely bless you and make your descendants as numerous as the stars in the sky and as the sand on the seashore. Your descendants will take possession of the cities of their enemies, and through your offspring all nations on earth will be blessed, because you have obeyed me." (NIV)

After another 200 years had passed – in about 1840 BC - the scriptures tell us about Jacob's encounter with God – *this in the form of a dream.*

Genesis 28:12-15 "He (Jacob) had a dream in which he saw a stairway resting on the earth, with its top reaching to heaven, and the angels of God were ascending and descending on it. There above it stood the LORD, and he **said**: "I am the LORD, the God of your father Abraham and the God of Isaac. I will give you and your descendants the land on which you are lying. Your descendants will be like the dust of the earth, and you will spread out to the west and to the east, to the north and to the south. All peoples on earth will be blessed through you and your offspring. I am with you and will watch over you wherever you go, and I will bring you back to this land. I will not leave you until I have done what I have promised you." (NIV)

Keep in mind that God's contact with individuals came at different times over many years But His most significant intervention with mankind (after Adam and Noah) came with Moses, with whom he had a long, direct relationship.

Most of you know the history of Moses, but let me remind you of some special instances of God's contact with Moses.

About 300 years after Jacob – about **1575 BC**, Moses' encounter with God came as a result of Moses drawn to a burning bush that didn't seem to burn up. He was very curious.

Exodus 3:5-10 "Do not come any closer," God **said**. "Take off your sandals, for the place where you are standing is holy ground." Then he **said,** "I am the God of your father, the God of Abraham, the God of Isaac and the God of Jacob." At this, Moses hid his face, because he was afraid to look at God."

The LORD **said**, "I have indeed seen the misery of my people in Egypt. I have heard them crying out because of their slave drivers, and I am concerned about their suffering. So I have come down to rescue them from the hand of the Egyptians and to bring them up out of that land into a good and spacious land, a land flowing with milk and honey -. And now the cry of the Israelites has reached me, and I have seen the way the Egyptians are oppressing them. So now, go. I am sending you to Pharaoh to bring my people the Israelites out of Egypt." (NIV)

Exodus 3:13-15 "Moses said to God, "Suppose I go to the Israelites and say to them, 'The God of your fathers has sent me to you,' and they ask me, 'What is his name?' Then what shall I tell them?"
God **said** to Moses, "**I AM WHO I AM.** This is what you are to say to the Israelites: 'I AM has sent me to you.'"
God also **said** to Moses, "Say to the Israelites, 'The LORD, the God of your fathers -- the God of Abraham, the God of Isaac and the God of Jacob -- has sent me to you.' This is my name forever, the name by which I am to be remembered from generation to generation." (NIV)

Exodus 20:1-7 And God **spoke** all these words: "I am the LORD your God, who brought you out of Egypt, out of the land of slavery."You shall have no other gods before me. "You shall not make for yourself an idol in the form of anything in heaven above or on the earth beneath or in the waters below.

You shall not bow down to them or worship them; for I, the LORD your God, am a jealous God, punishing the children for the sin of the fathers to the third and fourth generation of those who hate me, but showing love to a thousand [generations] of those who love me and keep my commandments. "You shall not misuse the name of the LORD your God, for the LORD will not hold anyone guiltless who misuses his name. (NIV)

After Moses died God spoke to Joshua about **1500 BC**. Joshua had been chosen to lead the "chosen people' into their new home land.

Joshua 1:1-11 "After the death of Moses the servant of the LORD, the LORD **said** to Joshua son of Nun, Moses' aide: "Moses my servant is dead. Now then, you and all these people, get ready to cross the Jordan River into the land I am about to give to them -- to the Israelites. I will give you every place where you set your foot, as I promised Moses. Your territory will extend from the desert to Lebanon, and from the great river, the Euphrates -- all the Hittite country -- to the Great Sea on the west. No one will be able to stand up against you all the days of your life. As I was with Moses, so I will be with you; I will never leave you nor forsake you.

"Be strong and courageous, because you will lead these people to inherit the land I swore to their forefathers to give them. Be strong and very courageous. Be careful to obey all the law my servant Moses gave you; do not turn from it to the right or to the left, that you may be successful wherever you go. Do not let this Book of the Law depart from your mouth; meditate on it day and night, so that you may be careful to do everything written in it. Then you will be prosperous and successful. Have I not commanded you? Be strong and courageous. Do not be terrified; do not be discouraged, for the LORD your God will be with you wherever you go." (NIV)

Joshua 13:1 When Joshua was old and well advanced in years, the LORD **said** to him, "You are very old, and there are still very large areas of land to be taken over."

After the Israelites had entered their new land, God's direct contact was reduced to a short contact with Balaam and Gideon until the time of the Kings. With King David there appears to have been a close relationship with God but no direct quotes are recorded.

The most direct contact with God for King David came through the prophet Nathan which seems to have been the approach God chose from then on. Most of God's directions for the Jews came through judges or prophets.

There is one instance, with King Solomon, about **1000 BC** which emphasized the other approach God made to men, and that was through a dream.

1 Kings 3:5 "At Gibeon the LORD appeared to Solomon during the night in a dream, and God **said**, "Ask for whatever you want me to give you." (NIV)

After Solomon had answered him,(**1 Kings 3:11-14**) God **said** to him, "Since you have asked for this and not for long life or wealth for yourself, nor have asked for the death of your enemies but for discernment in administering justice, I will do what you have asked. I will give you a wise and discerning heart, so that there will never have been anyone like you, nor will there ever be. Moreover, I will give you what you have not asked for -- both riches and honor -- so that in your lifetime you will have no equal among kings. And if you walk in my ways and obey my statutes and commands as David your father did, I will give you a long life." (NIV)

Alas, for the next 1000 years, the fate of the Jews became progressively worse so that they ultimately became subjects under the Roman Empire by the time Jesus was born.

So, what have we learned up to this point?

First, God spoke **directly** to man over many years – **almost 3,000 years**! God's words also came to men through prophets and dreams. God wanted men to know, love and serve Him as their Lord. That was made clear with the first of the Ten Commandments.

The contact God had with man is possibly better explained in **2 Peter 1:20-21** – "- - you must understand that *no prophecy of Scripture came about by the prophet's own interpretation. 21 For prophecy never had its origin in the will of man, but men spoke from God as they were carried along by the Holy Spirit."* (NIV)

Second, God revealed Himself to the Jewish people as the "I AM!" Further clarification of that is found in Revelations.

Revelation 1:8 "I am the Alpha and the Omega," (the beginning and the end) says the Lord God, "who is, and who was, and who is to come, the Almighty." (NIV)
In other words God exists today – always has - and always will!

Third, over the 4000 years from the time of creation, God demonstrated His love for man by **direct contact** with certain individuals who then communicated His message to others. Finally, God in His wisdom decided on a complete new course of action with regard to communicating with mankind.

He sent His son Jesus to us! In the Book of Hebrews we find it clearly stated.

Hebrews 1:1-3 "In the past God spoke to our forefathers through the prophets at many times and in various ways, but in these last days he has spoken to us by his Son, whom he appointed heir of all things, and through whom he made the universe. The Son is the radiance of God's glory and the exact representation of his being, sustaining all things by his powerful word. After he had provided purification for sins, he sat down at the right hand of the Majesty in heaven. "(NIV)

We know the history of Jesus but God still made His presence felt when John the Baptist baptized Jesus.

Matthew 3:16-17 "As soon as Jesus was baptized, he went up out of the water. At that moment heaven was opened, and he saw the Spirit of God descending like a dove and lighting on him. And a voice from

heaven **said**, "This is my Son, whom I love; with him I am well pleased."
(NIV)

God accomplished <u>three things</u> when He sent Jesus to earth. **First**,
Jesus, through His crucifixion and death, provided purification for all
of men's sins.

Second, *God's Message* for man was embodied in the teachings of
Jesus.

In **John 1:14** "The **Word** became flesh and made his dwelling
among us. We have seen his glory, the glory of the One and Only, who
came from the Father, full of grace and truth." (NIV)

Third, God provided to all mankind an advocate, in Jesus, so that
man could find his way to enter the kingdom of heaven for eternity.
Note Jesus' own words.

John 6:35-40 *"Then Jesus declared, "I am the bread of life. He who
comes to me will never go hungry, and he who believes in me will never be
thirsty. But as I told you, you have seen me and still you do not believe. All
that the Father gives me will come to me, and whoever comes to me I will
never drive away.*
*For I have come down from heaven not to do my will but to do the will
of him who sent me. And this is the will of him who sent me, that I shall
lose none of all that he has given me, but raise them up at the last day. For
my Father's will is that everyone who looks to the Son and believes in him
shall have eternal life, and I will raise him up at the last day." (NIV)*

The Jews were questioning who Jesus was, and He said to them
(**John 8:58**) "I tell you the truth," Jesus answered, "before Abraham was
born, **I am!**" (NIV)   Interesting that Jesus used the same expression
as God had in speaking to Moses.

Martha, at Lazarus resurrection, affirmed her belief in Jesus. **John
11:25-26** "Jesus **said** to her, "I am the resurrection and the life. He who
believes in me will live, even though he dies; and whoever lives and
believes in me will never die. - - -"(NIV)

Then too He gave us something that would help each one of us to learn about God's love for us and His wish for our future. He gave us the Bible – **His Word**!

Now we don't have to wait 300 or 400 years for direct contact through a prophet or God Himself. We have His word in our hands at all times. In fact, we have had the printed Bible for almost 500 hundred years. It is now the most constant presence of God's word in our lives.

When you think of it, doesn't it strike you as wonderful? God, who created us, has never given up on us and seeks a relationship with each one of us for eternity. His word makes that abundantly clear. But it does not end there. God still touches individuals in a direct way.

I have a question for you. Can **you** have direct communication with God (or Jesus)? Have you experienced such a contact? Do you have to be holy or a saint to have this contact? No – God has certainly proved that throughout the Bible. See Paul, originally named Saul, called to God's service on the road to Damascus. That is only one instance. There are many such as Jesus picking His apostles.

Have **you** been called into God's service through a voice, a dream or a sign? I have – several years ago. That's why I stand here now. You too, can be contacted. If you are, you need to examine what you have been told. Measure it against God's word so you can determine that it is not contrary to what God has taught us – another value of the Bible – God's written word.

If the message you received does not fit the teachings within the Bible, do not be dismayed. Realize the devil, too, can place thoughts in your mind – and does quite often. The answer, of course, is to pray, pray about it. Let God's word lead you.

Lastly, the great I AM has a promise for us found in Revelations.

Revelation 21:6-8

He **said** to me: "It is done. I am the Alpha and the Omega, the Beginning and the End. To him who is thirsty I will give to drink without cost from the spring of the water of life. He who overcomes will inherit all this, and I will be his God and he will be my son. But the cowardly, the unbelieving, the vile, the murderers, the sexually immoral, those who practice magic arts, the idolaters and all liars -- their place will be in the fiery lake of burning sulfur. This is the second death." (NIV)

Can you believe it? In my message to-day I have covered the whole Bible from Genesis to Revelations. What have we learned?

We have learned that God created us and made each of us in a fearful and wonderful way. He created the world we live in for our use and gave us stewardship over our planet.

We know that He loves us and has tried, throughout the existence of thinking man, to point us to the path through our mortal life that will lead to our souls rejoining Him in heaven for eternity. He has personally directed, influenced others and through the Holy Spirit, placed in men's minds and hearts, a desire to know Him.

But there is more – think about this. Without the Bible – God's word - those who would bring you a message in the Sunday service would have no grounding or basis for what they say – including me. We couldn't quote or direct you to meaningful passages in the Bible. Mankind has only had the printed Bible for a relatively short time. The best part is that God's word is available to everyone.

Often we hear of people, many who have everything there is to have, who still seek more out of life then they are getting. They have a hole to fill. Do you have a yearning? Do you desire to be a better person – a whole person? Are you a seeker? Even as a Christian, do you have a clear understanding of what God wants of you?

Understanding God, knowing who He is and how powerful He is, is crucial to realizing a truly awesome relationship with Him. God is an infinite being meaning He has always existed, does exist and will continue to exist forever – thus the great "I AM!" He wants that special relationship with you but it is your choice.

Do you want a closer walk with God? If you do, open your heart and mind and invite Him to dwell within you. Let Him strengthen you, comfort you and help you overcome the difficulties and hardships that besiege us all.

Let us pray – God is close to each of us – let Jesus come into our heart and mind and direct us in knowing, loving and serving God today – and for eternity.

Seek God's hand in looking after the ill, the sorrowing and those who are traveling. Finally, as our last act of devotion, let's praise God – stand and sing # 993 – How Great Thou Art!

Go in peace.

Devotional Title: **Who are you really when alone?** Devotional given on June 23, 2003
This short devotional draws attention to how easy your **soul** can be tempted and tainted.

Who are you really when alone?

What would you do in all these situations?

A little old lady leaves the bank and you notice she has dropped her wallet. No one else is around and you pick up the wallet and see there are several hundred dollar bills inside. You could catch her if you tried - -

You are in a store and find yourself looking at a very attractive watch in a counter-top display case. The case is easy to open and the watch must be worth $50.00. No one is around - you could reach in - -

A couple of ladies have stopped to have coffee in a small café. One places her purse on the empty chair beside her, right on the aisle, and is totally engrossed in a lively conversation with her friend. There must be money in the purse as the woman looks fairly well dressed. You walk quickly by the chair and - -

You are staying with some friends who have let you stay at their house. They have a lot of nice stuff in their home. They tell you to look after the house as they will be away for a couple of days. You assure them you will, realizing that this could be an opportunity, while you are totally alone, to really search out all their valuables. So you wait for a couple of hours and - -

What would you do?

It is said that the true character of a person is revealed by what he or she thinks and does when there is no one else around. Yes, all the examples I gave you are temptations - but they are more - they are tests of character and how you deal with each test will determine your life on earth <u>and</u> where your soul will spend eternity.

Consider these words from the word of God - the Bible. If you believe in God, - that there is a God Almighty, than these words from the scriptures will have a special significance for you. Listen carefully to the word of God and think!

Exodus 20:15 "Thou shall not steal." It is one of God's Ten Commandments!

1 Thessalonians 4:6-7 'that in this matter no one should wrong his brother or take advantage of him. The Lord will punish men for all such sins, as we have already told you and warned you. 7 For God did not call us to be impure, but to live a holy life."

1 Chronicles 28:9 "And you, my son Solomon, acknowledge the God of your father, and serve him with wholehearted devotion and with a willing mind, for the LORD searches every heart and understands every motive behind the thoughts. If you seek him, he will be found by you; but if you forsake him, he will reject you forever."

Psalm 139:1-4

"O LORD, you have searched me and you know me.
2 You know when I sit and when I rise; you perceive my thoughts from afar.
3 You discern my going out and my lying down; you are familiar with all my ways.

4 Before a word is on my tongue you know it completely, O LORD."

Hebrews 4:12-13 "For the word of God is living and active. Sharper than any double-edged sword, it penetrates even to dividing soul and spirit, joints and marrow; it judges the thoughts and attitudes of the heart. 13 Nothing in all creation is hidden from God's sight. Everything is uncovered and laid bare before the eyes of him to whom we must give account."

When your soul stands in judgment before God what will be the outcome?

Will you go to heaven or hell? You have a choice while here on earth - don't blow it!

Let us pray.

Sermon Title: **On Being Alone**   Sermon given on September 28, 2003
This is a talk on loneliness, seeking **God**, learning about God's
presence and Communication with God. The importance of
prayer

On Being Alone

How many of us know what being alone means? How many of us have
experienced the feeling of loneliness?

I remember going to camp as a very young boy and within a couple
of days I was totally 'homesick' so much so that I was sent home. It
was an awful feeling and in looking back now I realize that it was the
loneliness, despite all the other kids. It was a loneliness brought about
by severing all connection with my parents, friends and the familiar.
Some would say I was a 'wimp' but the feeling was 'real' and the term
homesick was really appropriate - I was sick.

But that loneliness is nothing compared to the loneliness experienced
by people as they go through life.

Let me first define for you the term lonely and alone. According to
the dictionary

World Book Dictionary

alone, *adjective, adverb.* 1. apart from other persons or things; quite
by oneself; solitary. (SYN) lone, isolated, unaccompanied, single. 2.
without anyone else. *Noun;* aloneness.

loneliness, *noun* .the condition or the feeling of being lonely; solitude, lonely,

1. feeling oneself alone and longing for company or friends; lonesome.

2. without many people; desolate, secluded

3a. alone; isolated. b. unaccompanied; solitary. .

Noun 1. a lonely person.

loneness, *noun*. = loneliness, loner, noun. (Informal.) 1. a person who is or prefers to be alone; one who lives or works alone. 2. an independent person. Noun. adjective 1. feeling lonely or forlorn. 2. making one feel lonely. 3. unfrequented; desolate. 4. solitary.

Noun lonesomeness. 1. (Informal.) a. a person who works or prefers to work alone. b. a person who remains to himself, especially in opinions.

Solitary adjective, *noun* 1a. alone or single; only. b. being the only one; standing by itself; unparalleled. 2a. without companions; lonely. b. away from people; remote.

Noun 1. a. person living alone, away from people. 2. a person who is left alone.

3. = solitary confinement. *Noun* solitariness. Solitary confinement, the separate confinement of a prisoner in complete isolation as a penalty for misbehavior.

Dictionary Random House Webster's Dictionary

Alone: apart from others; without another person; only; without equal.

Lone being alone; solitary; standing apart, isolated.

Lonely; affected with or causing a depressing feeling of being alone; lone, solitary (loneliness)

Lonesome; depressed because of the lack of companionship; attended with or causing such a feeling; remote or isolated.

Homesick: longing for home while away from it

Solitary; lacking or avoiding the society of others; marked by or done in the absence of companions; being the only one; sole; secluded, remote.

Solitude: the state of being alone, seclusion; lonely; unfrequented place

The Bible speaks of lonely and loneliness

From the Old Testament (NIV)
Genesis 2:18 The LORD God said, "It is not good for the man to be alone. I will make a helper suitable for him."

Ecclesiastes 4:11
"Also, if two lie down together, they will keep warm. But how can one keep warm alone? "

Psalm 25:16-17
"Turn to me and be gracious to me, for I am lonely and afflicted. The troubles of my heart have multiplied; free me from my anguish."

Psalm 69:20
"Scorn has broken my heart and has left me helpless; I looked for sympathy, but there was none, for comforters, but I found none."

Psalm 142:4
"Look to my right and see; no one is concerned for me. I have no refuge; no one cares for my life."

Lamentations 1:16
"This is why I weep and my eyes overflow with tears.
No one is near to comfort me, no one to restore my spirit.
My children are destitute because the enemy has prevailed."

From the New Testament
1 Timothy 5:5 "The widow who is really in need and left all alone puts her hope in God and continues night and day to pray and to ask God for help." (NIV)

And Jesus knew abject loneliness as He prayed in the garden.

Matthew 26:36-39 "Then Jesus went with his disciples to a place called Gethsemane, and he said to them, "Sit here while I go over there and pray." He took Peter and the two sons of Zebedee along with him, and he began to be sorrowful and troubled. Then he said to them, "My soul is overwhelmed with sorrow to the point of death. Stay here and keep watch with me."

Going a little farther, he fell with his face to the ground and prayed, "My Father, if it is possible, may this cup be taken from me. Yet not as I will, but as you will." (NIV)

How many of us see ourselves in those definitions of alone and loneliness?

Suffering from loneliness is not just a condition of present day life - it has existed as long as man has been on this planet.

Of course, we all seek our time of privacy and some even relish being alone. Some are their own best companions and do not seek the close companionship of others.

In fact many of us, especially when we are young, are so busy growing up, courting and getting married, having children, working to put bread on the table - so busy we never have time to be lonely. Until one day, we find ourselves in a situation where we lose a loved one - for whatever reason. Such a situation can sometimes be described as losing a part of yourself. *This can lead to a forlorn sense of loneliness!*

The thinkers here might even have contemplated the universe and placed themselves in the cockpit of a space capsule circling the earth while observing the billions of stars stretching as far as the eye can see and realizing that you are just a speck of dust in the great cosmos. *What a sense of loneliness!* Think about Neal Armstrong, the first man on the moon. Do you think he wondered whether the 'Lander' would lift him back to the space capsule?

In the midst of hundreds of people, you can be alone! Sometimes our pain is so great that we are oblivious to all those around us.

One definition of loneliness is this.

"Loneliness is a painful realization that you lack meaningful, close relationships with other people. This leads to emptiness, melancholy, isolation, and even to despair. A sense of rejection and a low self-image are present because you can't relate, or you feel left out and unwanted, no matter how hard you try to belong.

The nature of the society you live in contributes to loneliness. It is hard for some to maintain identity and meaningful relationships in the jungle of bureaucracy, specialization, regimentation and competition.

Loneliness can be self-inflicted. Some persons find it difficult to communicate with others or lack confidence because they have a poor self-image

Others yearn for togetherness, yet their demand for privacy and independence inhibits the development of meaningful ties with others. The fear of transparency of their inner being results in a kind of social paralysis."

Loneliness can lead to despair and a feeling of very low worth. - The very ingredients that can lead people to take their own lives. Isolation and loneliness can be a terrible burden for anyone to bear.

In the definitions we also learned that prisoners are placed in 'solitary confinement' as a form of punishment or a way of hurting them... They are taken out of "circulation" and isolated. They are forced to be 'alone'. The same feeling can be said about being ostracized. Hurtful!

What brings loneliness home to me is my wife. She looks out the bathroom window unto our neighbor's yard and sees a lovely little dog, on a chain, lying in the cold or rain and looking very sad and lonely. Even on a good day, with its master away at work, it looks lonely and she wants to comfort it. And many times, she does.

But the real concern she has about loneliness is the dying. My brother died in Toronto in the height of the SARS scare and no one was with him when he died because the hospital was closed to visitors. That really bothered her. She and her sister stayed with their mother until she died a year ago last July - so her mother was not alone.

Think of the loneliness of growing old. Family members, friends, acquaintances slowly die off leaving fewer and fewer to associate with.

We get older and feebler - possibly we can't drive anymore or get around and so we are confined to a smaller geographical area thus limiting our contacts and we get even lonelier. Finally, your life-long friend - your spouse - passes suddenly and now you are more alone than ever.

During a visit to MacKenzie Place a couple of years ago, I happened to greet a woman lying in a wheeled bed and took her hand to hold it for a minute. It was a very emotional moment as she whispered to me "she was so lonely!" My heart almost broke. I realized, then, that she was not unique as many on that ward were in the same boat.

So many people suffer from loneliness - even with the hustle and bustle and hectic pace of this world.

If we choose to be alone and we are comfortable with it - as many are - we do not suffer the pangs of loneliness as long as we are occupied and content. Curling up on the couch and reading a good book by oneself can be an enjoyable experience. Many of us need our 'private' time.

However, those who know or have known loneliness, for whatever reason, know how deep the feeling of loneliness can get. No wonder deep depression and despair are often present. You ask yourself - Does anyone care? Is there anyone to turn to for comfort when you're all alone and you need companionship?

The good news is there **is** someone who cares for you. Someone who loves you and will always be there for you.

In combating loneliness you can include the following

When you pray you can't be lonely because you are praying to – in communion with God or Jesus Christ who is your greatest friend of all. Jesus said, 'I call you not servants, but friends' (**John 15:15**).

Then again you are never lonely when you read the Bible - daily. You can become immersed in God's word thus dissolving your own loneliness.

You begin to change as you grow in a devotional relationship with God. The attitudes of loving and caring gradually develop a deepening of friendships between you and others.

Lonely people should seek a meaningful place of service in an active church. Giving attention to the needs of others will put your problems into perspective and make them seem a little less important.

Service helps us cultivate relationships with other Christians who serve and tends to increase your self esteem.

A comment from the Booklet "Our Daily Bread" is interesting. It states, "Our senior years can be viewed as a pleasantly useless era when we qualify for retirement benefits, senior discounts, and have a lot a free time to do nothing. Or we can see them as a time of great opportunity to be used for God. There is so much to do.

We can serve as mentors, teaching wisdom and virtue. Seniors can point to the ancient paths of holy living and encourage young believers to walk in them."

A leading evangelist says we should attempt to strengthen bonds within our family. Lonely people often have problems in regard to family relationships.

Working to communicate with our own family - learning to share, to respect and care, to integrate with each other - will do much to prevent loneliness.

Most of all we need to pray.

Luke 5:16 – "Jesus often withdrew to lonely places and prayed."

In **Matthew 26:36-39** where Jesus prays in the garden of Gethsemane, Jesus was alone and suffered the anguish of knowing that He was about to die. That sense of being separated and all alone was the human side of our Savior.

Concerning this passage, Charles Spurgeon wrote
"There are several instructive features in our Savior's prayer in his hour of trial. It was *lonely prayer*. He withdrew even from his three favored disciples.

Believer, be much in solitary prayer, especially in times of trial.
Lastly, *it was the prayer of resignation*. "Nevertheless, not as I will, but as thou wilt." Yield and God yields. Let it be as God wills, and God will determine for the best.
Be thou content to leave thy prayer in his hands, who knows when to give, and how to give, and what to give, and what to withhold. So pleading, earnestly, importunately, yet with humility and resignation, thou shalt surely prevail." Spurgeon, Charles H., *Morning and Evening,*

Thomas A. Kempis also commented on this passage of the Bible. He wrote -
"God our Father is here, and will be here all through the lonely hours; he is an almighty Watcher, a sleepless Guardian, a faithful Friend. Nothing can happen without his direction, for even hell itself is under his control. Darkness is not dark to him. He has promised to be a wall of fire around his people—and who can break through such a barrier?
Thomas A Kempis, *The Imitation of Christ,*

Jesus said to the Disciples, "But a time is coming, and has come, when you will be scattered, each to his own home. You will leave me all alone. Yet I am not alone, for my Father is with me." **John 16:32**

For the lonely, the Bible is a great source of comfort.

Listen - from **1 Peter 5:6-7** "Humble yourselves, therefore, under God's mighty hand, that he may lift you up in due time. Cast all your anxiety on Him because He cares for you."

In **Psalm 55:22** the psalmist says, "Cast your cares on the LORD and he will sustain you; he will never let the righteous fall."

From **Nahum 1:7** "The LORD is good, a refuge in times of trouble. He cares for those who trust in him."

One of the Bible's most comforting passages is **Matthew 11:28-30** Jesus says "Come to me, all you who are weary and burdened, and I will give you rest. Take my yoke upon you and learn from me, for I am gentle and humble in heart, and you will find rest for your souls. For my yoke is easy and my burden is light."

The answer then to loneliness is to turn to the Lord and spend time in prayer and reading the Bible.

Here is a little poem by Ackley that says it all to the lonely.
    I never walk alone, Christ walks beside me,
    He is the dearest Friend I've ever known;
    With such a Friend to comfort and to guide me,
    I never, no, I never walk alone.

It reminds me of the poem "Footprints in the Sand".

So for the lonely, the message is clear. You are never alone when you communicate with God. He is always there for you and wants your presence in heaven with Him. All you need to do is pray.

In a moment we will read the words from one of the hymns in the Hymn Book about learning how to pray.

But before we do that let me share with you a rather interesting thought mentioned in the fall 2003 Territorial Prayer Partner Newsletter. This comment is by Brenda Critch, newly appointed as Territorial Prayer Coordinator. She says, "This spring I read a particularly challenging article and felt the Lord challenging my heart with the simple words, "Lord, teach me to pray." I believe God was saying to me don't worry so much about the 'how' or the questions you might have, simply ask for the desire and discipline to pray more, and ask the Spirit's influence and guidance in your praying.

Now let's turn to the Hymn Book and hymn #625. Read (see box)

For those who know loneliness and for those who may someday know loneliness,

I encourage you to enter into a time or prayer and Bible reading daily and walk a little closer to God - a God who loves and cares for you - and who will never forsake you.

Turn to Hymn #633 - Sweet Hour of Prayer. Please stand and sing.

Let us pray –

Thanks, Blessings, Caring and Loving, Help us come to know you, and place our cares in your hands, help us to pray each day and learn from your word. Thank you for always being with us and being a comfort to us in times of loneliness.

Scripture Reading for this message

Psalm 25:16-17

> Turn to me and be gracious to me, for I am lonely and afflicted. The troubles of my heart have multiplied; free me from my anguish. (NIV)

Psalm 139:1-12

O LORD, you have searched me and you know me.

2 You know when I sit and when I rise; you perceive my thoughts from afar.

3 You discern my going out and my lying down; you are familiar with all my ways.

4 Before a word is on my tongue you know it completely, O LORD.

5 You hem me in -- behind and before; you have laid your hand upon me.

6 Such knowledge is too wonderful for me, too lofty for me to attain.

7 Where can I go from your Spirit? Where can I flee from your presence?

8 If I go up to the heavens, you are there; if I make my bed in the depths, you are there.

9 If I rise on the wings of the dawn, if I settle on the far side of the sea,

10 even there your hand will guide me, your right hand will hold me fast.

11 If I say, "Surely the darkness will hide me and the light become night around me,"

12 even the darkness will not be dark to you; the night will shine like the day,

for darkness is as light to you."

Psalm 34:15-22 "The eyes of the LORD are on the righteous and his ears are attentive to their cry; the face of the LORD is against those who do evil, to cut off the memory of them from the earth.

The righteous cry out, and the LORD hears them; he delivers them from all their troubles. The LORD is close to the brokenhearted and saves those who are crushed in spirit.

A righteous man may have many troubles, but the LORD delivers him from them all; he protects all his bones, not one of them will be broken. Evil will slay the wicked; the foes of the righteous will be condemned. The LORD redeems his servants; no one will be condemned who takes refuge in him."

From The Hymn Book – 'Prayer'

Prayer is the soul's sincere desire
Uttered or unexpressed,
The motion of a hidden fire
That trembles in the breast.

 Prayer is the burden of a sigh,
The falling of a tear,
The upward glancing of an eye
When none but God is near.

Prayer is the simplest form of speech
That infant lips can try;
Prayer the sublimest strains that reach
The majesty on high.

Prayer is the contrite sinner's voice
Returning from his ways,
While angels in their songs rejoice
And cry: Behold, he prays!

Prayer is the Christian's vital breath,
The Christian's native air,
His watchword at the gates of death;
He enters Heaven with prayer.

O thou by whom we come to God,
The life, the truth, the way!
The path of prayer thyself hast trod:
Lord, teach us how to pray!

James Montgomery (1771-1854)

Sermon Title: **Knowing, Loving Serving God** Sermon given on
September 11, 2005
A talk about how we are called to serve **God** with examples of
the many ways a church congregation can serve in individual
ministries.

"Knowing, Loving and Serving God"
Prelude - Brass Band

Thanks to our Brass Band led by Paul Rathke for providing our prelude
and service postlude music. The Brass Band has been an integral part
of The Salvation Army over many years.

Welcome, announcements, prayer & opening remarks
Welcome to The Salvation Army Grande Prairie Community
Church.

You're going to die! Well, that's what the doctor said. Let me explain

A man went to the doctor after weeks of symptoms. The doctor
examined him carefully, and then called the patient's wife into his
office. "Your husband is suffering from a rare form of anemia. Without
treatment, he'll be dead in a few weeks. The good news is it can be
treated with proper nutrition."

"You will need to get up early every morning and fix your husband
a hot breakfast—pancakes, bacon and eggs, the works. He'll need a
home-cooked lunch every day, and then an old-fashioned meat-and-

potato dinner every evening. It would be especially helpful if you could bake frequently. Cakes, pies, homemade bread—these are the things that will allow your husband to live.

One more thing. His immune system is weak, so it's important that your home be kept spotless at all times. No dust. Do you have any questions?" The wife had none.

"Do you want to break the news, or shall I?" asked the doctor.

"I will," the wife replied.

She walked into the exam room. The husband, sensing the seriousness of his illness, asked her, "It's bad, isn't it?"

She nodded, tears welling up in her eyes. "What's going to happen to me?" he asked.

With a sob, the wife blurted out, "The doctor says you're gonna die!"

Today, we commence our fall and winter program. Today's service is a special service to welcome newcomers, old friends and neighbors and, of course, our regular members.

Members - if you haven't noticed over the course of the last few weeks we have painted both the exterior and interior of our church. We've added new lighting fixtures. The grounds have been well kept and our parking lot has been spruced up for easier parking. Thanks to all those who helped, we present to you a clean and bright church.

A warm welcome to all - may you experience God's presence and be truly blessed today as we worship together.

Keep in your prayers today, our pastors Captains Dale and Jo Sobool who are holidaying in England. Our wish is that they will thoroughly enjoy themselves and return to us inspired and refreshed.

When you entered the church you received a bulletin with information about up-coming events in the church. Please read it carefully and feel free to ask any questions you may have.

The bulletin also contains today's order of service which will help you keep track of what is happening. I should point out that today's service is quite different from normal as we will present a cross-section of worship along with information about Church ministries that touch on personal spiritual growth, service to our community and our outreach programs.

Let us offer a special prayer for our service today and for those who will take part.

Today's Message is entitled "Knowing, Loving and Serving God"

What is a church?

Webster Handy College Dictionary says a church is 1st an edifice for religious worship; the chief services held there; 2nd - **a body or organization of Christian believers.**

Believer, as used here, is a person who believes in God.

My Desk Encyclopedia describes the church as a community of Christian believers, a society founded as such by Jesus Christ. The term is used both for the universal Church and for its national and local expressions.

Governed and served by its MINISTRY, the Church is established by the Holy Spirit through the Scriptures and the Sacraments.

Its life, ideally characterized by holiness, is expressed in worship, teaching, mission and good works.

Does that last statement describe our building - Nice as it is?

The church, as a building, is simply *a meeting place.*

I came from Toronto - in fact I was born and raised there. Back in the 1700's it was an open plain between two rivers on a large lake. There was no building except for the Indian teepees set up to house those visiting. The Huron Indian word for 'meeting place' is "toronto." That's how Toronto got its name. It is still a people place.

Our church then is about people - people who can be described as believers or seekers - all in various stages of learning, understanding and serving God.

Our church is very much about spreading the love of God through loving one another and loving our neighbors. We describe it this way - The Salvation Army exists to share the love of Jesus Christ, meet human needs, and be a transforming influence in the communities of our world. As a congregation, we serve with love "Heart to God and Hand to Man."

The church is also described as a 'house of worship'. Worship - an activity that believers want to do as a body or group and that is to focus on God in praise and worship through prayer and song.

Whether this is your first time here in our church or your hundredth time, we would like to share with you what our church body is all about. Jesus called on us to know, love and serve God. Let us share with you now, how we do that.

Before doing that let me direct your thoughts to an interesting bit of information that may affect your view of the Church and your own personal spiritual journey.

The information I am going to share with you will have more relevance if you believe that God exists, that you, as a mortal, have a soul, and that your soul will exist for eternity in either heaven or hell.

Someone has calculated how a typical life span of 70 years on earth is spent.

Here is the estimate of years spent on the following activities:

Sleep	23years	32.9%
Work	16years	22.8%
TV	8years	11.4%
Eating	6years	8.6%
Travel	6years	8.6%
Leisure	4.5years	6.5%
Illness	4years	5.7%
Dressing	2years	2.8%
Religion	**0.5years**	**0.7%**

Conclusion: The average person spends 183 days in 70 years attending a religious function or expressed another way - **1.2 hours is spent on religion per week - about the length of a Sunday church service.**

Interesting? Try this - if you believe in eternal life and you fit the typical mortal life span described then **you are spending .7% (less than 1 %) of your entire earthly existence in preparing your soul for eternity!**
Now that is something to think about.

What are your priorities in your life? Are you spending enough time with God – with the family of God? Is God calling you to become more involved?
Many of us spend a lot of our time in learning about Christianity – about Jesus – about the Bible – about how to live and follow in Jesus footsteps.

There are many ways we learn and grow spiritually.

PERSONAL SPIRITUAL GROWTH & DEVELOPMENT

Sharing - Knowing - learning - Bible Studies – Eva Scott - CSM
Fellowships & Worship services – Ryan Law – Youth Pastor
Scripture Reading – Psalm 100:1-5 – Myrna Colp

Loving God with
Praise & Worship with music and congregational singing
Special Song – "We Have Come Into His House" – Vicki Ying
Loving God with Praise & Worship with music and congregational singing
Worship Team

Sharing - use of personal talents in praise & worship – Michelle Davis
Hands of God and Timbrels

Youth & Sunday School – with kids – Deanna Scott
Scripture Reading – Galatians 6:7-10 – Henry Ying

Gospel Team

SERVING OTHERS
Sharing - serving God in our community –
Family Services – Pat Toyata
& Thrift Store – Dianne Chwyl

Offering – Music Interlude - Leah Colp
Scripture Reading – Romans 8:28 – Myrtle LaCroix
REACHING OUT TO OTHERS WITH LOVE
Sharing - reaching out - WOW, Community Care – Pat Toyata
Men's Retreat, Alpha – John Powers
Be an active part of the family of God – love each other – serve – volunteer

Concluding Comments – Know, love and serve God!

What you have heard and witnessed today, throughout our service, is the many ways that we, as believers, worship and serve the Lord. Each of us has been called to serve - each in a unique way.

Jesus tells us in Luke 10:27 "Love the Lord your God with all your heart and with all your soul and with all your strength and with all your mind'; and, `Love your neighbor as yourself."

I maintain that if you come to really know Jesus, and through Him, God, then you find that in knowing God, you will love Him. What do you do when you love someone deeply? Yes, you want to give to them - you want to serve them - you want to do their bidding! Because you love them!

Jesus says in John 12:26 "Whoever serves me must follow me; and where I am, my servant also will be. My Father will honor the one who serves me."

To serve the Lord - what do I have to give up? Do I have enough time? What about my many obligations? I am very busy.

I guess the answer must be in how much time you want to invest in where your soul will reside throughout eternity.

Do you know the day and the hour that you will be called? The victims of Hurricane Katrina had no idea of the ferocity of that storm - many have died. Are we close to end times?

In 2 Timothy 3:1-4, we find these words "But mark this: There will be terrible times in the last days. People will be lovers of themselves, lovers of money, boastful, proud, abusive, disobedient to their parents, ungrateful, unholy, without love, unforgiving, slanderous, without self-control, brutal, not lovers of the good, treacherous, rash, conceited, lovers of pleasure rather than lovers of God —"

Are end times just around the corner? Is our own lifetime near an end? None of us know the hour or day.

At this very moment God may be speaking to you. He has a message for each of you.

God wants you - God can use you!

God is calling you into His service. It doesn't matter how little or how much. It doesn't matter whether you are worthy.

Listen; there are many reasons why God <u>shouldn't</u> call you.
You are, however, in good company.

Moses stuttered. David's armor didn't fit. Timothy had ulcers. Jacob was a liar.
David had an affair. David was too young. Peter was afraid of death.
Paul was a murderer - so was Moses. Gideon and Thomas both doubted.
Elijah was burned out. Martha was a worry-wart. Samson had long hair. Noah got drunk. Did I mention that Moses had a short fuse? So did Peter, Paul - well lots of people do.

Come just as you are –
Today is the first day of the rest of your life! Make each day count.

If you would like to commit some of your time to helping out - in any of our ministries - just ask or let us know. If you would like to volunteer your time to help in one of our many endeavors - it could be at the soup kitchen, standing on a kettle at Christmas, helping out in Sunday school or with our worship teams - let us know.
If you want to know more about Jesus - what's it all about? You might want to sign up for our Alpha Course starting on the 20th. Or fellas, maybe you would like to experience something different in your life. Join us next Saturday for a special time of fellowship in Christ at our Men's Retreat. Register now!
"And we know that in all things, God works for the good of those who love Him, who have been called according to His purpose."
Romans 8:28
Do you feel the tug? Jesus is calling us - softly and tenderly - are we listening?
Do we feel that soft and gentle nudge - let's sing it!
Song: #264 – **Softly & Tenderly** – Leah Colp   **Closing Prayer**

Hymn
Softly & Tenderly

Softly and tenderly Jesus is calling,
Calling for you and for me!
Patiently Jesus is waiting and watching,
Watching for you and for me!

Come home, come home!
Ye, who are weary, come home!
Earnestly, tenderly, Jesus is calling,
Calling, O sinner, come home!

Why should we tarry when Jesus is pleading?
Pleading for you and for me?
Why should we linger and heed not his mercies,
Mercies for you and for me?

O for the wonderful love he has promised,
Promised for you and for me!
Though we have sinned, he has mercy and pardon,
Pardon for you and for me!

Will Lamartine Thompson (1847-1909)

Sermon Title: **Experiencing God**   Sermon given on January 29, 2006

This is a discussion about personal experience with God and how **God** calls us to perform a task within our lifetime.

Experiencing God

Before I talk to you about experiencing God I thought I would share with you a little humor about a pastor from another church.

One Sunday a pastor told his congregation that the church needed some extra money and asked the people to prayerfully consider giving a little extra in the offering plate.

He said that whoever gave the most would be able to pick out three hymns.

After the offering plates were passed, the pastor glanced down and noticed that someone had placed a $1,000 bill in the offering. He was so excited that he immediately shared his joy with his congregation and said he'd like to personally thank the person who placed the money in the plate.

And there sat our Rosie all the way in the back. She shyly raised her hand.

The pastor asked her to come to the front. Slowly she made her way to the pastor.

He told her how wonderful it was that she gave so much and in thanksgiving asked her to pick out three hymns.

Her eyes brightened as she looked over the congregation, pointed to the three most handsome men in the building and said, "I'll take him and him and him!"

Experiencing God – Part 1

I'm going to let some music play quietly in the background as I talk to you today.

You will hear the melody and even some of the words. I'll talk about that later but right now I have a few questions for you to think about.

Has God ever called you or talked to you directly?
Recently? Some time ago? Regularly?   Or never?

When I say God, I include Jesus or the Holy Spirit (or Holy Ghost).

Would you know it - if you had been called or talked to by God?

Has an angel or one of God's messengers ever made themselves known to you?

If you have been contacted how did it happen? Was it during a time of prayer? - Or during a church service? When someone was ill or dying?
Did it occur while you slept or in the middle of the day?

How did you feel after the encounter? Were you overcome with emotion? Elated? Were you in awe of the experience?

Did you know what was happening to you at the time? Were you scared? Did you feel inner peace afterwards?

Finally, what was the nature of the contact? Did God give you an answer to your prayers or desires? Did you feel uplifted? Did you feel that God was asking you to do something? - To serve Him?

Are you stronger in your faith because of your experience?

I've posed all these questions to you because I personally have experienced God's direct intervention in my life and I thought it is probably time to share this with you because of my own experience.

In fact, I have had innumerable reminders over the last little while that I need to do God's bidding and get on with it!

I now know that many others have had experiences with God - some barely perceptible - others very overwhelming. Each situation is different and affects us differently. So let me tell you about my experience.

I know I was feeling melancholy, listening to soft mood music for hours on end. I was probably in a depressed state for reasons I'll explain at another time. This was back in April 1992. I think I had a lost sense of time for a while as the words that started to appear in my mind came over a period of days. It was a message - a powerful message that caused me to virtually hold my breath. It was truly awesome and overwhelming!

At first, I could not believe what was in my head - where did it come from? Why were these thoughts in my head?

I had never had thoughts like these before - or since but I knew the message was directed at mankind - all of mankind - not just me!

Up until this time, I had always considered myself level headed, straight forward, a logical thinker and certainly not one to indulge in fantastical fantasies of the imagination. I have always been a so-called Capricorn character with deep roots and well grounded in good common sense.

I had more questions than I had answers. The first one being - why me? At that time, I did not have any relationship with God. In fact I had lived many years without giving Him a thought - at least, I think so.

I thought I was "losing it"! Losing my mind!

I assumed the message was from a divine source but I also knew that men can be fooled by the deceptions of the devil.

But the most powerful feeling I had was absolute fear - I was scared out of my wits, for myself, my wife and family. My thinking was this - if this was from God then the best way to stifle it or snuff it out was to cause the death of the recipient before the message could be made public.

To give you a sense of both the nature of the message and a taste of my fear, I felt compelled to write the whole message down, tape it and make several copies. Since I stand before, my worst fears were not realized.

It took me a while to tell members of my own family about what I had experienced but I knew very soon that the information I conveyed was not understood. I realized that to bring the message forward too soon might be counter-productive and I needed to become personally comfortable that God had indeed placed this matter on my heart and mind.

Very shortly after this experience, I came out of my melancholy state and actively pursued a thorough examination of the Bible to determine whether the information in the Bible confirmed the essential ingredients of the message I had received. Was it, in fact, of God?

At the same time, convinced that I had been called by God to fulfill some purpose, I became more involved in the church becoming a full-fledged soldier with The Salvation Army in 1996.

Since then I have tried to convey through my own sermons important parts of the Message that was imparted to me.

From time to time, I have looked at the Message I recorded and have not found any reason to change one word of it.

All these years, I have agonized over several things which I would like to share with you.

First, why me - I certainly was no saint - a sinner maybe but not that bad;

Second, I was not formally attached to any religion or religious belief at that time;

Third, although I had had a formal education in Catholic Christian Theology I was not a practicing priest, minister or pastor and this had occurred many years in the past. I had no formal training in the Bible and had read it from cover to cover only once;

Fourth, the Message seems to be aimed at both Christians and non-Christians;

Fifth, what am I supposed to do with it? I know that I am supposed to do something and I have agonized over how to do it and <u>when</u>?

Finally, I know through God's word - the Bible - to disobey God is a sin and I will suffer the consequences if I don't do His will and - - - last of all

How much time do I have left? How many years? - Or months? - Days?

So folks I'm in a quandary - what do I do?

And do any of you have the same problem?
Has God talked to you - has He asked you to do something?

In going through the Bible - searching for the answer to my problem, I came across the answer to why me.

Before I talk about that let us take a small break and thank God for His blessings and return to Him through our offering a small portion of the blessings He provides us. Let us pray.

Scripture Reading for today's message

Acts 8:3 - "Saul began to destroy the church. Going from house to house, he dragged off men and women and put them in prison."

Acts 9:1-7 - "Saul was still breathing out murderous threats against the Lord's disciples. He went to the high priest and asked him for letters to the synagogues in Damascus, so that if he found any there who belonged to the Way, whether men or women, he might take them as prisoners to Jerusalem.

As he neared Damascus on his journey, suddenly a light from heaven flashed around him. He fell to the ground and heard a voice say to him, "Saul, Saul, why do you persecute me?" "Who are you, Lord?" Saul asked.

"I am Jesus, whom you are persecuting," he replied. "Now get up and go into the city, and you will be told what you must do." The men traveling with Saul stood there speechless; they heard the sound but did not see anyone."

Acts 9:13-15 "Lord," Ananias answered, "I have heard many reports about this man and all the harm he has done to your saints in Jerusalem. And he has come here with authority from the chief priests to arrest all who call on your name."

But the Lord said to Ananias, "Go! This man is my chosen instrument to carry my name before the Gentiles and their kings and before the people of Israel."

Acts 9:17-18 Then, Ananias went to the house and entered it. Placing his hands on Saul, he said, "Brother Saul, the Lord -- Jesus, who appeared to you on the road as you were coming here -- has sent me so that you may see again and be filled with the Holy Spirit."

Immediately, something like scales fell from Saul's eyes, and he could see again. He got up and was baptized.

Experiencing God – Part 2

Before giving you the answer to my dilemma, let me touch on one of my other questions. When?

I think the time is now because of the continuing rise in crime, immoral behavior, the self-destructive use of drugs and alcohol, the declining influence of the church and finally a need to rekindle the awareness of God and Jesus in our world today as our source of strength in living out our mortal existence in preparation for eternity. It is time!

The scripture reading you just heard points to the solution of my problem and may even encourage you if God has called on you to follow Jesus.

Saul was worse than a sinner - he was a persecutor of Christians both men and women and even condoned Stephens death by stoning. Saul, later known as Paul was brought to his knees on the road to Damascus and blinded by Jesus.

The point here is that one does not have to be a Christian to be touched by God in a very forceful manner. You can be a total sinner!

Paul became, during his ministry, one of the main pillars of the new Christian church and was instrumental in spreading the word of God throughout the then known world.

Paul is a good example of being called by God into God's service, despite his background, and giving his all to teaching the gospel of Christ and the discipleship of many followers. He was totally and truly committed.

We also have our own example within The Salvation Army in William Booth who said of God "He will have all of me"! - And He did!

Those are but two examples of being called to God's service. There are thousands more. Let me elaborate. Turn to any page in the hymn book in front of you.

Pick a hymn (now don't think of the joke girls) – from the book!

Read the name of the song writer. Look at when they lived. Now look at some of the words. Tell me that they were not touched by God for both music and words.

Talking about music, think of the inspiration of Handel for "The Messiah".

Think of the inspiration of Michelangelo for the art in the Sistine chapel.

Think of all the Christian books that have been written. The videos and movies that have been made including Mel Gibson's "The Passion and The Christ".

Think of God's inspiration of the world famous evangelists over the years.

Think of the inspiration of Bill and Gloria Gaither in many of the beautiful songs and poetry they have composed - some of which you listened to earlier.

Many people have been touched by God - it is not unique. But each individual experience <u>is unique</u> - and personal! You can be deep in sin and still be called!!

I know that I have been blessed by the experience. I know that I am stronger in my faith and I know that I am commanded to know, love and serve God.

I also know that if you know God, you will love God and you will <u>want to</u> <u>serve God</u>!

If you have not already done so - sinner or saint - regardless of your present state, open your heart and mind to God. Let Him in!

Matthew 28:18-20 "Then Jesus came to them and said, "All authority in heaven and on earth has been given to me. Therefore go and make disciples of all nations, baptizing them in the name of the Father and of the Son and of the Holy Spirit, and teaching them to obey everything I have commanded you. And surely I am with you always, to the very end of the age."

Are you called to serve? Do you have a special calling? Do you have a special task to perform for your Lord?

If you are looking for God's will for you, you will find it in the Bible –
I encourage you to read your Bible daily.

Benediction from **Colossians 3:15-17**
"Let the peace of Christ rule in your hearts, since as members of one body you were called to peace. And be thankful. Let the word of Christ dwell in you richly as you teach and admonish one another with all wisdom, and as you sing psalms, hymns and spiritual songs with gratitude in your hearts to God. And whatever you do, whether in word or deed, do it all in the name of the Lord Jesus, giving thanks to God the Father through him."

Closing Hymn – Have Thine Own Way Lord

Devotional Title: **We are in God's World** Devotional given on August 20, 2006
The story of Brother Lawrence demonstrates that we need only look to know that **God** is with us.

We are in God's World

I would like to dwell for a moment on two phrases from to-night's Scripture Reading.

First, "The God who made the world and everything in it is the Lord of heaven and earth and does not live in temples built by hands."

Second, "God did this so that men would *seek him* and perhaps reach out for him and find him, though he is not far from each one of us."

The two verses made me think of Brother Lawrence – a monk in France in the year 1365 AD.

Before Brother Lawrence became a member of the Catholic Church he was like any young man growing up – alive, enthusiastic and ever seeking knowledge.

One wintry day he came upon a young tree – a sapling – standing alone – totally leafless – just a bare trunk and a few bare branches.

What caused him to gaze on that tree? What came out of that simple act was truly amazing. What did he see?

He started to think about what would happen in a few short months – the sap would start to flow, buds would come out, blossoms too, and the leaves would expand and grow.

The tree would be fully clothed in leafs and become, as it did every year, a growing vibrant plant until fall. Then it would shed it leaves and return to a dormant state and once again be a bare tree.

What did Brother Lawrence see? He saw God!! He saw God's creation, he saw God's love for mankind – he saw that the creation of earth and all that is in it as a magnificent manifestation of God's care in providing for mankind.

He knew from that single little tree that God is present all around us – He is always near us. We just have to look – to seek and you will find God.

What happened to Brother Lawrence? He became a member of a brotherhood and was the cook in a monastery. He gave his life to the service of God, through serving his fellow man.

He became famous because he was always praying and communicating with God – just as if God was in the same room as him. He did this all his life until he died.

Brother Lawrence's legacy was to demonstrate to all those around him that God is always present, and very close to each one of us.

The psalmist knew it hundreds of years before Brother Lawrence did.

Psalm 145:18 "The LORD is near to all who call on him, to all who call on him in truth. "

When people would complain about the condition the world was in, my grandmother had a stock answer. "My dear, it is not the world that is terrible, it is the people on it!"

Have you found God? If you haven't, try looking at a tree – you might be truly surprised by what you will find. Let us pray. Go in God's Grace.

Scripture for Devotional

Acts 17:24-28 "<u>The God who made the world and everything in it is the Lord of heaven and earth and does not live in temples built by hands</u>. And he is not served by human hands, as if he needed anything, because he himself gives all men life and breath and everything else. From one man he made every nation of men that they should inhabit the whole earth; and he determined the times set for them and the exact places where they should live. <u>God did this so that men would seek him and perhaps reach out for him and find him, though he is not far from each one of us.</u> 'For in him we live and move and have our being.' As some of your own poets have said, 'We are his offspring.' "

Psalm 145:18 "The LORD is near to all who call on him, to all who call on him in truth."

PART 5

The Soul and Life's Journey

Introduction

Because you have a soul and it is joined with a body, you are now fully embarked on a journey of life on earth. You will already know that life is full of obstacles and temptations—all of which will force you to exercise the free will that you have been given and make choices. That is your God-given right.

The next few sermons speak to the work of Satan, the role of angels, relationships, and the anxiety and frustration of your life—even as you seek happiness and satisfaction. They try to show you that your life is important and that God is very close.

Some say that your life on earth is a testing ground for your soul on earth. I think of life on earth as a learning experience, allowing us to make choices that will ultimately affect where our soul spends eternity. It is a unique experience, especially if you understand the message contained in *A Message for the Soul of Man*.

May you continue to be blessed by reading the sermons about your journey through life.

Sermon Title: **Defeating Satan** Sermon given on November 14, 2004

This Sermon discusses Satan and the battle being waged for each **soul**. Talk includes Sanctification and the soul as the temple of the **Holy Spirit**. You learn you always have choice.

Defeating Satan
Part 1

Bible reading in advance of Part 1 – **Revelations 12:7-9; & 17**

Let me announce that all scripture used in my message comes from the NIV Bible.

We are told to beware of the Satan and his evil forces let loose in this world. We are told he is all around us - ready to pounce. Who here believes there is a devil or Satan? Who believes there are angels? I presume everyone here believes there is a God - a God who created the universe and everything in it - including us.

I would like to spend some time today in explaining who is Satan, how he works and what his goal is. By the time I finish, I hope you will have a very clear understanding of Satan and what you need to do to defeat him - and defeat him you must!

First, who is Satan? Other names for Satan include the devil and the Evil One.

One can assume that the serpent that tempted Eve in the Garden of Eden was indeed the devil disguised as an upright animal. **Second,** where did the devil come from and why? **Third,** what does he want - and what means does he use to obtain what he wants? **Fourth,** where does he go to seek his goal? **Fifth,** how does he know if he has won or lost? Some of you may already know most of the answers - but - do you?

Interestingly the Old Testament has no mention of the devil or the 'evil one' throughout all its books. On the other hand, Satan is mentioned 14 times in the Old Testament. Satan is mentioned primarily in relation to Job in the Book of Job - about twelve times.

What does that tell us? It means that God relied on His message delivered directly and through prophets to the people of Israel to heed his teachings and acknowledge their fidelity to Him. After all, they were God's chosen people. They had no idea that a devil existed within their midst. Think of this - all the other people (non-Jews) of the then known world did not know about a living God and I presume had no knowledge of any evil forces.

We know from the Old Testament of the continuing "falling away" of the Jewish people and how they were punished for wrongdoing. Was it their sinful, disobedient nature or something else?

We learn more about Satan, the devil and the evil one from the New Testament. There are 32 references to the devil; 32 references to Satan; 32 references to demons and 12 references to 'the evil one'. Another interesting fact was 14 references to hell and 5 references to Hades in the New Testament but no references to Hades or hell in the Old Testament.

But, let us go on. Where did the devil come from? The Bible tells us in **Revelation 12:7-9** "And there was war in heaven. Michael and his angels fought against the dragon, and the dragon and his angels fought back. But he was not strong enough, and they lost their place in heaven. The great dragon was hurled down -- that ancient serpent called the devil, or Satan, who leads the whole world astray. He was hurled to the earth, and his angels with him."

In **Ezekiel 28:12-18** we find a possible picture of what transpired with Satan. God said, "Son of man, take up a lament concerning the king of Tyre and say to him:

`This is what the Sovereign **LORD** says: "'You were the model of perfection, full of wisdom and perfect in beauty. You were in Eden, the garden of God; every precious stone adorned you: ruby, topaz and emerald, chrysolite, onyx and jasper, sapphire, turquoise and beryl.

Your settings and mountings were made of gold; on the day you were created they were prepared. You were anointed as a guardian cherub, for so I ordained you. You were on the holy mount of God; you walked among the fiery stones.

You were blameless in your ways from the day you were created till wickedness was found in you. Through your widespread trade you were filled with violence, and you sinned. So I drove you in disgrace from the mount of God, and I expelled you, O guardian cherub, from among the fiery stones.

Your heart became proud on account of your beauty, and you corrupted your wisdom because of your splendor.

I threw you to the earth; I made a spectacle of you before kings. By your many sins and dishonest trade you have desecrated your sanctuaries."

The devil was originally an important and powerful angel in heaven and coveted God's position. Pride and selfish ambition were the reasons he was put out of heaven. Thus the battle ensued where the devil and his following were cast out of heaven, thereafter, to roam the earth.

The devil roams the earth as **Revelation 12:9 & 12** tell us; "--that ancient serpent called the devil, or Satan, who leads the whole world astray. He was hurled to the earth, and his angels with him." "Therefore rejoice, you heavens and you who dwell in them! But woe to the earth and the sea, because the devil has gone down to you! He is filled with fury, because he knows that his time is short"

What is Satan or the Devil like? Some of the names he has been called give a pretty good idea of his nature. He deceives transforming himself into an "angel of light" **(2 Corinthians 11:14)**; Satan tempts as seen in the contest with Jesus in **Matthew 4:1-11.** He blinds the minds of the unbelieving so that they may not come to the light. **(2 Corinthians 4:4)**

He is a murderer and a liar - the father of lies **(John 8:44)**.

What does the devil want? He has been cast out of heaven by God and he wants to thwart God's desire. What is God's desire? God wants every soul to acknowledge Him and come to know, love and serve Him and thereafter, to spend eternity in heaven with Him.

It is obvious, then, that the devil wants to defeat God's plan of salvation for each and every soul on earth - yesterday - today and tomorrow. So the prize for this great battle is your soul! And you are the battleground!

Let's talk about the soul for a minute,

When you arrived you were given a marble. Take this marble and hold it in your left hand - clench your fist. The marble represents your soul (as I have explained before and will do again sometime). Now slowly stretch out your hand to the left and slowly open your hand to reveal the marble in the palm of your hand.

Now the person to your left, using their right hand now takes the marble out of your hand.   *(Devil appears on screen)*

Symbolically you have just lost your soul! The opening of your hand - knowingly - allowed your soul to be exposed and taken.

In other words - *you all lost your marbles!* Please return the marble you took to your neighbor.

Seriously, you saw two things - the importance of your soul, the object of the devil's schemes, and how easily it can be taken from you by the mere power of suggestion.

Do you ever wonder why it is so hard to be good? God, in creating you, gave you certain attributes that are necessary for you to live. He gave you a desire to eat; He gave you the desire to quench thirst; He gave you the desire to procreate; He gave you the desire to seek knowledge and experiment; He gave you the desire to seek happiness, love and satisfaction; He gave you the desire to excel and succeed.

Notice that virtually all of these natural desires can be converted to the seven deadly sins of pride, envy, anger, sloth, avarice, gluttony and lust. All the devil has to do is encourage temptations to occur and let human nature take its course. Did the devil "make you do it"? Of course not, but, the great deceiver and father of liars did his very best to influence you and the actions of those around you. But you have always had the final choice!

You know that God hates sin but loves the sinner. He has warned you, through His word in **Romans 6:23** "For the wages of sin is death, but the gift of God is eternal life in Christ Jesus our Lord."

When and how does the Devil know he has won? He knows when he has stopped another soul from reaching heaven! Which cannot be counted until you leave your mortal body - why?

Because you no longer are able to do anything to change the result! Your soul has departed from your body.

You are dead!

How do you defeat the devil? I'll get into that in Part 2.

Let us pause to give back to God a portion of the blessings He has bestowed on us.

Defeating Satan - Part 2

Bible reading in advance of Part 2 – **Hebrews 10:26-31**

"If we deliberately keep on sinning after we have received the knowledge of the truth, no sacrifice for sins is left, 27 but only a fearful expectation of judgment and of raging fire that will consume the enemies of God. 28 Anyone who rejected the Law of Moses died without mercy on the testimony of two or three witnesses. 29 How much more severely do you think a man deserves to be punished who has trampled the Son of God under foot, who has treated as an unholy thing the blood of the covenant that sanctified him, and who has insulted the Spirit of grace? 30 For we know him who said, "It is mine to avenge; I will repay, "and again, "The Lord will judge his people. 31 **It is a dreadful thing to fall into the hands of the living God."**

Let me summarize. We know that there is a devil, who is determined to thwart God's desire to have every soul with Him in heaven. So **there is a major battle going on for your soul and the battleground is you!**

Some of you will say – "But I am already saved! – I don't have to worry."

Let's talk about Salvation for a moment. Those who have accepted Jesus Christ as their savior and acknowledge Him to be the son of God and have confessed and repented of their sins is saved through the grace of God (from hell).

Before you were saved - you were a sinner. **Romans 3:23** "for all have sinned and fall short of the glory of God,"

There are actually three phases in your walk towards eternal life with God in heaven. These could be described as pre-Salvation, Salvation and Post-Salvation.

The first phase (pre-salvation) is one of ignorance of God and His desire for you - your soul. Every person finds themselves wondering about God, especially during times of trials and tribulations.

The Holy Spirit is working to attract you to the word of God while the devil is busy trying to keep you occupied with your sins and vices.

One day you open the door to God's prompting and you seek more information. You have become a "seeker". Finally, through the convicting power of the Holy Spirit you accept Jesus as your Lord and Savior.

You have reached the **second phase.** You have experienced **Salvation!** You are now a Christian - a believer in and a follower of Christ. It is a time of wonderment and uncertainty. Your soul is saved! - from eternity in hell - and are promised eternal life in heaven!

The process I have just explained can take years. You may have accepted Christ very early in life or much later. At that point, becoming a Christian, you have initially defeated the devil – but that is only temporary. Now the devil is really ticked off!

Regardless, all Christians must go through the **third phase – post-Salvation.**

Keep in mind that you are never safe from the devil's devious ways. Let me explain

Paul states in **Colossians 1:21-23** "Once you were alienated from God and were enemies in your minds because of your evil behavior. But now he has reconciled you by Christ's physical body through death to present you holy in his sight, without blemish and free from accusation –if you continue in your faith, established and firm, not moved from the hope held out in the gospel. This is the gospel that you heard and that has been proclaimed to every creature under heaven, and of which I, Paul, have become a servant."

You will find that The Salvation Army states, "We believe that continuance in a state of salvation depends upon continued **obedient faith** in Christ." This is Doctrine 9 found in the back of the Hymn Book. Both Doctrine 9 and 10 deal with your Christian life after conversion.

Peter says in **1 Peter 1:3-9**
"Praise be to the God and Father of our Lord Jesus Christ! In his great mercy he has given us new birth into a living hope through the resurrection of Jesus Christ from the dead, and into an inheritance that

can never perish, spoil or fade -- kept in heaven for you, who through faith are shielded by God's power until the coming of the salvation that is ready to be revealed in the last time. In this you greatly rejoice, though now for a little while you may have had to suffer grief in all kinds of trials. These have come so that your **faith** -- of greater worth than gold, which perishes even though refined by fire - may be proved genuine and may result in praise, glory and honor when Jesus Christ is revealed. Though you have not seen him, you love him; and even though you do not see him now, you believe in him and are filled with an inexpressible and glorious joy, for you are receiving **the goal of your faith, the salvation of your souls.**"

When we are saved we move from darkness to light, from judgment to salvation, from death to life (of the soul). But we must also note that even in the case of the apostles (Peter, in particular), his theology changed gradually, and some of his sins and prejudices lingered on for a long period of time.

Salvation changes our status with God instantly, but it does not instantly eradicate all sin or error from prejudice. We are still prone to sin.

Peter is an apostle, but he is not infallible, nor is he free from all the errors of his past. So it is with us. God changes some things instantly and others gradually (through a process called Sanctification).

In other words in Phase three, we will find our faith is tested – and by whom?
You guessed it – Satan!

Those who have been saved can be tempted and fall away. We are told in **Revelation 2:10,** "do not be afraid of what you are about to suffer. I tell you, the devil will put some of you in prison to test you, and you will suffer persecution for ten days. Be faithful, even to the point of death, and I will give you the crown of life."

Besides Peter, Paul also suffered from the temptations to sin.

He says in **Romans 7:15-19** "I do not understand what I do. For what I want to do, I do not do, but what I hate, I do. And if I do what I do not want to do, I agree that the law is good. As it is, it is no longer I myself who do it, but it is sin living in me. I know that nothing good lives in me, that is, in my sinful nature. For I have the desire to do what is good, but I cannot carry it out.

For what I do is not the good I want to do; no, the evil I do not want to do – this I keep on doing."

Scripture does contain a dire warning.

Hebrews 6:4-6 "It is impossible for those who have once been enlightened, who have tasted the heavenly gift, who have shared in the Holy Spirit, who have tasted the goodness of the word of God and the powers of the coming age, if they fall away, to be brought back to repentance, because to their loss they are crucifying the Son of God all over again and subjecting him to public disgrace."

So the battle is now on! You must not fall away or your soul will be lost. The devil wants your soul to be lost and he is going to do everything he can to make that happen.

This is why The Salvation Army talks about Sanctification in Doctrine 10 and **it is the answer to defeating the devil!**

The Doctrine says" We believe that it is the privilege of all believers to be "wholly sanctified", and that their "whole spirit and soul and body" may "be preserved blameless unto the coming of our Lord Jesus Christ".

The basis of this doctrine is **1 Thessalonians 5:23** "May God himself, the God of peace, sanctify you through and through. May your whole spirit, soul and body be kept blameless at the coming of our Lord Jesus Christ. "

1 Thessalonians 4:3 "It is God's will that you should be sanctified: that you should avoid sexual immorality;"

Sanctified means to become holy. You have been filled with the Holy Spirit so God is close to you and the Holy Spirit dwells within you (in your soul which has been cleansed). That state can only continue if your soul does not become blackened with sin as God may love the sinner but He hates sin!

2 Corinthians 6:16
"For we are the temple of the living God. As God has said: "I will live with them and walk among them, and I will be their God, and they will be my people."

God wants you to be faithful to Him, abide with Him and walk with Him in your daily lives.

Study God's word daily and pray to Him always. Even if you stray you can seek forgiveness because He is a merciful God.

It is those who willfully and continuously disobey (sin) who will ultimately fall away and suffer the consequences promised in **Hebrews 6:4-6.**

In the New Testament, we have words of wisdom for the 'saved'.
1 John 2:24 "See that what you have heard from the beginning remains in you. If it does, you also will remain in the Son and in the Father."
1 John 1:9 "If we confess our sins, he is faithful and just and will forgive us our sins and purify us from all unrighteousness. We can always seek His forgiveness for our trespasses."
A good daily prayer is the Lord's Prayer – keep it in mind.

Ephesians 6:11, 13 "Put on the full armor of God so that you can take your stand against the devil's schemes. - put on the full armor of God, so that when the day of evil comes, you may be able to stand your ground."
This passage clearly demonstrates that God knows you will be attacked by the devil.

James 4:7 "Submit yourselves, then, to God. Resist the devil, and he will flee from you."

1 Peter 1:15-16 "But as He who called you is holy, you also be holy in all your conduct, because it is written, "Be holy, for I am holy.""

John 15:4 "Remain in me, and I will remain in you. No branch can bear fruit by itself; it must remain in the vine. Neither can you bear fruit unless you remain in me."

Finally, Jesus said in **Matthew 22:37** "'Love the Lord your God with all your heart and with all your soul and with all your mind.' In other words, totally commit yourself to God.

If you walk with God and abide in Him and He in you – **you will defeat the devil** and reach that which has been promised you – eternal life for your soul in heaven with God.

Let us sing song No 670 – Abide with Me (see box below)

Let us pray
Search us, Oh, God, and know our hearts today; cleanse us from every sin and set us free. Guide and bless us as we seek to walk daily with Thee and help us follow the teachings of your Son, the living Savior, Jesus Christ.

Help us, dear Lord, to defeat Satan and all his demons. May we be made holy through and through and may our whole spirit, soul and body be kept blameless at the coming of our Lord Jesus Christ. Amen

Go in Peace

Hymn
Evening - Abide With Me

ABIDE with me; fast falls the eventide;
The darkness deepens; Lord, with me abide!
When other helpers fail, and comforts flee,
Help of the helpless, O abide with me!

2 Swift to its close ebbs out life's little day;
Earth's joys grow dim; its glories pass away;
Change and decay in all around I see;
O thou who changest not, abide with me!

3 I need thy presence every passing hour;
What but thy grace can foil the tempter's power?
Who like thyself my guide and stay can be?
Through cloud and sunshine, O abide with me!

4 I fear no foe, with thee at hand to bless;
Ills have no weight, and tears no bitterness.
Where is death's sting? Where, grave, thy victory?
I triumph still if thou abide with me.

5 Hold thou thy cross before my closing eyes;
Shine through the gloom, and point me to the skies;
Heaven's morning breaks, and earth's vain shadows flee;
In life, in death, O Lord, abide with me!
                    Henry Francis Lyte (1793-1847)

Sermon Title: **Relationships and the Soul of Man**   S e r m o n
given on June 4, 2000
A talk on relationships through life; dealing with relationships
and choices through life affecting your **soul**'s ultimate destiny and
relationship with **God**.

Relationships and the Soul of Man

Several years ago, I believe the Lord lay on my heart, a special task. That
task was to lead people to a clear understanding of their soul and the
importance of their soul in the scheme of life on earth.

Why I should be asked to perform this task, I do not know. I do
know, however, how important it is. As a result, I have provided several
messages on the topic of the soul of man. Some of you may even
remember the marble.

Today, you see before you a nut! One of God's numerous creations.
Every one of God's creations has a purpose. So does this nut! Notice
it has a very hard outer shell which provides it with protection. It is
protected from many of life's hardships until it finds the proper place
in which it will play its role - the creation of a new life. We'll come back
to this lowly nut in a little while.

Today, I want to talk about human relationships and, again, the
soul of man.

"If you died right now, what three things would you miss most?"
I'm going to ask you to put your answers under Comments on the hand-

out page. Leave room to fill out answers to the some other questions as they come up. This will be like a memory test. You will not be asked to hand in your answers.

Now, I'm going to take you back in time to your own birth and upbringing. I am going to try to rekindle memories from your past about the relationships you have had with many, many people. While the circumstances will not be the same for everyone, it is my hope I will provide sufficient reminders that each of you will remember people and events in your life that became part of your life, however brief or long.

Now, just what do I mean by relationships? The dictionary definition describes **relationship** as a noun. 1. a **connection.** 2. the condition of belonging to the same family. 3. the state or condition that exists between people or groups that deal with one another. Example: a business relationship, a social relationship or a friendship.

Relationship comes from 'relation' a noun meaning 1. a **connection** in thought or meaning. 2. A **connection** or dealings between persons, groups, or even countries.

Relationships or connections can vary greatly in length, duration, intensity and meaning – they are as varied as life itself. They can be hurtful or joyful. Everyone's life is shaped by how they deal with each and every relationship and the choices made as a result.

Your relationships actually started in your mother's womb and while there will not be a recollection of that time, the relationship of mother and child was formed in the womb. The maternal love was nurtured in those few months while the child felt the warmth and security of the mother's womb as it grew.

We have all seen how rapidly children grow but from a child's point of view time passes very slowly - do you remember waiting and waiting for school to be let out for summer holidays? Or Christmas would never get here - **believing in Santa?**

Our childhoods are full of relationships. I can remember the playing and the fighting - with both boys and girls and the nonsense we participated in, sometimes, just to show off. Yes, our relationships as children often revolved around being better at something than the other guy. It was a time when we were learning about ourselves - our strengths, weaknesses - our likes and our dislikes.

We were, also, learning about our friends as they, too, sought out who they were. Can you remember how sensitive you were to a sarcastic remark about you or your appearance? Many of us, several times, were reduced to tears and made to feel very insignificant or inadequate. **Do you remember a person like that?**

The frustrations and the never-ending competition for acceptance by peers and parents alike created in each one of us a part of the character we are today. This was all brought about through our childhood relationships.

During this time in your life, do you remember what your mother and father and brothers and sisters were doing? Each played a part, however big or small - even teachers and church ministers played a role - they were there and each had their own idea of what you should be doing - either by direct order or by persuasion.

Then, we entered adolescence and life just got more complicated. Remember wanting to be 18 (it used to be 21) so that you could be your own boss? You wouldn't have to answer for your words or actions, and you could do whatever you wanted - ah such freedom! (Or so you thought!) **Who taught you to drive?**

This is the time that boys and girls noticed each other and special relationships sprung up. **Do you remember your first love?** It was also a time when true, long-lasting friendships were started that lasted many years as the trials and tribulations of growing up were shared. Think of those special relationships and how they helped influence the person you are today. **Can you remember your best friend** and how your lives were intertwined? Do you remember the stupid things you did?

Some of you may also have experienced working at a job, even part-time. The work gave you some money to spend - that allowance you got from your parents was never enough, was it? You learned the value of money, you learned the relationship between work and money and you, also, learned about - **the boss - remember?**

As your schooling progressed, you learned more and more about the world you live in, the many different countries and cultures on the globe, the many languages and religions and the many economic and political systems that exist - and war!

Your teachers were preparing you for your role in life - even though you may not have known it at the time. Some of the most important relationships anyone has ever experienced are that of loving and caring teachers - who, you recall, we really didn't appreciate at the time. We might not even remember their names. **Can you remember something a teacher did or said that somehow influenced you?**

About this time, you may have experienced, possibly not at first hand but close, the death of a dear one. Maybe it was a friend's father or your own grandfather or an aunt. How different everyone seems to be around death. **Do you remember?**

Then too, you may have experienced the role of the police and the court system as a friend of yours was arrested for some misdemeanor like shoplifting... **Can you remember being tempted to do 'naughty' things?** Did you?

What has been happening throughout your youthful years is that, through the influence of many people and relationships, the veil of ignorance - meaning the unknown - has been pulled aside and you have been "finding yourself" - your talents, your hopes and beliefs, your desires and even possibly a plan for your life with a goal to strive for. Without the influence and interaction with all those around you, you would probably not be the person you are today - good or bad. Yes, you may have picked up some bad habits along the way. Not all relationships are good and making a wrong choice can lead you into a life of sin and pain.

Do the hurts outweigh the happy times of your youth? Each person is different and each has had different experiences. But one thing is true.

The person we are - each one of us, throughout our life - at any moment of our life, - we are the sum total of all we have learned, thought, reasoned, experienced or done.

We are really something! But let me go on -

Now we are adults - we have found our true love and married. We have a job with good prospects and not a bad wage. We have a roof over our head and wheels to get around and life is settling into a routine of work, home and play. Now we balance our time between work and home, especially as the kids come along. It's nice to get away for a round of golf or a vacation. **Do you remember this change?**

Now we have a whole new spectrum of relationships. The first, of course, is our spouse - is this relationship working out? Or does it get rocky with financial pressures and emotional problems - - and the kids. How are we with the kids - more important, how are we as a parent with all the responsibilities of providing and caring for the children and our spouses? Are we having a hard time handling these family relationship pressures? **Is the relationship with the family a positive one - or is it a burden?**

What about the workplace? There is always someone trying to get the better of every situation. The political goings on within the company, you could write a book about. How do we relate to the other employees?
And then there is - the boss! How do we relate to the person who pays us and requires the full use of our abilities each and every day? Is it a drag? Is the pressure too much?

A good boss is worth their weight in gold! A good boss is a person who has learned to do the right things at the right time for the right purpose so as to achieve the right end .Notice - I said a good boss! From this person, you could learn a lot - even how to be a good boss yourself one day! I learned once to be a good boss, you, first, had to be a good employee! **How is your relationship with the boss?**
Obviously, I have not gone too deep into the whole spectrum of life. Many and varied relationships can be formed over many years,

under all kinds of circumstances. People's lives can be enriched by what they take and give in a relationship. The latter is the formula for a true relationship - giving and receiving. If you add love to that you will have a richer relationship.

Friendships are made of just such relationships - they are precious!

Well, where are we now? - we are getting older and life has thrown so many hardships our way we have developed a very tough defensive shell and you probably couldn't change us one iota if you tried. We are hard cases and life holds no surprises. We'll tough it out until the bitter end. **Can you identify with that?**

For some, life can become very bitter. Their heart is hardened - their ears are plugged and their eyes are blinded. Some may even feel that their whole life has been a waste. What is my life really all about? Why am I here on earth?

I have just covered some of the relationships with people. What about pets? What about your relationship with the material things around us. What about our ability to create something – a painting, a poem, a craft or even playing music?

Then there is the relationship with nature and the many faces of the seasons and the world around us? Do you appreciate God's handiwork in nature and how you relate to the world around you?

There can even be very special group relations that tie us to a movement (like politics), an idea or even the world through the Internet! There is so much more!

All of these are relations of one type or another, with one common denominator - simply put we, individually, are all **connected!**

Remember the definition - relation - connected! Through all our senses and intelligence we, continuously, all through life, have an open two way conduit to everything in this world. That is truer now, than ever, with the arrival of the communication age through the computer and the Internet.

I have always thought of life as a physics law. Newton's Law of Inertia states that an object moving in a straight line will continue to move in a straight line unless acted upon by an outside force. This law also states that an object at rest will stay at rest unless a force moves it. Every relationship is like a force as it 'affects' everything within the relationship or connection.

To complicate life even more, people relationships are influenced by color, creed, age, disposition, appearance, personality, language, even dress or hair style. Likes and dislikes surface quickly and first impressions are often lasting impressions. All of these affect our relationships with people.

As we proceed through life, we become steadfast in our opinions and convictions as learned through experience. This can harden us, keep a defensive shell around us and protect us from all the "slings and arrows" of life.

You have probably wondered - "Why am I going through all of this (life)? What is it all for?

Now ask yourself this question - what do you retain from every personal relationship you have ever had and those you continue to have? The answer is - you have the memory - right? If you have noted your memories on the paper, you will have proved that you do have the memory. And what memories we all have!

Did you, as a person, change as result of your relationships (connections)? What happened to you as a result of every relationship, occurred based on the choice you made at the time the relationship existed.

"What has this got to do with the soul?"

Every relationship, at one time, was real. But now they are memories.

As memories, they reside in the same place as your personality, your knowledge, intelligence, emotions - **they all reside in your immortal soul - now and forever!**

Your soul is the recipient of everything you have ever thought, said or done. Everything your soul is, and has stored away, will remain with you after the death of your body! Remember, your soul is indestructible and lives forever! - **So do your memories!**

Relationships happen in 'real time' (now) while past relationships exist in 'past' time. All relationships, good and bad, place before you opportunities for growth.

Everyone has the opportunity to seek out and find new relationships, anywhere in the world, and use these relationships to grow in maturity and intelligence. Life can be richer and more meaningful with every relationship experienced. Your maturity comes from the exercise of good judgment in any relationship. Your soul's eternal destiny is your choice!

How you have dealt with every relationship you have ever had, has helped make your soul what it is today?

Your **choices** in life have brought you to that point where you (your soul) is either good or evil which, in turn will dictate where your soul spends eternity - either in heaven or in hell!

You make the choice of your soul's destiny every day, every hour as you deal with every relationship and event that comes your way (in NOW time) - it may be as simple as the paperboy walking across your grass.

Let's go back to the nut. Can we say that this nut represents a person who has had a hard life and has created a hard defensive shell? Are you, too, like this hard nut?

Hard shell, a tough nut to crack - but watch........!

Inside the nut is a much softer substance - the meat... We are all like that nut as we are, inside our hard exterior, truly soft and fragile. We all seek comfort, love and security - just like in the womb. We've been searching for that all our lives.

The meat of the nut is like your soul. When it finds a place where it will be nourished, warm and comfortable in its environment, it will blossom and flourish.

Can you identify with the need for comfort, warmth, love and nourishment?

Such a place exists for every soul and it can be found through a very special relationship many never know exists unless they seek it out and find it!

But before I explain further, let me talk for a moment of two special relationships we have all experienced in this Church.

The first is the warm and loving relationship that each of us has for the other as members of the family of God. For many of us, that is a connection and relationship which are very meaningful in each of our lives and we cherish it. I pray it will always be there, for all of us, as we walk through life, on our spiritual journey.

The second relationship is that existing between our pastors, Dave & Lynn and family – and each one of us. They epitomize everything that is loving, warm and giving - and human as they minister to each of us as truly committed to God and His teachings. How can we not be affected by this wonderful relationship?

While it will soon become a memory in 'past' time, it will be, none-the-less, a 'living memory' that each of us will hold precious in our soul!

It is a memory that will continue to guide us as we seek a home in heaven for our souls. Dave and Lynn have helped each us so much in our spiritual journey. We ask God's blessing and protection for the Grice family, wherever they go.

Finally, the most important relationship of all is the spiritual connection with a loving Father in Heaven and His Son, Jesus Christ.

Do you have any idea, the number of times, during your life that God, your Creator, has sought you out? - has wanted to 'connect' with you? Every day!

Have you any idea how much, He loves each one of you and wants to have a deep, spiritual relationship with you - not just here on earth but, for all eternity?

Because He gave us a **'free will'** under which we can exercise **"free choice"**, He does not impose Himself on us, but, does send us a lot of reminders.

A good example of that occurred to me about 10 years ago when my grandson came home from church one Sunday and said, "You know what, Gramp?" Of course, I said "no" to which he responded with, **"God loves YOU!"**

That came in the midst of a very trying time in my life. I was a hard case nut but I was cracked and made vulnerable and that is when God placed on me a very special burden. We entered a very special relationship - one, I hope I can live up to.

He asked me to tell you that you must recognize the importance of your own soul - **your soul is immortal** - that no matter what the world holds out for you, there is only one thing that should be important to you.

God wants each and every soul to have a right relationship with Him, thus, assuring your soul will be with Him in heaven, after it has departed your body.

Of all the relationships you will experience in your life, none are more important than a loving relationship with God! Such a relationship will guarantee that you will spend your eternal life in the love and comfort you have been seeking in this life. But it is a lonely journey. Each must make this spiritual journey on their own.

Yes, your mortal life is shared with those who love you - that IS a special relationship. But no one knows you like God does - He knows your every thought and deed - past, present and future. He knows your most innermost fears and feelings. He knows you better than you know yourself and He loves **YOU**!

Because of His great love for all souls, He sent His son, as a sacrifice, to pay the penalty of man's sinfulness and to guide each one of us during our mortal life. It is, through Jesus, that you will come to know the Father. It is, through Jesus, your soul (you) will come to know eternal happiness in heaven.

Some of you already have a very strong relationship with God and are blessed with the indwelling of your soul by the Holy Spirit. You are truly blessed. You know the Holy Spirit helps you in your daily walk while you seek to know, love and serve God and follow in the footsteps of Jesus.

Because Jesus became man, died and returned to His Father's throne, He knows what it is to be mortal, the stress and strain of living, all the afflictions we, as humans, endure. He knows life is not easy and much of it clouds the most important quest your soul has - the goal of eternal happiness found in heaven.

That is why Jesus said, "Come to me, all you who are weary and burdened, and I will give you rest. Take my yoke upon you and learn from me, for I am gentle and humble in heart, and you will find rest for your **souls.** For my yoke is easy and my burden is light." **Matthew 11:28-30** (NIV)

To help you live a right life, .Jesus told you how - in His Word; "'Love the Lord your God with all your heart and with all your soul and with all your strength and with all your mind'; and, 'Love your neighbor as yourself'". **Luke 10:27** (NIV)

What is important here, beside your relationship with God, is your relationship with all mankind recognizing that, like you, every person in the world has a soul and was created by God. That should be reason enough to love them.

If you do not now have that special relationship with God, Jesus will help you. All you have to do is have the desire - you must make the first move - it's your choice!

Jesus says; "So I say to you: Ask and it will be given to you; seek and you will find; knock and the door will be opened to you. **Luke 11:9** (NIV)

It is that simple - you and Jesus. Jesus is asking you to come to the Father through Him. "As the Father has loved me, so have I loved you. Now remain in my love. If you obey my commands, you will remain in my love, just as I have obeyed my Father's commands and remain in his love. I have told you this so that my joy may be in you and that your joy may be complete.

My command is this: Love each other as I have loved you. Greater love has no one than this that he lay down his life for his friends. You are my friends if you do what I command. I no longer call you servants, because a servant does not know his master's business. Instead, I have called you friends, for everything that I learned from my Father I have made known to you. You did not choose me, but I chose you and appointed you to go and bear fruit -- fruit that will last. Then the Father will give you whatever you ask in my name. This is my command: Love each other". **John 15:9-17** (NIV)

If you were one of Jesus' disciples and you heard these words, would you not think this was truly a wonderful relationship?

He is calling you - Jesus is calling you to that same kind of relationship that He had with the apostles. Will you meet Him now? You and Jesus - in the garden as dusk is falling - alone with Jesus - just you and He -

If you do not know Jesus as Lord and Savior, will you open your heart to HIM now? As we sing the words to this beautiful music, why don't you resolve to give your whole heart, mind and soul to Jesus - how?

Easy - just say, "Dear God I love you, I believe in Jesus and I am sorry for all my sins. Please forgive me and cleanse my soul and let the Holy Spirit dwell in me the rest of my life. Please help me have a right relationship with You, dear Lord. In Jesus' name, I ask it."

Relationships exist for varying lengths of time. Some come to us, others we seek out.

Relationships, ultimately, become personal memories of times and events in which we participated. We will have become a better or worse person and our soul will reflect this forever.

May Jesus show us the way to an eternal loving relationship with Him and may God bless us and have mercy on our souls. Amen

Let us sing "I come to the garden alone"

Sermon Title: **Love and your Soul** Sermon given on August 11, 2002
A discussion on love's value and God's unconditional love. Object
of **God**'s love - the **soul**.

Love and your Soul

As you get older you tend to become a little forgetful and need to write
things down. This story may help you understand.

Mistaken Identity

Two ministers were discussing the advisability of writing down the
names of brides and grooms to aid their memory at the ceremony. One
minister said, "I once called the groom by the wrong name,"

The other minister said, "1 once started a ceremony and realized I
couldn't remember whether the groom was John or James. I whispered
to the groom, 'is your name James or John?' 'James,' he replied. Then
the bride nudged the groom and said your name is John."

Please forgive me than if I refer to my notes on the subject of **Love
and your soul.**

Ten years ago I was brought to my knees by God to receive a
message that I immediately wrote down and even taped. This message
entitled, "A Message for the Soul of Man" troubled me - even scared me
as I could not understand why I was the recipient of such a message -
nor what I was to do about it At the time, I was not a really committed
Christian .. 'Lukewarm' is probably an apt description.

However, from that day, I have earnestly studied the Bible seeking confirmation of the content of the **"Message for the Soul of man."** I can honestly say that in re-reading three of four times since I received that Message, I cannot change one word.

In the meantime, 1have tried to impart to members of this congregation the details of that 'Message' and have done so through sermons over the last six years.

Some of you may remember the marble when I talked about the soul in July and October 1996. Some may remember the discussion on Salvation, Relationships- and Understanding through 1997 to 2000.

Today, I would like to continue this journey with you - a journey to appreciate the real significance of each individual soul on this earth. Today, I would like to talk about each soul and the importance of love.

Where do I start? Everybody knows what is meant by love - or do we?

Let me tell you one of two short stories about love -

For Richer or Poorer
Author Unknown

The wives who lived within the walls of the Weinsberg Castle in Germany were well aware of the riches it held: gold, silver, jewels, and wealth beyond belief.

Then the day came in 1141 A.D. when all their treasure was ·threatened. An enemy army had surrounded the castle and demanded the fortress, the fortune, and the lives of the men within. There was nothing to do but surrender.

Although the conquering commander had set a condition for the safe release of all women and children, the wives of Weinsberg refused to leave without having one of their own conditions met, as well. They demanded that they be allowed to fill their arms with as many possessions as they could carry out with them. Knowing that the women couldn't possibly make a dent in the massive fortune, their request was honored.

When the castle gates opened, the army outside was brought to tears. Each woman had carried out her husband.

The wives of Weinsberg, indeed, were well aware of the riches the castle held.

Now that is love!

Let us return to the present.

Before going on, try this - look at each other and try to visualize that person next to you as a soul without a body - can you do it? [Pause] That is how God sees us - as an individual soul!

Yes, we have a mortal body but that is temporary! Our soul is His creation and it is immortal - it will never die. Keep that thought in the back of your head.

Let me ask you a few questions.

Do you know the *purpose* of your mortal life on earth?
Do you *really* know that God loves you *unconditionally?*
Do you know *why* and what that kind of love is called?

Do you know what love is - *really?*
Do you love God with *all* your heart, mind, soul and strength?
Do you love yourself... *truly?*

Finally, do you love your neighbors, friends and your fellow man?
Do you love your enemies?

No matter what your answers to the foregoing questions I think you will be surprised by some of the information I will give you to-day.

Let us look at what the Bible tells us about love... specifically what Jesus says to us in the New Testament. Let me read you a few very explicit and moving verses from the Bible...

Matthew 22:37-39 - from the New Testament

Jesus replied: "'Love the Lord your God with all your heart and with all your soul and with all your mind. This is the first and greatest commandment. And the second is like it:' 'Love your neighbor as yourself'!" (NIV)

Now, listen to this from the Old Testament -

Deuteronomy 6:4-9 "Hear, 0 Israel: The LORD our God, the LORD is one. Love the LORD your God with all your heart and with all your soul and with all your strength. These commandments that I give you today are to be upon your hearts. Impress them on your children. Talk about them when you sit at home and when you walk along the road, when you lie down and when you get up. Tie them as symbols on your hands and bind them on your foreheads. Write them on the door frames of your houses and on your gates. "(NIV)

The Old Testament is full of phrases like God's *"unfailing love"* and, as you heard earlier in Psalm 136, God's *"love endures forever"'*!

Let us turn back to the New Testament for more scripture on love.

John 13:34-35

Jesus said; "A new command I give you: Love one another. As I have loved you, so you must love one another... By this all men will know that you are my disciples, if you love one another." (NIV)

John 15:9-13

Again, Jesus says; "As the Father has loved me, so have I loved you, now remain in my love. If you obey my commands, you will remain in my love, just as I have obeyed my Father's commands and remain in his love. I have told you this so that my joy may be in you and that your joy may be complete. My command is this: Love each other as I have loved you. Greater love has no one than this that he lay down his life for his friends." (NIV)

1 John 4:7-12

John says to us: "Dear friends, let us love one another, for love comes from God. Everyone who loves has been born of God and knows God. Whoever does not love does not know God, because God is love. This is how God showed his love among us: He sent his one and only Son into the world that we might live through him. This is love: not that we loved God, but that he loved us and sent his Son as an atoning sacrifice for our sins. Dear friends, since God so loved us, we also ought to love one another. No one has ever seen God; but if we love one another, God lives in us and his love is made complete in us." (NIV)

John 3:16-17

"For God so loved the world that he gave his one and only Son, that whoever believes in Him shall not perish but have eternal life. For God did not send his Son into the world to condemn the world, but to save the world through him. (NIV)

Does anyone doubt that God loves us? What do we mean by us? Do you feel God's love specifically or do you just know it? If so, how do you respond?

Before I answer those questions, let me raise another question and tell you of a concern I have. Think of the words of Jesus when He says, "Love your neighbor as **yourself**." My question is - what if you don't love yourself? There are many who have a very low esteem of themselves - some even feel that they are not worthy of love for many reasons - sinning against God among those reasons.

Jesus words presume that each of us love ourselves - many of us thankfully do. But there are those who would destroy their body because of despair, loneliness, depression, despondency, self-hate, a feeling of being unlovable or unloved. This is tragic and much too prevalent in our society. Much as we are all sinners, we need to establish clearly, not only that God loves us, but why He loves us! When I say "us", I mean each soul - individually and collectively.

God created each soul and, as His creation, we are perfect. We were created in the image of God and He loves each and every one of his 'children'. We are His whether we know it or not. But - He has freed us and placed each soul on this earth so that we may come to know Him, love Him and hopefully, ultimately serve Him and know eternal life with Him in His Kingdom. That's His purpose!

God created the universe and everything in it. God created man and He gave us a beautiful world and an equally beautiful body to look after. Listen to the Word.

Psalm 139:13-16

"For you created my inmost being; you knit me together in my mother's womb praise you because I am fearfully and wonderfully made; your works are wonderful, I know that full well. My frame was not hidden from you when I was made in the secret place. When I was woven together in the depths of the earth, your eyes saw my unformed body. All the days ordained for me were written in your book before one of them came to be. "(NIV)

Hebrews 2:5-8

"It is not to angels that he has subjected the world to come, about which we are speaking. But there is a place where someone has testified: "What is man that you are mindful of him, the son of man that you care for him? You made him a little lower than the angels; you crowned him with glory and honor and put everything under his feet." In putting everything under him, God left nothing that is not subject to him. Yet at present we do not see everything subject to him."(NIV)

We are unique because God made us! Each one of us!

So God gave us domain over the world and gave us special gifts with which to deal with our stewardship. He gave us intellect, the power to reason and think, to feel and remember - he gave us a body especially equipped for our soul to direct.

Here are some examples of the unique nature of our body - It is said that all we have to do is examine ourselves to know the universe as God's creation.

In the last few years we have been learning a lot about DNA. DNA is estimated to contain instructions that if written out would fill 1000 six hundred-page books.

The DNA is so narrow and compacted that all the genes in all the body would fit into an ice cube; yet if the DNA were unwound and joined together end to end, the strand could stretch from the earth to the sun and back more than four hundred times. Listen to this -

Your eyes have 100 million receptors with which to see.

Your body has 500 hundred muscles, two hundred bones and seven miles of nerve fiber so you can stand and move about.

Your heart beats thirty-six million times a year and pumps your blood through more than sixty thousand miles of veins, arteries and tubing ... pumping more than six hundred thousand gallons each year - year in and year out.

Within your five quarts of blood are twenty-two trillion blood cells and within each cell are millions of molecules and within each molecule is an atom oscillating at more than ten million times each second.

Each second two million of your blood cells die to be replaced by two million more in resurrection that has continued since your birth.

Your brain is the most complex structure in the universe. Within its three pounds are thirteen billion nerve cells. To assist your brain in the control of your body you have dispersed, throughout your form, four million pain-sensitive structures, five hundred thousand touch detectors, with more than two hundred thousand temperature detectors.

Indeed, your body is one of God's finest creations! Do you doubt He has every reason to love each one of you as His own? More important, should you, mindful of who made you - both body and soul - not love yourself, as God loves you?

But, there is more - He, also, gave you (soul) the ability to choose - to make choices. He gave you, as well, a desire to know - about everything. Your choices in going through life dictate where your soul is going to spend eternity.

God loves you so much that He has done everything He can to direct you to know Him - and continues to do so. He has provided you with His word (the Bible) which survives to this day. He sent His Son, Jesus to this earth, to teach and lead and ultimately make the sacrifice of His life and establish a dear message of what we are to do.

Most of all, Jesus re-iterated that God's greatest desire is for *each soul* to be saved and return to Him and enjoy eternal life with Him.

1 Corinthians 2:9
However, as it is written: "No eye has seen, no ear has heard, no mind has conceived what God has prepared for those who love him" -- (NIV)

Does God love each one of us? Absolutely "yes" and *unconditionally!* In other words, we don't have to do anything. His love is there!

The answer to ""Do you love yourself? The answer should be a resounding "yes!" And should you love your neighbor and even your enemy - again a resounding "yes" because God not only made each soul but always loved you before you even knew it!

There is another term to describe God's love for us - it is God's grace.

Webster's dictionary does well in defining grace. It is the *unconditional love* of God, which not only forgives, but transforms. It is God's grace, not His law that makes people live more ethical lives. It is God's grace, not the fear of His judgment that makes people holy"

1 think I have answered all the questions asked earlier except - do you know what love is - *really?* '"

So what is love?

The New Testament describes what love is in - **1 Corinthians 13:4-7**

"Love is patient, love is kind. It does not envy, it does not boast, it is not proud. It is not rude, it is not self-seeking, it is not easily angered, it keeps no record of wrongs. Love does not delight in evil but rejoices with the truth. It always protects, always trusts, always hopes, always perseveres."

It is said that love is the cornerstone of Biblical ethics! Jesus said all the law and the prophets can be summarized in this one word: Love (**Matthew 22:34-40**).

The Apostle Paul said there are only three things that last faith, hope, and love; and the greatest of these is Love. (**1 Corinthians 13:13**)

John defined love this way: "It is not that we love God, but that God first loved us."(**1 John 4:10**)

To truly love, one must be connected to the source - God. One must understand the love that comes from God for each person - for each soul.

Here is how love is described in the New Testament. This should help you understand what is meant when the word 'love' is used by Jesus and others in the Bible.

The language of the New Testament, Greek, has three words that mean love: Eros, Phileo, and Agape. Each word defines a particular type of love, although they sometimes overlap.

Eros is passion. It can be sexual, erotic, romantic love. It is the kind of love that we say a person is "in". Eros grabs hold of a person, rather than the person grabbing hold of it. It has been used outside of the Bible to describe being overcome by a passion for God. Even though

Eros is not found in the New Testament, being overwhelmed by the love of God is.

Phileo is family love or the love between friends. It can also be translated affection. Like Eros, there is a feeling that Phileo depends on. When that affectionate feeling goes, so goes Phileo.

The third Greek word for love is **Agape**. Unlike the other two, Agape is not a feeling. It is an action. The Apostle Paul says that Agape is patient and kind, not envious, boastful, arrogant, or rude (l Corinthians 13:4-13). These qualities are not feelings. They are types of behavior. They are controllable. They are controlled by the will. Feelings are not. People cannot make themselves feel passionate or affectionate, but they can decide to be more patient, to treat kindly and not be rude"

Agape is the kind of love that Jesus calls us to have for our neighbor (**Mark 12:31**)" It is also the kind of love Jesus demands we have for our enemies (**Matthew 5:45**). Because Agape is not dependent upon feelings, it can be unconditional. He wants our love for our neighbor to be the same!

Summarizing:
Eros is: I love you because 1 can't help it
Phileo is: I love you if I feel affection for you.
But
Agape is: I love you unconditionally because that is the way God loves, and I want to love - like God"

You can see the translation of the Bible - in this case Greek to English clearly makes a difference on how love is expressed. You can more readily separate how we love our spouses, family and friends and how we *can love* mankind including our enemies. In English, we use only one word to describe all the forms of love.

My grandmother use to say, rightly, when referring to people she didn't like - "They are all God's creatures!"

Let me tell you the second story of love.

The Golden Box
Author Unknown

We sometime learn the most from children.

Some time ago, a friend of mine punished his three-year-old daughter for wasting a roll of gold wrapping paper. Money was tight, and he became infuriated when the child tried to decorate a box to put under the Christmas tree.

Nevertheless, the little girl brought the gift to her father the next morning and said, "This for you, Daddy." He was embarrassed by his earlier overreaction, but his anger flared again when he found the box was empty.

He yelled at her, "Don't you know that when you give someone a present, there's supposed to be something inside of it?"

The little girl looked up at him with tears in her eyes and said, "Oh, Daddy it's not empty. I blew kisses in the box. I filled it with my love. All for you, Daddy."

The father was crushed, He put his arms around his little girl, and he begged her for forgiveness. My friend told me that he kept that gold box by his bed for years.

Whenever he was discouraged, he would take out an imaginary kiss and remember the love of the child who had put it there.

In a very real sense, each of us, as parents, has been given a gold container filled with unconditional love and kisses from our children. There is no more precious possession anyone could hold.

God, too, has given each one of us a Golden box; filled with His love for each of us.

How do we receive this wonderful gift of God's unconditional love or - do we ignore it or wave it away as worthless? Let us come closer to

God and become like Jesus in our daily lives! Let us love one another as God loves us!

We need to practice the 'Presence of God and His love' to be comfortable knowing that He loves each and every one us.

Think of these words from Chorus No 121 of our Hymn Book - entitled "God is love."

God is Love

God is love
I feel it in the air around me;

God is love,
I see it in the heaven above me;

God is love
All nature doth agree;

But the greatest proof of his love for me is Calvary.

Let us pray

Benediction: **2 Corinthians 13:14**
"May the grace of the Lord Jesus Christ, and the love of God, and the fellowship of the Holy Spirit be with you all."(NIV)

Sermon Title: **Peace** Sermon given on January 30, 2005
A discussion on peace - what is it? Where is it found? and the nature
of Peace for the **soul** within **God**'s word.

Peace

Before I get into the subject of to-day's message, let me first tell you a little story about one of the frustrations of life and what can happen to any of us – anytime.

Cowboy Boots
Anyone who has ever dressed a child will love this one!

Did you hear about the Texas teacher who was helping one of her kindergarten students put on his cowboy boots?

He asked for help and she could see why.

Even with her pulling and him pushing, the little boots still didn't want to go on.

Finally, when the second boot was on, she had worked up a sweat.

She almost cried when the little boy said, "Teacher, they're on the wrong feet."

She looked and sure enough, they were.

It wasn't any easier pulling the boots off than it was putting them on.

She managed to keep her cool as together they worked to get the boots back on - this time on the right feet.

He then announced, "These aren't my boots."

She bit her tongue rather than get right in his face and scream, "Why didn't you say so?" like she wanted to.

And once again she struggled to help him pull the ill-fitting boots off his little feet.

No sooner they got the boots off and he said, "They're my brother's boots. My Mom made me wear 'em." Now she didn't know if she should laugh or cry.

But, she mustered up the grace and courage she had left to wrestle the boots on his feet again.

Helping him into his coat, she asked, "Now, where are your mittens?"

He said, "I stuffed 'em in the toes of my boots." Her trial starts next month.

To-day in Iraq, general elections are taking place which hopefully will result in that country ultimately finding peace for its people. Elsewhere, Palestinians and Israelis may be moving to a position of peaceful co-existence with each other. If nothing else, the turmoil in those countries emphasizes the value of peace – at least within a country and with neighboring countries.

Today I would like to talk about peace. You all know the concept of peace. You know of it in the world, even nationally. What about peace in your world? Or even personal peace?

So I ask. What is peace? Do you know what peace is? I mean 'real' peace? How many here have experienced 'real personal peace'?

If you have, raise your hand. How long did your peace last? Drop your hand as I mention different periods of time. 1 day? 2 days? 1 week? 1 month? 6 months? 1 year? Over a year?

How many would like to experience 'peace' for a long, long time?

What is Peace?

The World Book Dictionary says that 'peace' is the state of being calm, quiet and free of disturbance, or freedom from strife of any kind.

How elusive is real peace in the world? My research brought forth some rather interesting statistics.

The world has been in turmoil for many years – since the beginning of recorded history!

A former president of the Norwegian Academy of Sciences and historians from England, Egypt, Germany, and India has come up with some startling information: Since 3600 B.C. the world has known only 292 years of peace! (That is 292 out of 5,600 – 5.2%)

During this period there have been 14,351 wars, large and small, in which 3.64 billion people have been killed. The value of the property destroyed would pay for a golden belt around the world 97.2 miles wide and 33 feet thick.

Since 650 B.C. there have also been 1656 arms races, only 16 of which have not ended in war. The remainder ended in the economic collapse of the countries involved.

More than 8000 peace treaties were made - and broken.

It has been said that true peace in the world will only occur when Jesus returns to reign on earth. (Revelations)

Peace in the world in our day is precious especially when we think of the fighting in Iraq. The poor Iraqi people must really long for peace. Will it happen? We need to pray for them.

Another word that has been used to denote peace is the word 'harmony'.

The Webster College Dictionary has another definition for "peace" which states "it is harmony in human relations."

The World Book Dictionary describes harmony as the agreement of feeling, ideas, or actions; getting along well together.

On a personal level, with family, friends and even business associates, peace or harmony can be equally elusive.

How many times in your lifetime has your 'peace and tranquility' been upset by fights and strained relations with family members or friends. There are times when you feel there is no escape from the bickering and pettiness of others. How can you find 'peace of mind'? Or should we be saying "happiness"? .

Duke University did a study on "peace of mind". The following information seems to suggest a relationship between peace, peace of mind and happiness based on emotional and mental stability. Some of the factors found to contribute to emotional and mental stability were:

1. The absence of suspicion and resentment. Nursing a grudge was a major factor in unhappiness.
2. Not living in the past. An unwholesome preoccupation with old mistakes and failures leads to depression.
3. Not wasting time and energy fighting conditions you cannot change. Cooperate with life, instead of trying to run away from it.

4. Force yourself to stay involved with the living world. Resist the temptation to withdraw and become reclusive during periods of emotional stress.
5. Refuse to indulge in self-pity when life hands you a raw deal. Accept the fact that nobody gets through life without some sorrow and misfortune.
6. Cultivate the old-fashioned virtues—love, humor, compassion and loyalty
7. Do not expect too much of yourself. When there is too wide a gap between self-expectation and your ability to meet the goals you have set, feelings of inadequacy are inevitable.
8. Find something bigger than yourself to believe in. Self-centered egotistical people score lowest in any test for measuring happiness.

Can you have peace when those around you, and even the world, is full of trials and tribulation? Can you ever know real peace within your world or environment?

Are you dependant on others to bring you "peace"?

Matthew Henry once said "Peace is such a precious jewel, that I would give anything for it but truth."

I once heard a Chinese proverb about harmony which was attributed to the Chinese philosopher Confucius who said;
"If you want harmony in the world you must have harmony in the government; if you want harmony in government, you must have harmony in your home; and if you want harmony in your home, you must have harmony within yourself."

Substitute the word peace for harmony.
As a matter of fact, President Franklin D Roosevelt, in a speech August 14, 1936, said "Peace, like charity, begins at home."

I ask you again – what is peace?

Let me tell you a story of a Perfect Picture of Peace.

Long ago a man sought the perfect picture of peace. Not finding one that satisfied, he announced a contest to produce this masterpiece. The challenge stirred the imagination of artists everywhere, and paintings arrived from far and wide.

Finally the great day of revelation arrived. The judges uncovered one peaceful scene after another, while the viewers clapped and cheered. The tensions grew. Only two pictures remained veiled. As a judge pulled the cover from one, a hush fell over the crowd. A mirror-smooth lake reflected lacy, green birches under the soft blush of the evening sky. Along the grassy shore, a flock of sheep grazed undisturbed. Surely this was the winner.

The man with the vision uncovered the second painting himself, and the crowd gasped in surprise. Could this be peace? A tumultuous waterfall cascaded down a rocky precipice; the crowd could almost feel it's cold, penetrating spray. Stormy-gray clouds threatened to explode with lightning, wind and rain.

In the midst of the thundering noises and bitter chill, a spindly tree clung to the rocks at the edge of the falls. One of its branches reached out in front of the torrential waters as if foolishly seeking to experience its full power.

A little bird had built a nest in the elbow of that branch. Content and undisturbed in her stormy surroundings, she rested on her eggs. With her eyes closed and her wings ready to cover her little ones, she manifested peace that transcends all earthly turmoil.

Can you visualize that type of peace for yourself? Are you surrounded by the turmoil and uncertainty of life? Are you anxious about what the future holds for you?

If you want a special kind of peace – an inner peace – like the bird exhibits in the picture I just talked about, I believe I have the answer for you.

Your desire for a lasting and continuous inner peace is found in God's word – the Bible.

Let me give you some examples from the NIV Bible.

From the Old Testament -

Psalm 4:8 "I will lie down and sleep in peace, for you alone, O LORD, make me dwell in safety."

Psalm 34:14 "Turn from evil and do good; seek peace and pursue it."

Job 22:21 "Submit to God and be at peace with him; in this way prosperity will come to you."

It is in the New Testament that we find the answer to how we can know a lasting peace.

There is where we find out how each person or soul can experience the glorious joy of an inner peace that defies description.

Simply – <u>inner peace for your soul</u> is found through acceptance of Jesus Christ as our Lord and Savior!

Acts 10:36 "You know the message God sent to the people of Israel, telling the good news of peace through Jesus Christ, who is Lord of all."

When we confess our sins and acknowledge Jesus Christ as our Lord and Savior – our Redeemer, we are filled with the Holy Spirit, which immediately changes our lives.

Galatians 5:22-23 "But the fruit of the Spirit is love, joy, <u>peace</u>, patience, kindness, goodness, faithfulness, gentleness and self-control."

Romans 5:1 "Therefore, since we have been justified through faith, we have peace with God through our Lord Jesus Christ."

The Book of Revelation Chapter 20 teaches us that Christ will come again to earth. Paul's prayer to the Church of Thessalonia was,

1 Thessalonians 5:23 "May God himself, <u>the God of peace</u>, sanctify you through and through. May your whole spirit, soul and body be kept blameless at the coming of our Lord Jesus Christ."

2 Thessalonians 3:16 "Now may the Lord of peace himself give you peace at all times and in every way. The Lord be with all of you."

What is the <u>nature of this peace</u> that you will find through accepting Jesus Christ?

You saw already that you will be blessed with the "fruit of the Spirit" when you accept Jesus. Your peace will consist of a quiet conscience – you've confessed your sins and have been forgiven. This is <u>peace with God</u> – the peace of salvation where you are brought into a right relationship with God through faith in Jesus Christ.

You will have the <u>peace of a restful mind</u> (soul).

Philippians 4:6-7 "Do not be anxious about anything, but in everything, by prayer and petition, with thanksgiving, present your requests to God. 7 And <u>the peace of God</u>, which transcends all understanding, will guard your hearts and your minds in Christ Jesus."

(Keep in mind that heart and mind are synonymous with soul: Author)

This is a <u>peace of assurance</u> – the peace that comes from knowing that God is in control.

A peace that settles our nerves fills our minds and allows us to relax even in the midst of uproar around us. Does that describe the little bird in the painting?

You will have the <u>peace of a surrendered will</u> as you have forsaken your old life for a life centered on Jesus Christ, your Redeemer.

You will have the <u>peace of a hopeful heart</u> as you have been promised eternal life in eternity. This is a peace of fellowship with God – a personal peace that God gives each one who walks in accord with God's word.

You will have the <u>peace of harmony</u> with others within the body of Christ. This is a peace and unity – of oneness and purpose.

God reaps a harvest of peace where there are believers sowing and watering their minds with the Word. But Satan, the agent of disunity and strife, seeks to reap a harvest of discord through hurt feelings, unwillingness to forgive, and selfish ambition when people refuse to operate on the principles and promises contained in God's word.

Can there be <u>public peace</u>? Yes. It would have to be a society without war or turbulence. It would come through good rulers or government acting in accord with the principles of the Word and through a strong nucleus of godly citizens who apply and live by the truth of Scripture.

Summarizing

Each of us can know the joyous <u>peace of God</u> in our lives which includes

The peace of eternal security with the assurance of our salvation;
The peace of good conscience, of no known sin unconfessed;
The peace of knowing God's will, of God's direction; and
The peace of knowing that God will supply – He is always there for us.

Can you think of yourself to be like the little bird in the picture?

To know the nature of the peace that you can have in your life and for eternity, you need to recognize and acknowledge the source of this wonderful peace.

The Bible tells us very clearly the source of the personal peace we seek.

You have peace <u>with God</u>.

Romans 5:1 "Therefore, since we have been justified through faith, we have peace with God through our Lord Jesus Christ,"

He is the <u>God of Peace</u>

Romans 15:33 "The God of peace be with <u>you</u> all."

You will have the <u>peace of God</u>

Philippians 4:7 "And the peace of God, which transcends all understanding, will guard your hearts and your minds in Christ Jesus."

And finally, He is the <u>Lord of Peace</u>

2 Thessalonians 3:16 "Now may the Lord of peace himself give <u>you</u> peace at all times and in every way. The Lord be with all of you."

The secret of inner peace is found in God. God loves each soul. God's heart is so full of love for each of us; He wants us to know the peace of quiet rest, comfort and safety – a place where you will know the greatest joy and peace.

We have already song that song that so aptly describes God's peace. Let us stand and sing that song again # 973 – **Near to the Heart of God.**

While you sing, think of the words of the song. Think of how Cleland McAfee must have known God's peace to describe it so beautifully. Congregation sing.

If you are seeking the wondrous, joyous peace of God that I have talked about just ask Jesus to come into your heart as your personal Savior sent from God, renounce your sins and seek God's forgiveness and you can claim the peace of God that transcends all understanding not just for now but for eternity!

As I have talked about peace have you thought that I might even be describing happiness? Let us pray.

My prayer for you as we bring our service to a close is found in **2 Thessalonians 3:16** which says. "May the Lord of peace himself give you peace at all times and in every way. The Lord be with all of you."

We have had a particularly nice choral benediction in this church over the years. Many of you will remember it. It's prayer of God's light, love and peace - certainly appropriate for closing our service today.

Let's stand and sing our benediction.
(See box)

Benediction

May the light of God shine on us today
May the light of God shine on us today,
May it show us where to travel
Lead us back if we should stray
May the light of God shine on us today.

May the love of God live in us today
May the love of God live in us today
May the warmth we feel within us
Show in all we do and say
May the love of God live in us today.

May the peace of God be with us today
May the peace of God be with us today
May it guide us and protect us
As we go our sep'rate ways

May the peace of God be with us
May the love of God live in us
May the light of God shine on us today
Author Unknown

Sermon Title: **You are never Alone** Sermon given on May 22, 2005
A talk about **God**'s angels; their ministry and the knowledge that
angels are always close to each **soul**. Angels are always present.

You are never Alone!

As you can tell I like a good story – even better a good joke. I think
it must be my Irish ancestry. The Irish, especially the black Irish, are
known for their love of telling and hearing some pretty far-fetched tales.
Part of my ancestry is black Irish.

When I was much younger – about 15 or 16 I used to make up
stories. I remember many a warm, summer night when it was pitch
black out, sitting on my girl friend's veranda railing and spinning rather
tall tales to five or six of my friends – boys and girls who just sat around
listening. They always seem to encourage me to get me started and these
stories could last maybe an hour at a time.

Even later in life, with our kids, we made up stories and taped them.
The kids would 'play' various parts like hoot owls and wolves, little girls
and boys, sometimes in a dark forest and sometimes in a beautiful castle
with lots of pageantry and all set to a background of music. It was rather
fun and I know the kids all enjoyed it.

But let me get on with my topic today. We are never alone! Do
you believe it? Even when you are at your very loneliest – you are not
alone!

Do you believe in fairies and elves? How about a tall tale?

I don't know about you but I enjoy the quiet and peacefulness of the forest with a warm sun and gentle breeze blowing.

I used to visit my first mother-in-law's cottage in the Halliburton Highlands, up in northern Ontario when I was married to my first wife. It was a lovely 3 bedroom cottage situated on one of the many small lakes that dot that area of Canada – part of the Cambrian Mountain range – actually more like rock hills.

It was there that I would take a hike in the woods, following old logging trails and deer trails. This particular day was warm and you could see through the trees the sparkle of the water. The sun shone through the leaves making portions of the forest very bright while other areas were patches of shadow.

It was so pleasant and peaceful. Suddenly, I heard a rustle in the underbrush - just ahead of me in some dark overgrown underbrush. I thought for a minute it was a big furry jack rabbit but no – I was astounded to see a little dwarf of a fellow sit up a rub his eyes while looking right at me. He jumped up and was about to run when I yelled "stop" which he did.

This gnarled gnome-like creature had a weather-beaten face and was obviously quite old as he hung on to a short stumpy cane that he held in his withered little hand. His clothing is hard to describe as it seemed to be made of rabbit fur and didn't fit very well.

"Hi" I said to him. I smiled and added, "I didn't mean to scare you – can you sit for a bit and tell me who you are and where you come from?" I looked around and found a large rotten old tree trunk that had fallen by the wayside and sat down.

In a raspy voice he said to me that I had surprised him and would not have let me see him under ordinary circumstances. He added he had lived in this forest nearly all his life and had for his home a little burrow about a kilometer away in the side of a rocky outcropping, overlooking a small valley.

He tried to tell me his name but I couldn't understand it – the closest I could make out was "Rufolus" and he lived on roots and berries that he gathered throughout the year.

As we talked – he sat on the ground – I on my log – it was either the sun or the breeze through the tree leaves – a feeling of peace and contentment spread throughout my body.

I remember him telling me of wondrous things about his world and the earth that we live on. Things that we, in our busy lives, know virtually nothing about – no one takes the time to see or hear – even touch and feel.

To this day, I am sure that while he talked there was melodious music somewhere around me that seemed to wrap me in a cloak of warmth and loving – it seemed so strange – and wonderful - -

I woke up with a start – the air had turned chilly and dark clouds were coming over. I looked around but no one was there – did I dream my encounter with the little old man?
How long had I been there?
I headed back to the cottage as I suddenly felt very hungry.

You are not alone! Let me return to my message.

We live in an age of instant communication, an age of science, an age of information overload and, at the same time, an age of constant change where one never knows what is going to happen next.

We are or are becoming desensitized to the spectacular, the grotesque, and the unbelievable. With the rapid changes that have taken place over a life-time, it would seem that science fiction has caught up with real life.
The question becomes what is believable? What is unbelievable? Do the unbelievable have an impact in our lives when we come face to face with it?
You have heard or read four stories (See Scripture Box for other three) – did you believe what you heard or read?

As you saw, three of the stories were taken right from scripture – the Bible – the unassailable 'word of God'! Each story – taken by itself, has an element of the supernatural or science fiction about it which we would normally associate with fables or science fiction stories.

My concern is that the emotional and even intellectual impact of what we would normally consider miraculous has become mundane in this day and age – hardly worth noticing. Note the excitement over the release of the last Star Wars movie Thursday.

To establish my statement that you are never alone, I must tell why I say you are never alone and then I must get you to believe what I'm telling you.

Simply put – you are never alone because angels are always near you!
Let me repeat that - you are never alone because angels are always near you!

Strangely both Christians and non-Christians believe in angels! That even includes those who follow Islam, Buddhism and Hinduism.

A recent poll in the United States found that 69% of respondents believed in angels. Further, 46% believed in a personal guardian angel. This poll, as I understand it, was not a poll directed to only Christians. It was a general poll.

Where do you belong? Are you a believer in angels?

If yes, would you share that belief with anyone who asked? To help you do that, let me point out a few things you should know about angels.

What is an angel? Where did they come from? What do they do?

Before I go on let me make a very special point. The Bible has about 300 references to angels, either directly or indirectly. About half of these references are found in the Old Testament and the other half in the New

Testament. Of those in the New Testament about 30 are found in the last book of the Bible – the Book of Revelations written by John with the help of an angel.

What is important to note is that your soul and your eternal life is very connected to that unseen realm where angels dwell. Do not be surprised that upon leaving this earth, you will be surrounded by angels who number in the thousands.

Hebrews 12:22 *tells us*
- "You have come to thousands upon thousands of angels in joyful assembly,"
This company of angels is in addition to the many souls who have realized the goal of their salvation – namely eternal life in heaven. Can you picture that? Can you picture that - right now – you are in the company of many angels? – All invisible!

Where did angels come from?
God created them just as He did the universe and all the souls in it.

Colossians 1:16 *says –*
"For by him all things were created: things in heaven and on earth, visible and invisible, whether thrones or powers or rulers or authorities; all things were created by him and for him."

What is an angel? An angel is described as a supernatural personality of the unseen world employed as a messenger in the service of God. They belong to a heavenly court as part of the heavenly host and serve God. Their mission in heaven is to praise and worship God. You will find this described in Revelations.

Revelations 5:11 It *is mind boggling to consider the number of angels that exist.*
"Then I looked and heard the voice of many angels, numbering thousands upon thousands, and ten thousand times ten thousand. They encircled the throne and the living creatures and the elders. "(That I believe is about 100 million angels)

Billy Graham, the famous evangelist thinks of angels as God's secret agents.

The Bible is loaded with references to angels and their role. Many of us learned of angels when we were very young. Often we think of angels as our own personal guardian angel. There are hundreds of stories out there that would seem to support that thought. Books like Billy Graham's book "Angels" or the book entitled "A Rustle of Angels" by Marilynn and William Webber provide many accounts of human encounters with angels. Some of you may even have had such an experience. But I really want to concentrate on the tremendous support the Bible gives to the presence of angels in our lives.

Those who are familiar with the Old Testament will remember some of these instances where angels were present. Let me give you some examples.

Genesis 28:11-13 (*This is about Jacob – often referred to us Jacob's ladder.*)
"When he reached a certain place, he stopped for the night because the sun had set. Taking one of the stones there, he put it under his head and lay down to sleep. He had a dream in which he saw a stairway resting on the earth, with its top reaching to heaven, and the angels of God were ascending and descending on it. There above it stood the LORD, and he said: "I am the LORD, the God of your father Abraham and the God of Isaac. I will give you and your descendants the land on which you are lying."

Jacob wrestles with some one – an angel?
Genesis 32:24-28 "So Jacob was left alone, and a man wrestled with him till day-break. When the man saw that he could not overpower him, he touched the socket of Jacob's hip so that his hip was wrenched as he wrestled with the man. Then the man said, "Let me go, for it is daybreak." But Jacob replied, "I will not let you go unless you bless me."

The man asked him, "What is your name?" "Jacob," he answered.

Then the man said, "Your name will no longer be Jacob, but Israel, because you have struggled with God and with men and have overcome."

Joshua had led the Jews across the Jordan to attack Jericho. The first step in taking possession of the land promised them by God.

Joshua 5:13-15 " Now when Joshua was near Jericho, he looked up and saw a man standing in front of him with a drawn sword in his hand. Joshua went up to him and asked, "Are you for us or for our enemies?"

"Neither," he replied, "but as commander of the army of the LORD I have now come." Then Joshua fell face down to the ground in reverence, and asked him, "What message does my Lord have for his servant?"

The commander of the Lord's army replied, "Take off your sandals, for the place where you are standing is holy." And Joshua did so.

Daniel had been thrown to the lions and explained why he had not been eaten.
Daniel 6:22 "My God sent his angel, and he shut the mouths of the lions. They have not hurt me, because I was found innocent in his sight. Nor have I ever done any wrong before you, O king."

2 Kings 19:32-35 *This scripture is an example of the power of the angels.*
"Therefore this is what the LORD says concerning the king of Assyria:

"He will not enter this city or shoot an arrow here. He will not come before it with shield or build a siege ramp against it. By the way that he came he will return; he will not enter this city, declares the LORD. I will defend this city and save it, for my sake and for the sake of David my servant."

That night the angel of the LORD went out and put to death a hundred and eighty-five thousand men in the Assyrian camp. When the people got up the next morning -- there were all the dead bodies!

What a sight that must have been. But think about the destruction of Sodom & Gomorrah. You find that story in Genesis.

Let us look at the New Testament for a moment in which it is reported that the angels played a prominent role with regard to Jesus and His life on earth.

John's (The Baptist) birth promised

Luke 1:11-20 "Then an angel of the Lord appeared to him, standing at the right side of the altar of incense. When Zechariah saw him, he was startled and was gripped with fear. But the angel said to him: "Do not be afraid, Zechariah; your prayer has been heard. Your wife Elizabeth will bear you a son, and you are to give him the name John.

He will be a joy and delight to you, and many will rejoice because of his birth, for he will be great in the sight of the Lord. He is never to take wine or other fermented drink, and he will be filled with the Holy Spirit even from birth. Many of the people of Israel will he bring back to the Lord their God. And he will go on before the Lord, in the spirit and power of Elijah, to turn the hearts of the fathers to their children and the disobedient to the wisdom of the righteous -- to make ready a people prepared for the Lord."

Zechariah asked the angel, "How can I be sure of this? I am an old man and my wife is well along in years."

The angel answered, "I am Gabriel. I stand in the presence of God, and I have been sent to speak to you and to tell you this good news. And now you will be silent and not able to speak until the day this happens, because you did not believe my words, which will come true at their proper time."

The angel Gabriel is thought to have been the most important of God's messengers.

Here is another example with Joseph's concern about taking Mary as his wife.

Matthew 1:20-21 "But after he had considered this, an angel of the Lord appeared to him in a dream and said, "Joseph son of David, do not be afraid to take Mary home as your wife, because what is conceived in her is from the Holy Spirit. She will give birth to a son, and you are to give him the name Jesus, because he will save his people from their sins."

Jesus warns his listeners about the end times and what the angels will do.

Matthew 13:40-43 "As the weeds are pulled up and burned in the fire, so it will be at the end of the age. The Son of Man will send out his angels, and they will weed out of his kingdom everything that causes sin and all who do evil. They will throw them into the fiery furnace, where there will be weeping and gnashing of teeth. Then the righteous will shine like the sun in the kingdom of their Father. He, who has ears, let him hear.

This is the announcement of the return of Jesus

Matthew 24:30-31 "At that time the sign of the Son of Man will appear in the sky, and all the nations of the earth will mourn. They will see the Son of Man coming on the clouds of the sky, with power and great glory. And he will send his angels with a loud trumpet call, and they will gather his elect from the four winds, from one end of the heavens to the other.

The angels even helped Jesus in the Garden of Gethsemane

Luke 22:43-44 "An angel from heaven appeared to him and strengthened him. And being in anguish, he prayed more earnestly, and his sweat was like drops of blood falling to the ground."

Angels serve mankind

John 1:51 He then added, "I tell you the truth, you shall see heaven open, and the angels of God ascending and descending on the Son of Man."

This is the passage that many believe suggests that every child has a guardian angel

Matthew 18:10 "See that you do not look down on one of these little ones. For I tell you that their angels in heaven always see the face of my Father in heaven."

The angels have a special role when it comes to those who have accepted the Lord Jesus as their Savior, have confessed their sins and have accepted the salvation of their souls.

Hebrews 1:14 "Are not all angels ministering spirits sent to serve those who will inherit salvation?"

The Bible tells us exactly where we stand in relation to God and His angels. We are special – we are subject to the perils of this world and the temptation to sin. For this reason, we are blessed to have the assistance and guidance of the angels – even our own personal angel – if there is one.

We have the opportunity to be with the angels in heaven –

Hebrews 2:1-8

"We must pay more careful attention, therefore, to what we have heard, so that we do not drift away. For if the message spoken by angels was binding, and every violation and disobedience received its just punishment, how shall we escape if we ignore such a great salvation? This salvation, which was first announced by the Lord, was confirmed to us by those who heard him. God also testified to it by signs, wonders and various miracles, and gifts of the Holy Spirit distributed according to his will.

It is not to angels that he has subjected the world to come, about which we are speaking. But there is a place where someone has testified: "What is man that you are mindful of him, the son of man that you care for him? You made him a little lower than the angels; you crowned him with glory and honor and put everything under his feet. In putting everything under him, God left nothing that is not subject to him."

God loves you and has placed his angels in this world to help us grow and mature as Christians - knowing, loving and serving God through Jesus and all the saints.

As in all things created by God, there is a purpose. Angels have a purpose as you have learned. They are God's creations – just like us. They have a special place in our lives. They are not to be adored or prayed to. Your prayers should be directed to Jesus or God – they will tell the angels what to do.

You are never alone! – No matter where you are – what conditions exist – whether you are 'down' or 'up' – whether life is just terrible or wonderful. Regardless of what may be wrong or right with your life, you know always, first – that God loves you – his creation.

Second, in loving you, He has provided the means to guide and assist you in your life on earth through the ministry of His angels. You are indeed, blessed!

Now it is up to you. Do you believe in God? Do you believe in angels? Do you (your soul) feel closer to God at this moment? Can you feel His peace and comfort? My prayer is that you do.

Let us stand and sing that wonderful song # 973 – Near to the Heart of God

Special Scripture for this Sermon. Three appearances of an Angel of the Lord

---

Appearance One: Daniel 3:10-12 & 19-28

You have issued a decree, O king, that everyone who hears the sound of the horn, flute, zither, lyre, harp, pipes and all kinds of music must fall down and worship the image of gold, and that whoever does not fall down and worship will be thrown into a blazing furnace. But there are some Jews whom you have set over the affairs of the province of Babylon—Shadrach, Meshach and Abednego—who pay no attention to you, O king. They neither serve your gods nor worship the image of gold you have set up."

19 Then Nebuchadnezzar was furious with Shadrach, Meshach and Abednego, and his attitude toward them changed. He ordered the furnace heated seven times hotter than usual and commanded some of the strongest soldiers in his army to tie up Shadrach, Meshach and Abednego and throw them into the blazing furnace. So these men, wearing their robes, trousers, turbans and other clothes, were bound and thrown into the blazing furnace. The king's command

---

was so urgent and the furnace so hot that the flames of the fire killed the soldiers who took up Shadrach, Meshach and Abednego, and these three men, firmly tied, fell into the blazing furnace.

Then King Nebuchadnezzar leaped to his feet in amazement and asked his advisers, "Weren't there three men that we tied up and threw into the fire?" They replied, "Certainly, O king."

He said, "Look! I see four men walking around in the fire, unbound and unharmed, and the fourth looks like a son of the gods."

Nebuchadnezzar then approached the opening of the blazing furnace and shouted, "Shadrach, Meshach and Abednego, servants of the Most High God, come out! Come here!" So Shadrach, Meshach and Abednego came out of the fire, and the satraps, prefects, governors and royal advisers crowded around them. They saw that the fire had not harmed their bodies, nor was a hair of their heads singed; their robes were not scorched, and there was no smell of fire on them.

Then Nebuchadnezzar said, "Praise be to the God of Shadrach, Meshach and Abednego, who has **sent his angel** and rescued his servants! They trusted in him and defied the king's command and were willing to give up their lives rather than serve or worship any god except their own God."

Appearance Two: Numbers 22:26-35

"Then the angel of the LORD moved on ahead and stood in a narrow place where there was no room to turn, either to the right or to the left. When the donkey saw the angel of the LORD, she lay down under Balaam, and he was angry and beat her with his staff. Then the LORD opened the donkey's mouth, and she said to Balaam, "What have I done to you to make you beat me these three times?"

Balaam answered the donkey, "You have made a fool of me! If I had a sword in my hand, I would kill you right now." The donkey said to Balaam, "Am I not your own donkey, which you have always ridden, to this day? Have I been in the habit of doing this to you?" "No," he said.

Then the LORD opened Balaam's eyes, and he saw the **angel of the LORD** standing in the road with his sword drawn. So he bowed low and fell facedown.

The angel of the LORD asked him, "Why have you beaten your donkey these three times? I have come here to oppose you because your path is a reckless one before me. The donkey saw me and turned away from me these three times. If she had not turned away, I would certainly have killed you by now, but I would have spared her."

Balaam said to the angel of the LORD, "I have sinned. I did not realize you were standing in the road to oppose me. Now if you are displeased, I will go back."

The angel of the LORD said to Balaam, "Go with the men, but speak only what I tell you." So Balaam went with the princes of Balak."

Appearance Three: Acts 12:5-10

"So Peter was kept in prison, but the church was earnestly praying to God for him.

The night before Herod was to bring him to trial, Peter was sleeping between two soldiers, bound with two chains, and sentries stood guard at the entrance. Suddenly an **angel of the Lord** appeared and a light shone in the cell. He struck Peter on the side and woke him up. "Quick, get up!" he said, and the chains fell off Peter's wrists.

Then the angel said to him, "Put on your clothes and sandals." And Peter did so. "Wrap your cloak around you and follow me," the angel told him. Peter followed him out of the prison, but he had no idea that what the angel was doing was really happening; he thought he was seeing a vision. They passed the first and second guards and came to the iron gate leading to the city. It opened for them by itself, and they went through it. When they had walked the length of one street, suddenly the angel left him."

Sermon Title: **Our Journey through Life** Sermon given on August 14, 2005
This is a talk about the meaning of life for the **soul** in man and the recognition that **God** is the giver of all material blessings. Some personal experiences. The case for making God number one in your life.

Our Journey through Life!

Joke

I must tell you a quick cute joke before we get started.

This is a tale of unselfishness and its rewards.

There were 11 people hanging on to a rope that came down from a helicopter. Ten were men and one woman.

They all decided that one person should get off because if they didn't, the rope would break and everyone would die. No one could decide who should go.

Finally, the woman gave a really touching speech on how she would give up her life to save others, because women were used to giving up things for their husbands and children and – giving in to men.

All of the men started clapping.

Prelude

Before I go further, let me share with you a thought I have had over the years while attending church. I often wondered who is the minister or priest addressing with their sermon.

In my mind I have broken down the listeners into two main groups and two sub-groups.

The first main group is made up of Christian "believers" – those who have been saved. This group is further broken down into those who continuously seek holiness and to serve the Lord during their lifetime. The second group are those who want to worship within the body of believers expressing their acknowledgment and devotion of God. This entire group loves the Lord.

The second main breakdown is the "unsaved" – those who have not experienced salvation. This group is broken down into two sub-groups also. The first sub-group is what I call "seekers".

These are people who are looking for something meaningful in their lives – something they feel is 'missing'.

The second part of the 'unsaved' group is those who just don't believe in Jesus Christ or salvation. Obviously, it is a rare occasion that you find members of the latter group in church - probably at weddings and funerals.

So I ask the question – who do we direct our sermons to - The converted or the unconverted? My answer is simply - both. Let me tell you why.

For the believers, the message is to help them with their spiritual walk with the Lord so that they will aspire to be good examples of Christ's teaching as they go through life.

Secondly, a message should provide Christians with information that can be shared with others and hopefully create an interest in the 'unsaved' about Christ and God. This can be useful for non-attending family members.

For the 'non-believers' who may attend a church service, the message will hopefully create a continuing interest in finding out more about God and Jesus – as a seeker. They are the ones who find that their journey through life leaves them 'empty". They want something more meaningful.

Finally, there is the last group of non-believers. All of us need to be equipped with enough knowledge about God and Christianity so that we may, in some small way, encourage them to look at God's word. After all, this is the group that 'seekers' come from.

So, as we minister to you, it is our hope that God and the Holy Spirit will work in wondrous ways to bring each of us closer to God and eternal life with Him as we walk our journey through life.

Let us pray!

Our journey through life! - Part 1

Questions

By now you probably have guessed that I have a 'questing' mind. One of the earliest questions I posed to everyone was "Does the mind age?" I won't get into the responses at this time.

Lately, two questions have come to my mind and have influenced what I am going to talk about today. Firstly, can a person be a 'good' Christian in today's "Me" society. A society that seems to have grown up from the 'hippy' days where people were encouraged to do their own thing!

The "me" society I define simply as 'me' first – you last! My interests always supersede yours!

The second question is this. Did God provide sufficient time for each of us (souls) to experience life and to find the purpose and meaning of our lives on earth? Is 3 score and ten years (70) enough time?

Time on earth – scripture

Scripture provides some thought about our life ending and our time on this earth.

In **2 Samuel 14:14** a wise lady said to King David, "Like water spilled on the ground, which cannot be recovered so we must die." The same thought is found in **2 Timothy 4:6** "For I am already being poured out like a drink offering, and the time has come for my departure."

Both scriptures talk about the finality of death – you cannot recover your life once it is spilled.

Both of my questions are addressed somewhat in The Book of Ecclesiastes – especially Chapter Three.

Ecclesiastes 3:1 says, "There **is** a time for everything and a season for every activity under heaven" You can read the list of activities verses 2-9 for yourself."

Ecclesiastes 3:17 - "I thought in my heart, "God will bring to judgment both the righteous and the wicked, for there will be a time for every activity, a time for every deed."

In thinking about the amount of time we have been given to live on this earth, I began to think about the experiences I have gone through over the years. I wondered what brought me to be the person I am today.

It is said that, at this moment, I am the sum total of all that I have experienced, done, thought, felt, failed to do, the impact of all those who have had anything to do with my life – their influence, their thinking – character and even the conditions of where I grew up and lived during the course of my life.

So the question is – who am I and what is my purpose in life? Do you ask yourself that question?

Do we have enough time in our journey through life to learn what is important? To do what is important?

I am hoping the lesson found in the Book of Ecclesiastes will enlighten us. I encourage you to read it. My message is based on all of Chapter 3.

Before going further, I was struck by the words of the choral benediction we sang last Sunday after Henry Ying's service. This is a benediction that has been a favorite of this congregation for years and I would like to sing it now before going on with my message. Please pay special attention to the words.

Choral Benediction - May the Love of God Shine on Us

My life experiences

In my life I have experienced many things. Let me tell you some of the nasty things that have occurred through my life. This is a litany of some of my experiences brought about by the affects of abuse by others. You will have had your own experiences and some may be worse than others. I know that everyone goes through trials and tribulations. We are all different and will deal with the adversities of life in different ways. None of us are unique in our life experiences.

I was a boy while the WW II was being fought; I saw the affects of war through rationing of things like butter, sugar, bread and more; I saw horse-drawn streetcars; I lived in poverty in low-income housing where the conditions were terrible – it was a slum; I saw drunkenness and fighting – all kinds of abuse; I experienced the pain of my mother when she was beat up by my drunken father; I ran from my drunken father when he tried to kill me with a knife; I turned down drinking as a saw the effects; I tried smoking but that didn't work; I played around with girls but didn't like many of them – many of them were loose and dirty.

One time, I fought with my father who attacked me and threw him around until he quit – I didn't hurt him – just his pride. I saw my father try to make my grandmother (his mother) drink beer on her death-bed – his idea - she'd feel better. Then the parting when my grandmother died. I married my first wife – we had four children – then she left us all – I saw the pain of rejection in the kids' faces.

My brother Ed, having had too much to drink, fell over a railing and broke his back and lived the rest of his life in a wheel chair until he died just a couple of years ago. I experienced a crazed man pointing a 303 rifle at my stomach. I experienced the long-term mental illness and depression of my mother and her attempted suicide – jumping from a 3 story apartment building. After living in a convalescent home for several years, she too died.

Even though my brother Bob and I tried to help him, my father wouldn't change his addiction to alcohol. My father died but we didn't know it until 3 months later. They had found him in a cold abandoned house in downtown Toronto where he had died from alcoholism.

I saw the affects of drugs and alcohol in our kids – one son is a physical mess. One of our daughters is also a physical mess – our other kids have gone through varying degrees of addictive substances and all have paid a price.

I have seen the abuse – emotional, mental and physical brought about by people who cared only for their own needs and wants and victimized those around them.

But despite all that I have just said – believe this – I know that I personally have been blessed. I have been blessed in many ways.

I know that God has protected me in ways that even I cannot fathom. The most powerful way He has protected me is keeping me from falling into the pit of misery that I see in so many lives.

My grandmother had a saying when talking about people who were less fortunate or who had succumbed to the temptations of life. "There, but for the grace of God, go I." I totally identify with her statement.

My journey through life has not been easy – and I have not had all the riches that some have had.

The Bible tells us about Solomon who is thought to have written the Book of Ecclesiastes.

When you read the Book of Ecclesiastes and I hope you will, you will think that Solomon has nothing but a pessimistic view of life. That living is a hopeless mess.

King Solomon had everything anyone would ever want in life. He had riches, wisdom, power, beautiful women in his huge harem. He was revered throughout the land. But he tells us it was all meaningless!

If you look at the beginning passages of Genesis, you will find the creation of the world and everything in it described. After the completion of each day, God looked at what He had done and said "It is good!"

Everything God created and then gave to man to be under his domain was good! God has given man things of this earth that in themselves are good. Listen to the words spoken earlier from **Ecclesiastes 3: 11-14**

11 "He has made everything beautiful in its time. He has also set eternity in the hearts of men; yet they cannot fathom what God has done from beginning to end. 12 I know that there is nothing better for men than to be happy and do good while they live. 13 That everyone may eat and drink, and find satisfaction in all his toil -- this is the gift of God. 14 I know that everything God does will endure forever; nothing can be added to it and nothing taken from it. God does it so that men will revere him"

From this passage you can see that God has no difficulty with people enjoying pleasure and happiness and has even given them the means to do so. God has made everything beautiful in its time.

Ecclesiastes 5:18-19 says it this way -

"Then I realized that it is good and proper for a man to eat and drink, and to find satisfaction in his toilsome labor under the sun during the few days of life God has given him -- for this is his lot. 19 Moreover, when God gives any man wealth and possessions, and enables him to enjoy them, to accept his lot and be happy in his work -- this is a gift of God."

What are we saying here? What is Ecclesiastes 3 telling us? It is simple. All material things were placed on this earth by God for our use and we are to enjoy the benefits of our toil and labor. This is all good. Abuse of these good things is where men become sinful and wrapped up in their own excesses.

What really happens is, that in our journey through life, we become immersed in the material things of life and we cannot fathom what God has done. It is extremely easy to forget about God.

When I come back I will try to help you understand what God has done and provide the answer to the meaning of Solomon's cry of "meaninglessness" and "striving after the wind."

Meanwhile let us give thanks for God's blessings we enjoy as we take up our offerings. Prayer

Piano Interlude

Reading - Scripture **Ecclesiastes 3:18-22**

"I also thought, "As for men, God tests them so that they may see that they are like the animals. 19 Man's fate is like that of the animals; the same fate awaits them both: As one dies, so dies the other. All have the same breath; man has no advantage over the animal. Everything is meaningless. 20 All go to the same place; all come from dust, and to dust all return. 21 Who knows if the spirit of man rises upward and if the spirit of the animal goes down into the earth?"

22 So I saw that there is nothing better for a man than to enjoy his work, because that is his lot. For who can bring him to see what will happen after him?"

Our journey through life! - Part 2

Ecclesiastes 3:22 says

"So I saw that there is nothing better for a man than to enjoy his work, because that is his lot. For who can bring him to see what will happen after him? "

What is Solomon telling us through the Book of Ecclesiastes?

Bob Deffinbaugh, author of '**On Wings of Eternity**" offers the following thoughts about the intent of the Book of Ecclesiastes.

"However, there is one more thing he *(Solomon)* wants us to remember: *the meaning of life cannot be found in anything under the sun – be it our material possessions or other immaterial things like human wisdom or intellect. Everything of this world is vain and futile in the ultimate sense, as it cannot fulfill the human desire for meaningfulness.*

One after another Solomon takes all the things that we usually consider good and points out their futility and meaninglessness: futility of all human endeavor (1:3-11); futility of pleasure and possession (2:1-11); futility of human wisdom (2:18-23); and futility of wealth (5:8-17). He sets forth the vanity of everything in this world of which he can think. He tries everything under the sun that is supposed to be capable of making man happy, but to his utter dismay, he finds that all is vanity and vexation of spirit, that every effort in acquiring happiness in whatever way it may be ends in sorrow. The greater the capacity of the object to give enjoyment, the deeper and wider is the experience of disappointment and vexation of spirit.

Solomon has brought out the meaninglessness of everything under the sun, as we noted above, to lay up the foundation for his final thesis. If nothing is permanent, if nothing under the sun can give real and lasting happiness, how can man fulfill his desire for the meaning of life? Where can he find the things that can give real and lasting happiness and fulfill the quest for the *meaning of life?* "

Solomon says certainly not under the sun, but he can surely find it from beyond the sun.

Eternity in Their Hearts

Here is the key to understanding the Book of Ecclesiastes Chapter 3 Mr. Deffinbaugh writes

"Although everything under the sun is temporal, <u>God has set eternity in man's heart</u> (3:11b).

Every culture, no matter how primitive or developed, has a concept of eternity, of something that will last forever. Because of this sense of eternity in his heart, man is looking for something that will last forever, most of all, something that will make him last forever.

In summary, what Solomon is saying is this: enjoy all the material things of the world. There is nothing wrong in that. They are gifts from God. However, remember that these things cannot last forever nor can they give real lasting happiness. The purpose and meaning of life cannot be found in any of these things. *So, acknowledge God as the source of all enjoyment; He alone can give meaning to life; He alone can give eternal significance to our temporal works.*

Solomon learned from his own experience that all material things are his to use and fully enjoy, but he realized that he can enjoy them only if he has first established a relationship with God, who is the Giver of all material blessing and the source of real joy and happiness. Without that primary relationship to God, all things are vain and empty.

That is why he raises the question: **"For who can eat and who can have enjoyment without Him?"** (2:25)."

Augustine said, "No man can find peace except he finds it in God."

Similarly, Pascal said, "There is a God-shaped vacuum in the heart of every person. And it can never be filled by any created thing. It can only be filled by God, made known through Jesus Christ.""

This is the message of Ecclesiastes; this is the message of the Bible. This is what Jesus said: **"Seek first His kingdom and His righteousness, and all these things will be given to you as well" (Matthew 6:33).**

The simple conclusion that we have to come to is this. To find meaning and purpose in our lives we must seek beyond our earth, the moon, sun and stars. We must seek it from God Himself.

Ecclesiastes 3:11 God has made everything beautiful in its time. He has also set eternity in the hearts of men, yet they cannot fathom what God has done from beginning to end.

We need to understand what God has done and realize His purpose.

God says all material things are good – He made them! Abuse He does not condone.

King Solomon soon found out that no matter what you own or possess – all the beautiful wives, all the riches and wealth in the world means nothing. If all the things of this world distract you from finding the real meaning of your time on earth, you have or are wasting your time in futility. This you may only realize on your death bed.

This little poem sets it out very well

"The Four Calls" from the Booklet **"Our Daily Bread"**

The Spirit came *in childhood* and pleaded, "Let me in,"
But oh! The door was bolted by thoughtlessness and sin;
"I am too young," the child replied, "I will not yield today;
there's time enough tomorrow." The Spirit went away.

Again He came and pleaded *in youth's* bright happy hour;
He came but heard no answer, for lured by Satan's power
the youth lay dreaming then and saying, "Not today,
not till I've tried earth's pleasures." The Spirit went away.

Again He called in mercy *in manhood's vigorous* prime,
but still He found no welcome, the merchant had no time;
No time for true repentance, no time to think or pray,
and so, repulsed and saddened, the Spirit went away.

Once more He called and waited, *the man was old* and ill,
and scarcely heard the whisper, his heart was cold and still;
"Go leave me; when I need thee, I'll call for thee," he cried;
then sinking on his pillow, without a hope, he died!

Now that is a picture of meaninglessness and hopelessness. How many do you know fit the description in that poem? I suspect too many.

If <u>you</u> have found the true meaning of your life, will you share it with others?

God has set eternity into men's hearts (souls). Only in God will we find what we are looking for.

How does this message relate to the four groups I mentioned earlier?

For the believers, you can know a sense of fulfillment for having chosen God over sin.

For the unsaved or non-believers, the message gives you the sense that you can find happiness and fill that vacuum you feel within you. You need to learn more about Jesus and God and the promise that Christians share as God's people.

Finally, there is one message I would like to leave with everyone.

If we seek to rejuvenate Christianity and Christians as a whole and individually – all we have to do is – and I say this knowing that we live in a very self-centered, selfish 'me' society - all we have to do is

Make God Number One in your lives! Can you do that?

You say it – God is number one in my life!

As you follow your journey in life let God, be number one in your heart, thoughts and deeds - your souls!

I will guarantee you – your soul will be blessed!

Prayer of thanks and supplication

Let us end our service today with a fitting song for all Christians – "Onward Christian Soldiers"

Go with God!

Bible Study Title: **Quest of Life**   Study took place November 16, 2006
Given at Willow Place. A check list and time line for seeking eternal
happiness for the **soul**.

Quest of Life

*Your quest in life is to unlock the secret of finding happiness for your
soul in heaven before 4 score years (80) has expired.*

Note: There is no guarantee that you will be granted this length of
life nor is it a given that you will have the full use of all your faculties
including full mobility.

To seek your 'quest' you must have taken certain steps.

> **First** (a time of learning from birth) - You must get
> to know and, yes, experience the playing field of life
> that your body has been introduced to. This means, as
> you grow from childhood, you remove the veil of the
> unknown while seeking to expand your awareness of
> who you are and your many talents and attributes.
>
> You soon become a member of the society you
> were born into and work to fulfill your needs and
> responsibilities. Hopefully your involvement in society
> will be a positive one - not negative. i.e.: a productive
> member of society.

Second (a time of meaningful seeking) - You must continue to learn and seek answers to questions like "Why am I here on earth?", "What is my purpose in Life?" - At this time you should discover the Bible.

Third - (a time of spiritual learning) - Through the Bible and possibly with assistance from those who believe in the Bible, you must come to know God and all about Him along with the story of creation and God's love for each one of His creations - specifically mankind.

Fourth - (a time of understanding) - You must realize why Jesus, the Son of God, came to earth - You must understand His ministry and why He died and what His resurrection meant to all mankind.

Fifth - (a time of acceptance and dedication) - You must accept Jesus as your Lord and Savior renouncing all evil in your heart and follow His teachings which are founded on God's will.

Sixth - (a time of realization and wisdom) - You come to realize your purpose in life and your role and finally

Seventh - (a time of walking with God with the promise of eternal happiness in heaven for your soul) - If you have been successful in your quest and have unlocked the secret of eternal happiness, you (your soul) will experience the peace of God as you bask in the presence of God and wait your turn to step into eternal life in heaven.

Question: Have you been given adequate time to pursue all these steps?

It can take a lifetime or it can be accomplished long before you life on earth comes to an end. It all depends on how soon you reach step six.

You have had no control over when and where your soul was introduced into this world; nor do you have any control as to when and where your soul will depart this world. Do not get side-tracked on your quest - you may not have the luxury of time to complete your quest.

You have God-given abilities and talents along with the full unhindered right to choose what you will do with your life. It is an awesome responsibility as the destiny of your soul for eternity is squarely in your hands. God has given you the intelligence to comprehend and understand this responsibility. After all you were made in the image of God!

Pray constantly to God to assist you in finding your way in life while you seek the object of your quest - eternal happiness in heaven for your soul.

May you be blessed in your endeavor.

PART 6

God's Plan and Man's Purpose

The Soul's Purpose

Finding Your Purpose in Life

My journey started out as an obligation to God to emphasize the importance of the soul and the importance of the soul to each person on earth. In the course of my studies, it came to me that God also wanted to convey to each soul that there was, indeed, a purpose for each soul within the mortal body. God has a plan, which includes the reason each body and soul was created. Now it is time to take a look at the soul's purpose.

Comment on the Exclusion of Jesus from the Message

Before going further, I feel that I need to comment on the perception that Christians may have of the message so far. In explaining the message to my wife, she observed that there was no mention of Jesus. Christian readers may have the same observation. In my mind, at the time of receiving the message, this wasn't important because the message conveyed to me made no mention of Jesus. I've come to learn since that the message really focused on why God provided His message, which demonstrated He cared for all souls. In caring, God was demonstrating His love for all souls, which ultimately led back to Jesus.

A Message for the Soul of Man talks about creation, man's creation, the creation of each soul, and what happens to that soul. The entire message was not aimed at any particular segment of mankind. Rather, it is meant for all of mankind, regardless of their spiritual affiliation. All major Abrahamic religions came into existence after the creation. God is very much aware of each religion. The message does not detract from any belief system.

I believe that the message will strengthen each soul's understanding of their mutual relationship with the God each serves and worships.

Learning More about the Soul

In the intervening years, as God opened my eyes to the real ramifications of his created soul, it struck me that every person had some gift, some talent, and some ability that they needed to discover as they grew older.

I remember distinctly learning in school that it was like pushing the veil of ignorance aside to peer beyond and learn what was there. When you went back to the same area of learning, it seemed easier as you understood it better and it was no longer the challenge originally encountered. I wondered when that process ever stopped. It doesn't— as long as we have an inquiring mind and a deep-seated desire for knowledge. The latter I believe is a further gift of God placed in every soul—that and a need to seek love, acceptance, acknowledgment, and approval.

Expanding My Understanding of God's Creation of the Soul

It became obvious that God had a purpose for all of these gifts and talents. My mind was directed to the inventions of man from the very beginning of time. Man has always sought methods of doing things more efficiently and using less energy. This desire to improve on man's inventiveness has led to marvelous discoveries in all fields of life. Man is more efficient at what he does. The best example I can think of is man's ability to feed himself. What is so wonderful is that over the years our planet can support more people as our food supplies have increased to meet the growing needs of an expanding world population. One hundred years ago, we could not have supported six billion people on this planet (soon to be seven billion).

Man's Evolution over the Centuries

Man's evolution since the beginning of time is also something to consider. Examining the role of inventions in man's development naturally leads to how man has evolved over the centuries. The history of man is fantastic to say the least. So many different civilizations have come and gone, leaving a lasting legacy in all fields of man's endeavors, such as medicine, architecture, science, law, economics, government, and more.

What is really fantastic is that all of man's existence on earth has been God-directed from the very start with our souls. Each and every soul was given attributes that, if and when fully developed, could lead to certain achievements on earth, which could advance man's stewardship over this earth. God gave man stewardship over all of the things on earth and he wanted man to fulfill this duty.

Soul Really Has Two Purposes

It became apparent to me through God's message that God really had two purposes for man's soul.

God's first purpose for man is to help the world achieve the ability to utilize all the resources of this world while finding the best method of bringing about peace on earth and goodwill to all men. That message is no mistake.

God truly wants each individual to use all their God-given abilities, including intelligence, to become the best person they can. In the process, they will become either an asset or a liability to themselves, their families, their community, country, and world. This is man's main purpose on earth. It is your purpose for living. It is your combination of knowledge, talent, skills, and ability that make you unique to learn and undertake your purpose in life.

Think of the individuals from all generations and backgrounds who have contributed to the sum total of man's knowledge and history and will continue to do so. We have often heard the expression that the times produce men and women who come forward to meet the needs of the times. Again, we have seen many examples of that in man's history.

The examination of man's soul and its purpose is therefore a look at what God intended when each soul was first created.

Examining Your Soul

To see the progression of the soul through life, two areas must be examined:

- What the soul has done as part of its existence as a person in this world. Is the soul, within the body of man, an asset or a liability to mankind?
- What the soul has become (evil or holy) spiritually, which will dictate its place in eternity. The second is not dependent upon the first area. You can be an abject failure in life and still find a place in heaven.

God's Purpose for Releasing His Message

Finally, God's purpose in releasing his message for the soul is to clearly lay out his desires for man while man is entering the most challenging period in human history. God made man in his image, which automatically endowed mankind with the ability to create great achievements in all fields.

God's Future Plans for Mankind

Even now, we continue to roll back the veils of darkness that exist on the border of every new endeavor. No one can predict the future, but God's plan for mankind promises to be challenging and exciting. God wants each and every soul to reach its full potential. Individuals must exercise discipline over their own development as they make choices for the future. The choice is still theirs.

Think of the tremendous potential of all mankind harnessing and using all their God-given gifts and talents for the betterment of mankind and the earth.

A Special Note to the Reader—Examine Your Life

As you read this, start examining your own life. Pay particular attention to those areas where a decision was required—a fork in the road. Look at the rationale (if any) behind the decision and continue noting where that led you. Sometimes we would like to go back in time, but we can't. The moment of choice is gone forever—only new choices lay ahead.

You direct the path of your life and your life's journey. God gives you nudges every once in a while, which you may recognize or not and to which you may respond or not. Understanding God's purposes for your life can make you more aware of your calling.

Experience God and Achieve the Second Purpose for Your Soul

This is where you touch the spiritual part of your life. If you listen for God and become aware of His presence, you may slowly undertake that spiritual journey that will bring your soul closer to Him. God's second purpose is to have your soul return to Him for eternity. Understanding His message and living your mortal life accordingly can bring about the spiritual goal that all souls should seek. Having been given a free will, what you do with your life will always be your choice!

Rereading your Bible will give you a new perspective with God's message in mind.

A New Revelation for the Soul
—the Formative Years

Humans have inhabited the earth for thousands of years. There have been very clear periods of time when the evolution of man on earth has come to definite turning points. One cannot compare the life of a present human being on this earth with the man who existed 6–8,000 years ago. Some would say life was simpler then—maybe so, but it was also harder.

The Evolvement of Man

Man has evolved over the years. I don't think there is any question about that. It's a fact.

When man was a caveman, he hunted. His tools were fashioned to help accomplish his desire. These included sharp, shaped stones fastened to a stout branch that served as a spear, then a cutting or scraping tool for tanning a hide. Fire was a major discovery. Many years passed.

Man then evolved further when he found that he could domesticate certain animals and keep them close so as to possess his food as he needed it. This led to growing crops. We then entered into the Age of Agriculture where man produced sufficiently to feed his family and barter the remainder to others for other items, such as clothes. Interestingly, the sources of energy in this era were water and wind. Windmills ground grain for cooking and baking. Horses and oxen also played major roles as they were used for tilling the soil and harvesting.

Continued Evolvement Included Inventiveness

Some of the great inventions of this period included the plow, wheel, harness, wagon, and more.

As man continued to evolve, he entered the Age of Industrialization. Factories started to employ hundreds of people. This age completely revolutionized how man lived. He began to use fossil fuels for many things such as the heating of homes (with coal), operating of steam engines (wood and coal), running of cars (gasoline), trucks (diesel fuel), and more.

We are now in the midst of the Age of Computerization and Miniaturization or the Information Age. Huge amounts of our energy are required for electricity and transportation and to run the many machines and equipment that we have come to rely on. Our energy sources include renewable and non-renewable resources.

The evolvement of mankind has taken many years and thousands of people have lived on this earth in those years.

Another way of describing the evolution of man over time is to mentally place a man from the twenty-first century into the 1800s to find out what would be different. Would there be a motor vehicle, TV, CD, DVD, or iPod? Would he see an electric stove, refrigerator, or indoor plumbing?

One of our luxury homes today is grander than a castle was then!

How did this all come about?

The Importance of Inventions

It is worth looking at inventions and inventors. How important were they then and are they now? Inventions such as the stirrup, the printing press, and the cathode ray tube. Now we hear about a new invention almost every day. Man's inventiveness, using his God-given gifts and talents, has fueled his continuing development on earth. Continuing to do so is all part of God's plan for the soul and man.

God's Presence

God is always with you! Do you believe that? Do you have to be a Christian for God to always be with you? I say definitely not!

In the past, we have talked about the destination of the soul. We recognize that each person has an indestructible and eternal soul.

If we know the soul will last for eternity, then it is reasonable to expect that it has already existed since God first created it.

That statement attests to the power of God since He created the world, the universe, and everything in it—including your soul.

God's Role and Man's Gifts

God knew you before you were born!

Proverbs 16:9 says, "A man's heart plans his way, but the Lord directs his steps."

When I tell you that God has played a very definite role in every life throughout many thousands of years, you should not be surprised. He has planned in advance that man should evolve on this planet, which we know is unique in the universe. He set in motion everything and when it was to be.

In each soul, he has given various gifts, which will be available in human form. He has given many souls certain talents. He has given certain souls special gifts that when activated will impact how man evolves.

Everyone in the world has been given certain gifts, talents, and tasks that can advance the role of man in this world—regardless of their beliefs. God's first priority has been to the growth of mankind since man was created in His image.

God's Purpose

What is God's purpose? It is obvious that God placed gifts and talents in every soul long before they were born. He had their roles as humans in mind when He bestowed these gifts. Each soul, when joined with the body, has inherent qualities and desires to utilize the gifts and talents given.

Ultimately, God's plan was to equip those souls in such a way that they would fulfill a need on earth or have the necessary know-how to complete a certain project. Whichever was true, the ultimate benefit was for the advancement of mankind on earth. Think of all the inventions that have been made since the earliest days of man.

Think about this. No man has ever decided when or where he or she was to be born into this world. God, in His great wisdom, chooses the time and place—presumably to provide the people of that particular place in the world with the gifts and talents of the newborn. For proof, all you have to do is look at all of the inventors and inventions over time to discover the contributions to man's evolvement all over the world and from which we have all benefitted.

Finally, as part of God's purpose, I suspect that man will become so intelligent that he cannot ever refute or ignore the existence of God. With the knowledge man will have by that time, man will know (not guess or surmise) that God is the Supreme Being and worthy of our total love and adoration.

When will that occur? What year of man's existence on earth? What conditions will apply? Will we have controlled our tendency for war or to damage our planet by exhausting all of our resources?

Fitting in with God's Plan

Does this plan fit in with God's overall plan? He wants you (your soul) to know, love, and serve Him—now and forever!

Finally, what gift has God given you that you have not used or become aware of? Could the application of this gift or talent help bring about the further evolution of man and the salvation of his soul?

God's Revelation is More Important Now

Is the revelation of God's purpose for man and his soul more important than ever? Does it not tie in with the very thinking that has started to become prevalent as we try to understand and deal with our environment, the need to curtail the growth of weapons of mass destruction (man's destruction), reducing starvation, and seeking peace and mutual cooperation among nations?

I believe that this is why I am moved by God to place this message of God's revelation about the soul and the soul's purpose before you.

Sermon Title: **Man Revealed**   Sermon given: July 1, 2007
A discussion about the evolution of **man** on earth and God's role;
man's progress through invention and how the soul is equipped to
serve **God**'s Plan and His calling.

Man Revealed

Preamble

Before touching on the subject of my message today, I would like to review with you a few givens.

The first of these is personal. Over the years that I have provided Sunday messages, I have emphasized the importance of the <u>soul of man</u> as God has directed me to do. The rationale for this is simply this – if you know and understand that you have a soul and you know it is eternal, then you will focus on the important things that you can do here on earth to ensure that your soul reaches and resides in heaven with your Creator.

Second, to fully understand the foregoing, you must **totally** (heart, soul & mind) believe in God and really know and understand the power of God - which has no limits.

Mark 10:27 - Jesus looked at them (the disciples) and said, "With man this is impossible, but not with God; all things are possible with God."

Finally, you must believe that God created everything, including souls and angels and sent His Son to earth to demonstrate His love and concern for the eternal salvation of every soul.

All Christians believe that God is always present – He is close and He has the power to know our every thought and deed. Please keep in mind as I talk to you that with God - <u>all things are possible</u>!

Part 1 – The impact of changes in our lives

Over the last few weeks we have been going through a period of great emotional upset with the retirement of Dianne, Supervisor of the Thrift Store and Captains Dale and Jo Sobool leaving us, after seven years, to go to their next posting in the Northwest Territories. Conversely, we will be welcoming Captains Gordon and Karen Taylor to their new posting here in Grande Prairie at the end of July.

While Dianne retired, the officer changes, within The Salvation Army have come about at the direction of Headquarters in Toronto. Officers have very little say in their new posting.

This is not true of many of us in our world. We look for opportunities in employment and, if we think the job is right for us and the pay is attractive, then we make a decision to leave our present job and take on the new. What prompts us to do that? Is it the money? The challenge? The opportunity for recognition? Is it a career move?

The same thought process might be involved in choices of where we live, the type of home, who should we marry – do we want a family?

In other words, whatever direction we take, the road ahead of us is unknown and we rely on our own intellect (and sometimes gut-feeling) to see us through to our new path in life. Hopefully we have made the right choice – but only time will tell.

So the question is – why do we make one selection over another? Why did Headquarters in Toronto decide to make the change of officers for Grande Prairie when they did? What prompted them – the decision makers - to do so?

History will record what change was a good or bad one. What decision has had the most beneficial impact?

I raise this question because there is a bigger picture I would like you to see. Very often "things happen for the best"! How often have you heard that expression? Even over very hurtful situations.

Keep in mind that what I have just mentioned is happening right now to thousands of people right around the world. They are in the throes of making decisions about their life.

Part 2(a) – The Evolution of mankind and God's Role

God is always with you! Do you believe that? Question - Do you have to be a Christian for God to always be with you?

The scripture verse **Proverbs 16:9** is very appropriate – "In his heart man plans his course but the Lord determines his steps. Note – this verse comes from the Old Testament and before Christianity.

The verse implies that God, who we know is ever present, is directing our steps – everyone!

The next verse states even more. **Philippians 2:13** – "for it is God who <u>works in you</u> to act according to His good purpose. Saint or sinner – He works in everyone."

My question for you is this? What **is** God's good purpose? As Christians, we have a tendency to have 'tunnel vision'. We think His purpose for all of us is simply an eternal life in heaven with Him for our soul. While true, that is only part of His good purpose.

Let me tell you a few things that may surprise you about man's progress over the years.

<u>Part 2(b) – Man's progress through invention</u>

The invention of the stirrup transformed the political picture. Few inventions have had such an influential effect. Why? A man on horseback without stirrups is insecure. If he strikes a blow with his sword and misses he will probably fall off and then be killed by his enemy before he can regain his feet. Moreover, by using a lance, the energy of the horse's gallop is added to the impact of the blow.

'The stirrup welded horse and rider into a single fighting unity capable of a violence without precedent: stated the American historian Professor Lynn White. 'The fighter's hand no longer delivered the blow, it merely guided it.' Stirrups thus made the horseman dominant over unmounted opponents in a period when few could afford to maintain a horse.

In their individual countries, the mounted knights became a professional brotherhood, and from this arose chivalry (from the French cheval, or horse).

So vital was the horse in power politics that Charles Martel, the eighth-century Frankish ruler, and his immediate successors seized ecclesiastical properties to endow the cavalry they needed to repel a Muslim invasion. Thus the foot stirrup, originally a Chinese invention of the 5th century or earlier, laid the foundations of the feudal system which dominated the life of Europe for nearly 500 years.

The invention of the printing press in the mid 1500's allowed for the printing of the Gutenberg Bible and subsequently saw the proliferation of many printing presses and the flooding of printed material throughout Europe. For the first time, man was able to obtain and read for himself the whole Bible.

The broadening of the mind and the incentive to learn fueled the Reformation changing the history of man forever.

An article from Reader's Digest – **"The Roots of Invention"** by Gordon Rattray Taylor stated,

"From man's inventiveness has arisen the vast difference between his way of life and that of animals. Who are the geniuses who made our civilization possible? From all the tens of thousands of millions of men and women who have peopled the earth, only a few thousand - say .00001 per cent - have had the creative genius to conceive something new and useful.

Their inspiration did much more than raise our standard of living. It changed the size and distribution of population, brought about great shifts in the location of political power, created new class systems, transformed education and much else, in ways which few of us fully appreciate.

Who, then, are the inventors? What motivates them? How can they be encouraged? What have they got that others have not? These are questions of more than philosophical interest."

There are hundreds of examples of how man has progressed through inventiveness both in creation of objects as well as in thought. The whole concept of democracy has come about primarily in the last couple of centuries. Men have embraced it just like the Fathers of Confederation did in creating the Dominion of Canada 140 years ago.

And the process has escalated with the discovery and use of the computer which now helps us in discovering even more ways of getting things done and improving our lives.

Man's inventiveness continues today at an accelerated rate! Here are three of the new inventions announced just over the last while (note Sermon date) – each will have an impact on our lives.

June 8, 2007 Massachusetts Institute of Technology researchers made a 60 watt light bulb glow by sending it energy wirelessly – from a device seven feet away potentially heralding a future in which cell phones, I pods and other gadgets get their juice (charge) without having to be plugged in.

June 23, 2007 <u>Just thinking moves toy train with new technology from Hitachi</u>. A new technology in Japan could let you control electronic devices without lifting a finger simply by reading brain activity.

The "brain-machine interface" developed by Hitachi Inc. analyzes slight changes in the brain's blood flow and translates brain motion into electric signals. A cap connects by optical fibers to a mapping device, which links, in turn, to a toy train set via a control computer and motor during one recent demonstration at Hitachi's Advanced Research Laboratory in Hatoyama, just outside Tokyo.

The technology could one day replace remote controls and keyboards and perhaps help disabled people operate electric wheelchairs, beds or artificial limbs. Initial uses would be helping people with paralyzing diseases communicate even after they have lost all control of their muscles.

June 26, 2007 IBM and Sun Microsystems' new supercomputers have broken the "petaflop" speed barrier, the companies said separately at the International Supercomputer Conference in Dresden, Germany.

A petaflop equals one-quadrillion floating point operations per second, or 100,000 times faster than a home computer.

IBM's Blue Gene/P operates more than three times faster than its forerunner - the Blue Gene/L - during continuous operation. The company said it can work at speeds up to three petaflops.

Sun's new supercomputer, the Constellation, claims up to 1.7 petaflops of power.

"Blue Gene/P marks the evolution of the most powerful supercomputing platform the world has ever known," said Dave Turek, an IBM vice-president.

"A new group of commercial users will be able to take advantage of its new, simplified programming environment and unrivaled energy efficiency," said Turek.

So how does all of man's inventiveness tie into God's good purpose?

As man has evolved on this earth he has progressively improved his ability to become productive through the use of tools and his own ability. Both his ability and the tools appear to have improved over a long period of time stretching from the earliest days of man on earth to the present day with changes occurring virtually daily. How can this be?

For instance, why wasn't the steam engine invented at the same time as the plow and yoke? Why wasn't nuclear power discovered before we found out about the burning qualities of coal? Why were wooden sail boats developed before huge steel hulled ocean liners?

The answer is that everything starts at a certain point and progresses as man, materials and know-how (inventiveness) combine to create further advancement. The one thing you can be sure of is this. Behind every new thought or invention there is a human being (man or woman) and they live anywhere in the world and are not necessarily a Christian. (Most probable they are not.)

God, besides creating the earth and universe and all the things in it or on it, also gave it all to man to look after. Man became the manager of his own destiny and that of the thousands of people who would follow him. This means that of the billions of people who have lived on the earth many have contributed in some manner to the advancement of mankind. Some have played a more important role than others. Some have been the catalyst behind the work of an inventor.

God's good purpose has included guiding the orderly advancement of mankind on earth - to what end? Can you see the hand of God in what I have described and I've only just touched on the subject?

Part 3 – Review

Humans have inhabited the earth for thousands of years

There have been very clear periods of time when the evolution of man on earth has come to definite turning points. One cannot compare the life of a present human being on this earth with the man who existed 6 - 8,000 years ago. Some would say life was simpler then - maybe so, but it was also harder.

Man has evolved over the years. I don't think there is any question about that - it's a fact.

When man was a cave man, he hunted. His tools were fashioned to help accomplish his desire. These included sharp, shaped stones fastened to a stout branch that served as a spear, then a cutting tool or scrapping tool for tanning a hide. Fire was a major discovery. Many years passed.

Man then evolved further when he found he could domestic certain animals and keep them close so as to have his food on hand as he needed it. This led to growing crops for feed. Then man entered into the Age of Agriculture where he produced sufficient food to feed his family and barter the remainder to others for other items such as clothes, shoes and tools. Interestingly the source of energy in this era was water; wind with water and wind mills grinding grain for cooking and baking. Horses and oxen also played a major role as they were used for tilling the soil and harvesting. Thousands of horses and oxen were utilized by man in those days.

Some of the great inventions over this period included the plow, wheel, harness, wagon and more.

As man continued to evolve, he entered the age of industrialization where factories started to employ hundreds of people. This age completely revolutionized how man lived. He began to use fossil fuels for many things such as the heating of homes (with coal), operating of steam engines (wood & coal), running of cars (gasoline), trucks (diesel fuel) and more.

We are now in the midst of the age of computerization and miniaturization – the information age. A huge amount of our energy needs are required for electricity and transportation to run the many machines, appliances and equipment we have come to rely on. Our energy source includes renewable and non-renewable resources.

The point I'm making here is that the evolvement of mankind has taken many years and, thousands of people have lived on this earth in those years.

Another way of describing man's progress over time is to mentally place a man from the twenty-first century into the mid eighteen hundreds to find out what would be different Would there be a motor vehicles, a TV or even CD, DVD or I pod; would he see an electric stove or refrigerator, indoor plumbing? Conversely, a man from the 18th century would be astounded by what he would find in our world today.

As we have seen, man has utilized all this world's resources, his intelligence and ability, through inventions and the comprehension of, and an understanding of how things can work. Man's quest has always been to find the right tool or method to accomplish a perceived goal -to make work easier and quicker to accomplish while reducing man's level of physical involvement.

How did mankind reach his present level of accomplishments? Where is mankind headed?

Part 4 – Let's turn to God's Role

God created every soul that has or will live on this earth – thousands upon thousands until when – we don't know.

In the past we have talked about the destination of the soul. We recognize that each person has a soul - an indestructible soul - an eternal soul.

If we know the soul will last for eternity then it is reasonable to expect that it has already existed since God first created it.

That statement attests to the power of God in that He created the world, the universe and everything in it.

So when I tell you that God has played a very definite role in <u>every life</u> throughout many thousands of years you should not be surprised. You may, however, have trouble believing it. He has planned in advance that man should evolve on this planet which is unique in the universe we know. He set in motion everything and when it was to be.

To each and every soul He has given certain gifts and talents. These may or may not be used by the soul within the mortal body with which it is ultimately joined.

The soul within the mortal body is YOU! You may have certain talents that the Lord wants you to use on this earth. He might have endowed you with a keen desire to find a cure for the common cold. Or he may have placed in you a mechanical ability that finds expression through the Lego set you played with as a boy.

You may have a musical talent such that you are invited to play with The New York Symphony Orchestra.

You may have developed a keen interest in how to identify one human from the next and became the discoverer of the value of the human fingerprint.

Keep in mind that God knows you better then you know yourself.

Jeremiah 1:5 "Before I formed you in the womb I knew you, before you were born I set you apart; I appointed you as a prophet to the nations." (NIV)

Psalm 139:13-16 "For you created my inmost being; you knit me together in my mother's womb. I praise you because I am fearfully and wonderfully made; your works are wonderful, I know that full well. My frame was not hidden from you when I was made in the secret place. When I was woven together in the depths of the earth, your eyes saw my unformed body. All the days ordained for me were written in your book before one of them came to be." (NIV)

As you heard in **Proverbs 16:9** <u>"In his heart a man plans his course but the Lord determines his steps."</u>

As God's plan for mankind unfolds, **you** may be an important part of that plan and while you may not know it **Philippians 2:13** tells us <u>"for it is God who works in you to will and to act according to his good purpose."</u>

Each soul (or person) has been given certain gifts and talents and even tasks which when used will advance the role of man in this world - regardless of their beliefs or where they live on this earth!

God's first priority has been the evolution of man as he (man) was created in God's image which means that man can accomplish almost miraculous achievements as man continues to progress and inhabit this earth and even beyond.

Paul, in his letter to the church at Corinth, prophetically said the following –
1 Corinthians 12:4-7 "There are different kinds of gifts, but the same Spirit.
There are different kinds of service, but the same Lord.
There are different kinds of working, but the same God works all of them in <u>all men.</u>
Now to each one the manifestation of the Spirit is given for the <u>common good.</u>

What is God's purpose? *For all men*, I suspect that man will become so intelligent that he cannot ever refute or ignore the existence of God and with the knowledge man will have by that time, man will know (not guess or surmise) that God is the Supreme Being and worthy of our total love and adoration.

When will that occur? What year of man's existence on earth? What conditions will apply - will we have controlled our tendency to war or damage our planet by exhausting all our resources?

For Christians, He wants you (your soul) to know, love and serve Him - now and forever! If you personally can help with man's advancement <u>and</u> also save souls, then it can be said you are doing God's work.

Finally, what gift has God given you that you have not used and become aware of? Could the application of this gift or talent help bring about the further evolution of man and the salvation of souls?

Think about it –

It is why I stand here today speaking about God's presence in the life of every person living on this planet.

Have you an inner voice speaking to you? Do you have a hidden desire to do something very special with your life – for God, for mankind? Is God calling you to serve?

Let us pray.

Dear God, we are truly thankful that you love each of us and that you are constantly in our presence. Help us, dear Lord, to know and understand you and your purpose for our lives.

Help us be good stewards of all that you have given us and help direct us in the path that you wish us to go. Let us make a positive difference in the lives of all those around us and help us show others that your love is there for them as well. Help us show the way to Jesus Christ, your son, who died to save all mankind from eternal damnation while showing them the way to you dear God in heaven. Amen

Closing Hymn – "Near To the Heart of God" (See box)

Near To the Heart of God

There is a place of quiet rest,
Near to the heart of God.
A place where sin cannot molest,
Near to the heart of God.

Refrain
O Jesus, blest Redeemer,
Sent from the heart of God,
Hold us who wait before Thee
Near to the heart of God.

There is a place of comfort sweet,
Near to the heart of God.
A place where we our Savior meet,
Near to the heart of God.

Refrain

There is a place of full release,
Near to the heart of God.
A place where all is joy and peace,
Near to the heart of God.

"I Appointed You - - - !"

Psalm 139:13-16 (NIV)
"For you created my inmost being; you knit me together in my mother's womb. 14 I praise you because I am fearfully and wonderfully made; your works are wonderful, I know that full well. 15 My frame was not hidden from you when I was made in the secret place. When I was woven together in the depths of the earth, 16 your eyes saw my unformed body. All the days ordained for me were written in your book before one of them came to be."

Jeremiah 1:5
"Before I formed you in the womb I knew you, before you were born I set you apart; <u>I appointed you as a prophet to the nations."</u> *(Underline my emphasis)*

How many here this evening believe that we each have a soul and it will exist forever (in other words, it is eternal)?

Let us go back to before the beginning of your life on earth – when you were just a soul waiting to be joined up with a new growing baby in a mother's womb somewhere here on earth.

We talk often about the soul <u>after</u> it leaves the body but I can't recall any literature that speaks about the soul before it enters the body. So bear with me as I let my imagination run wild.

Now I don't know if there is a special school (if so, probably run by the angel Gabriel) somewhere in the cosmos where new unattached souls are given instruction as to what they can expect when they take over the reins of a functioning human body.

I can imagine that it would cover subjects like **God's love** for each and every soul along with a strong suggestion that God wants to welcome them back into his loving arms – to enjoy heaven with him and to be eternally happy. Letting them have a sense of how much they are loved.

On top of that, each soul is reminded that they have been given certain **talents and attributes** which will integrate with the human body's own internal assets and thus they will be able to contribute to the world in which they will live. Some may be given very **special gifts** that will have a tremendous impact on how life on earth develops after they have returned to their soul's spirit form. (An Einstein, Socrates or Beethoven come to my mind and, there are many more)

Each soul will be told that when they take over the body to which they have been assigned they will slowly learn about their new environment and will have **freedom of choice** of how they deal with every challenge put before them. They alone will decide each situation, without any interference from God, although probably protected in some instances by God's angels.

Finally, I can imagine that each soul is told that they will enter human life and will not have any conscious remembrance of their past or their indoctrination as a soul about to embark on a very special journey in the land that had been created by God for them to inhabit.

Let us pray as we consider God's plan for each of us.

Sermon Title: **Back to the Future**   Sermon given on: July 6, 2008
Talk on how God's Plan encompasses all **man**kind and that **God**
has a purpose for every person (soul) born. There is a dual purpose
for every soul as we are called to serve a common God.

Back to the Future
Part 1

I am sure most of you are familiar with the movie "Back to the Future"
where our young hero travels back in time to visit places that existed
before his time. Another movie like this is "The Time Machine" based
on a novel by H. G. Wells written in 1895. He also wrote The Invisible
Man (1897), War of The Worlds (1898), First Men on The Moon
(1901).

There is a fascination about going back in time to see the past.
Sometimes it is a good idea to reflect on the past, particularly where
we came from. I know my wife has always liked going back to her
old neighborhood in Calgary to revisit those times in her memory.
Revisiting the past can give us different perspectives on the future –
even provide us with a new insight as to what we should do with the
remainder of our lives.

Right now your future is only seconds away. This is the first day of
the rest of your life! Yesterday is history, today is the present – the now
- and tomorrow is the future. This is the way it has always been since
the beginning of the world.

From the Book of Genesis

1:1 "In the beginning God created the heavens and the earth."

1:26-30 " Then God said, "Let us make man in our image, in our likeness, and let them rule over the fish of the sea and the birds of the air, over the livestock, over all the earth, and over all the creatures that move along the ground."

So God created man in his own image, in the image of God he created him; male and female he created them.

God blessed them and said to them, "Be fruitful and increase in number; fill the earth and subdue it. Rule over the fish of the sea and the birds of the air and over every living creature that moves on the ground."

Then God said, "I give you every seed-bearing plant on the face of the whole earth and every tree that has fruit with seed in it. They will be yours for food. And to all the beasts of the earth and all the birds of the air and all the creatures that move on the ground—everything that has the breath of life in it—I give every green plant for food." And it was so."

Wouldn't it be wonderful if we could have witnessed God's awesome power in creating the universe, our world and everything on earth, including the creation of man?

Later in the Book of Genesis we learn that God called Abram to leave Haran with all his family and all of his possessions and go to the land of Canaan. God called Abram to a new future in a new land.

In the **Book of Genesis, Chapter 17:1-8** we are told.

"When Abram was ninety-nine years old, the LORD appeared to him and said, "I am God Almighty; walk before me and be blameless. I will confirm my covenant between me and you and will greatly increase your numbers.

Abram fell facedown, and God said to him, "As for me, this is my covenant with you: You will be the father of many nations. No longer will you be called Abram; your name will be Abraham, for I have made you a father of many nations.

I will make you very fruitful; **I will make nations of you, and kings will come from you. I will establish my covenant as an everlasting covenant between me and you and your descendants after you for the generations to come, to be your God and the God of your descendants after you.** The whole land of Canaan, where you are now an alien, I will give as an everlasting possession to you and your descendants after you; and I will be their God."

Abraham was the father of three religions. An Abrahamic religion is a monotheistic religion (belief in the existence of a single god) that includes Abraham (Hebrew): Arabic: Ibrahim) as part of its history.

Prominent examples are Christianity, Islam, Judaism, and the Baha'i Faith. Other, smaller religions that identify with this tradition—such as Druze—are sometimes included. Abrahamic religions account for more than half of the world's total population. Today, in a world with a population just over 6 billion people, there are around 3.8 billion followers of various Abrahamic religions.

Eastern religions form the other major religious group, encompassing the "Dharmic" religions of India and the "Taoic" East Asian religions—both terms being "parallels" of the "Abrahamic" category.

Islam is a monotheistic Abrahamic religion originating with the teachings of the Islamic prophet Muhammad, a seventh century Arab religious and political figure. The word Islam means "submission", or the total surrender of oneself to God (Arabic: Allāh). An adherent of Islam is known as a Muslim, meaning 'one who submits (to God)'. There are between 1 billion to 1.8 billion Muslims, making Islam the second-largest religion in the world, after Christianity. (1,400 years)

Judaism is the original religion of Abraham and is still practiced today (4,000 years)

Christianity came about with the birth and death of Jesus Christ 2,000 years ago.

The point of all the foregoing is this. God said to Abraham **"I will be your God and the God of your descendants after you." God is the God of all Jews and all Muslims as well as all Christians!**

Three religions share one Almighty and Powerful God!

This visit back to the beginning would not be complete without acknowledging God's creation of man.

Genesis 1:27 "So God created man in his own image, in the image of God he created him; male and female he created them".

The descendants of Abraham knew the power and wonder of God. You find that expressed in
Psalm 8:3-9 "When I consider your heavens, the work of your fingers, the moon and the stars, which you have set in place, **what is man that you are mindful of him, the son of man that you care for him?**

You made him a little lower than the heavenly beings and crowned him with glory and honor.

You made him ruler over the works of your hands; you put everything under his feet: all flocks and herds, and the beasts of the field, the birds of the air, and the fish of the sea, all that swim the paths of the seas.

O LORD, our Lord, how majestic is your name in all the earth!"

Let me repeat – (this is part of a prayer to God acknowledging His gift to us)
"**What is man that you are mindful of him, the son of man that you care for him?"**

This question is posed long before Jesus came to earth and relates to man as he then existed. (That is - in Old Testament times)

Have we got an answer to that question? Are we aware of how important we (each of us) are to God? Do we have a sense of God's presence in our lives? If so, why should that be? We'll talk about that when we come back.

Back To the Future – Part 2

This sermon is about going back in time to see the future. But right now let us look at the present and who we are.

We are Christians or followers of Christ. As Christians we believe in the following - Jesus, the son of God, was sent to earth to show and teach man how to live their lives so that their souls might reside in heaven with God forever. To accomplish that, God gave his Son, as a sacrifice (through crucifixion), paying the penalty for all of the sins of mankind. This act was a manifestation of God's great love for all men. To be a Christian, all we have to do is acknowledge God's love, repent of our sins as offenses against God and affirm Jesus as Lord and Savior,

Romans 10:9-10 sums it up nicely.
"That if you confess with your mouth, "Jesus is Lord," and believe in your heart that God raised him from the dead, you will be saved. For it is with your heart that you believe and are justified, and it is with your mouth that you confess and are saved."

We come to know Jesus through the Bible. The story of Jesus is told in the New Testament along with the record of how the early church came to be.

Do you believe in God? Does God exist? As Christians, we <u>know</u> God exists. A recent poll of Canadians state that only 78% thought God exists.

As Christians, we know that God is always present with us - the Bible says so. Do you believe that? God is always close to us! He has a purpose for each of us! Do you believe this?

Finally, we know that God loves each and every one of us - He knows our every thought and deed! We cannot hide from Him! How do we know that? - The Bible tells us so!

Can we agree that God is all-powerful, all knowing, and always present? He is the Alpha and Omega - the beginning and the end!

Do you doubt He made you? He made your soul - and your body with all its parts?

But God has done more.

As a Christian you know he has blessed each follower of Christ with spiritual gifts that they can use to fulfill a ministry in serving God. We are told that we should go into the world preaching the message of Jesus - we should do our best to bring the message of salvation <u>to all nations</u> on this earth.
What are we talking about? We are talking about saving souls! Right?

Christians, by definition, stand for and represent the salvation of the soul through the grace of God, the teachings and example of Jesus Christ and the crucifixion of Christ and ascension. We, as Christians, are guided by the teachings (God's word) recorded in the New Testament.

Our duty as Christians is found in the **Great Commission.**
Matthew 28:18-20 (Jesus, after His resurrection, speaking to the eleven apostles) "All authority in heaven and on earth has been given to me. Therefore go and make disciples of **all nations**, baptizing them in the name of the Father and of the Son and of the Holy Spirit, and teaching them to obey everything I have commanded you. And surely I am with you always, to the very end of the age."(NIV)

We are also influenced by the **Great Commandment** Jesus gave us.
Matthew 22:36-39 Jesus was asked - "Teacher, which is the greatest commandment in the Law?" Jesus replied: "Love the Lord your God with all your heart and with all your soul and with all your

mind. This is the first and greatest commandment. And the second is like it: 'Love your neighbor as yourself."

The result of following the dictates of our faith, Christianity means that we virtually pass over the message of the Old Testament although we acknowledge its place within our belief system and use the various books and chapters of the Old Testament to clarify who God is, His Nature as well as our own beginnings.

The 4,000 years encompassed by the Old Testament is still extremely important as is evidenced by the continuing faith of the Jews and Muslims relating to the teachings of God Himself beginning with Abraham and then the patriarchs and prophets. Three major religions of the world share an almighty God as the focus of their religion. The Old Testament is common to all three and over thousands of years (now 4,000 years for the Jews) has become deeply established as part of their religious beliefs.

Other religions acknowledge a Supreme Being or something similar.

Being Christian sets us apart from all other belief systems and makes it difficult for us to relate to their beliefs. We believe in Jesus Christ as Lord and Savior – no one else does!
We have the New Testament – no one else does!

Stated simply, <u>from our perspective</u>, Christianity is made up of the "in" group of mankind while all other members of the human race belong to the "outside" group. The latter group is made up of those who we (the "in" group) are called on to bring into the fold of Christianity so that their souls, too, may be saved. ("All nations")

If you want an example of how powerful Christianity is just consider this. We imposed our calendar on the rest of the world by changing the start of our Calendar to coincide with the birth of Christ.

The Mix of Mankind: Up to and around the time of Christ 2,000 years ago many nations existed. At various times the world was populated and even ruled by Sumerians, Assyrians, Babylonians, Persians, Amorites, Hittites, Chinese, Egyptian, Greek and Roman – all empires encompassing hundreds of thousands of people of various languages, over many years. To get a full sense of man's history on this world you could start with the "Outline of History – Volume 1 and 2" written by the same H.G. Wells in 1923 – the same person who wrote the Time Machine.

What stands out is the extent of civilized human population throughout the world including the Aztecs in the Americas, Hindus in India, Chinese, Indians of North America and so much more. The Jewish nation was but a very small part of the total makeup of the total civilized world.

When you examine the history of mankind, how man developed from the very beginning to now you should realize that God has had a major role in providing the talent, the ability and desire to achieve the advancement of mankind step by step over many centuries. Since God created this world He has had a plan for mankind.

By visiting the past we see that God created man, told him to multiply and have dominion over all the things of earth and we saw how God arranged for a small segment of mankind to develop a special nation that were to be His people and ultimately produce a savior for all mankind. This ultimately included the birth of a new religion called Christianity. Those of the Jewish people who did not convert to Christianity retained and continued their religious practice.

So, we know about us – Christians but what about the rest of the world? What about the other part of mankind. The people of all other nations who were not approached by God directly?

We are now talking about the future of all mankind from the very beginning. All men were created by God and He has a purpose for them within His plan for mankind.

In the beginning, none of them were approached and told that they had God in their lives. At least, not until Abram who was told he would be the father of great nations, whose people would all have God as their one and only God.

So we have 3 groups of people in the world -Those who do not have God in their lives; those who have one God, and those that have one God and a Redeemer. The first group can include those that are aware of a supreme being or a powerful being but have no name for it – spirit, enlightenment – they don't worship a single deity.

Soon our world will have seven billion people on it.

Christians (about 2.1 billion) are but a part of the total world population and, as you know, God has a special mission for us. A divine mission – to save souls! How do we accomplish our mission when we even have difficulty getting close family members to accept the Lord in their lives?

The answer lies in understanding God's purpose for our individual existence and the purpose for **all** mortal lives.

God has a purpose for every person ever born!
In visiting the past, we know God created all mankind – not just a select few. He gave each person abilities and talents – some very special gifts – and through their choices made during their earthly existence, they would have a major influence on what happened around them in their world. Great moments of history have occurred because of individuals from many different eras and nations.

Some were/are inventors, decision-makers (politicians?), generals, composers, poets, artists, teachers, administrators, scientists, doctors, nurses, lawyers, engineers, counselors, clergy, communication experts, even janitors and office workers.

The world that God created has evolved as man has applied his God-given talents to make our planet a productive entity capable of supporting billions of people and giving each person every chance to be a part of a productive society while providing for their individual and family needs. All part of God's plan!

The history of man on this earth is a record of the many successes and failures he has had in developing a highly functional and effective society for the advancement of all mankind. Just read the history of man and his inventiveness to know that God has always been present and provided a guiding hand in all of our endeavors.

Man has overcome many obstacles in the development of this world. Much of the development can be traced back to individuals from all walks of life and all nationalities – many are not Christian as one would assume considering the amount of advancement man made before Christ was born. Can we say, then, in looking back that man, in fact, was made in the image of God and through man's creativeness has taken on the task of managing all the resources of this world just as God intended. (See Genesis)

Man, individually and collectively, through the choices he makes, is the author of his own **earthly** destiny and in some way influences development of mankind. At the same time, each individual man, through his choice, is the author of his own personal **eternal** destiny. Successfully fulfilling both areas of responsibility meets God's purposes placed in the soul of every person prior to their journey on earth.

Back from the past – let's look at the "now" as we enter the future!

> **First**, is there any doubt in your mind that God has a dual purpose for your life whether you are a Christian or not?

> **Second**, can you understand that every person – no matter what nationality, religion or moral persuasion is God's creation and God has a purpose for their life?

> **Third**, can you see that God's plan encompasses all of mankind for the betterment of our existence while on earth and ultimately in heaven?

> **Fourth**, can you see the common factor that unites all people is that each is God's creation, He loves each one, **is mindful of them,** has given each talents and a task

and desires our obedience in helping each other live on this planet and ultimately in heaven with Him?

The future? With the understanding we have of man's creation and that God has had a purpose for every person ever born in this world, as Christians, we can help others to understand God exists personally in their lives (right now!) and He has given them the means to help mankind grow and prosper in the world God created for man to inhabit.

Can we remove the barriers that exist between us replacing it with an understanding of our common heritage and love of God, our mutual Creator, ever present with all of us?

Be always joyful in the Lord for you are His child and <u>He has placed His trust in you</u> to find your way through life helping others and joining Him in His world of love, peace and joy in heaven!

May God be with you as you continue your journey through life!

Let us pray.

PART 7

How Do We Now Live?

Concluding Remarks

I would like to review some of the points made through the message and the many sermons and devotionals in this book. The primary focus of the original message is the soul—each and every soul—and then God and His relationship with our souls and mankind. He has given each soul gifts, abilities, talents, and basic intelligence, which is available for use by the body through the exercise of choice. Finally, He has given us His word along with His presence to guide us to the fulfillment of His purpose for mankind on earth and the eternal destination of each soul.

Creating Awareness of the Soul

Since *A Message for the Soul of Man* is about the soul of man, it is meant to emphasize the soul and what that means. This is to make everyone aware of his or her soul, its immortality, and the need to seek direction for the soul so that it may enjoy everlasting happiness in heaven.

Putting the message out was interesting, but it called into question a few things. For instance, to be believable one had to really:

- Believe in God
- Believe in God's almighty power and wisdom
- Accept that God was the creator of all things
- Believe that God provides His life force for every human being, which begged the question—why? What was God's purpose?

The purpose of the sermons and devotionals was to focus on the details of the message, which included much of the above. It is obvious that in order for the message concerning the soul to be accepted, there needs to be a strong acceptance of who God is. Despite many books being written about God, the consensus seems to be that people get a better grasp on who God is by talking about what he is not. It is difficult for people to accept that God is all-powerful and can do anything to anyone at any time. Don't cross him if you don't want to experience his wrath. See the Old Testament. We need to be in awe of God.

Accepting God has been an integral part of the ongoing development of *A Message for the Soul of Man*.

God's Provision of Gifts and Talents

It became clear to me that there was a lot more to it. The message talked about providing gifts and talents to each and every soul created—every soul that became attached to a body on earth. The bestowment of these gifts occurred before birth and people need to understand that God did this for a reason.

The more that one examines the soul scenario, the more a person can see the science fiction aspect of the situation. Because of the high degree of interest in science fiction in our society, it is possible that God felt that mankind might be ready to accept what is now being presented.

Nevertheless, it seems apparent that God had a plan that involved all souls. It also meant that it included all of mankind.

God's Plan and Purpose

God has had a purpose for everything. He created the universe and our planet. Why? He created all the things that exist on this planet. Why? He provided for the ever-changing nature of our planet, its cycles, and weather. Everything was created for a reason. Why? In this case, only one reason presents itself—a habitat for man including his soul! Why?

Because God is so mighty, powerful, and all knowing, we don't really know. However, there are clues about the reasons for man's existence. The first starts with the history of mankind on earth. When you examine history, you see that the advancement of man on earth has occurred in an orderly manner due to the inventiveness of men and women in every corner of this earth over hundreds of years.

Individual Goals and Choices

The inventions and ideas that were necessary for man's progress in his environment came about because of man's gifts, talents, and working with his hands and mind.

God had two purposes in placing man on earth: development of mankind and each soul. It calls into question the individual's goals in life as he or she completes their education. What choices will they make? Will they be an asset or liability to mankind and the advancement of mankind?

Strangely, the progress to this point started to make sense because the message, directed to the soul of man, was now providing a reason for every soul to develop their talents and abilities for mankind. The rewards could be huge satisfaction or great wealth. Certainly a feeling of having contributed to the improvement of mankind can make one's life very worthwhile.

We have learned what the soul is and now know its purpose!

One other thing that has come to my attention is that passages from the Bible can be read with a person getting even greater meaning, making the Bible truly instructive of God's wishes for man. Each person can see themselves as important in God's eyes.

A Challenge

There is a challenge within the messages that has to be dealt with. *The message was directed to all souls*—everyone—no matter what their religious affiliation and is intended to set aside (for the moment) the religious beliefs of post-Christ and post-Mohammed followers. The message does not detract from their beliefs. If nothing else, it should strengthen them since the message implies that God placed in everyone the abilities, gifts, and talents to become what they have as an influence on those who follow—even to the extent of extolling the virtues of living a virtuous life.

God wants the world of man to understand who they are, their relationship with God, and the final destiny of their individual souls.

God's Presence

In my talks about God, I have attempted to get across that God is present with each of us at all times.

This starts with God's life force within us—keeping the body alive. The second is the presence of God close to us. Angels—or an angel—may be a part of this. Finally, God enters our mind (soul) to place a thought or idea there for us to become aware of. Each one of us is a work in progress up until we die.

God's Role

I know that I am an example of God's relationship with every individual soul on earth.

He provided the gifts and talents I was born with. He helped direct my experiences as I matured. He helped set me on a path in life where I would come to a point where He would call on me to do something that would be beneficial for all those around me—in the material world. He also called on me to find him so that I would come to know, love, and serve Him in my spiritual walk on earth.

Each of us is called—some in minor ways and others to major works that affect the world. The election of a president in the United States could qualify for the latter.

What is so striking is that you can go back in history and find the acknowledgment of God's presence in the lives of both ordinary and famous people.

One should not be surprised by God's close proximity since it was recorded in the Old Testament that God made himself directly known to chosen people. He even spoke directly to a few.

God's Purpose in His Current Message

The message God provided is serving two real purposes. The first is that each man, woman, and child should be aware of their soul and who they are. Each needs to realize that the ultimate destiny for his or her soul is decided by themselves through the choices they make in life, starting at a very early age. Should you take the cookie from the cookie jar that you were forbidden to touch?

Knowing that your soul is a creation of God, it probably is a good idea to get a real sense of who God is and discover why God made you in the first place. Your soul and God's purpose for you go hand-in-hand. In other words, you are something very special and you won't know it until your life is over.

The Parable of the Talents (Matthew 25:14–30) is a good one to go by when considering what you do with your life!

About Your Religion

Every religion has a single purpose. Each of us is encouraged to acknowledge God as the creator of all things, including us. We are asked to worship and obey God and to follow His wish that each of us live in a holy manner, loving God and all mankind so that we will enjoy eternal life with Him. It is all about overcoming the sins of the flesh, loving and worshiping God in a world strewn with temptation. Ultimately, each soul joins God for eternity.

Each religion has come about with God's full knowledge. Just as God set the example in the Old Testament, he also has set the example within the New Testament in sending Jesus to bring the message of salvation to the world for all to hear and see. The Jewish people have seen fit to follow the Old Testament and the teachings of the prophets, the Muslims have chosen to follow the teachings of Mohammed as related through the Koran and, of course, Christians believe in Christ and follow his teachings as gathered within the New Testament.

All have one goal—to be with God. The ideal final destination of each soul for eternity is with God. All major religions direct our attention to one God!

As a follower of Christ, much of the material within this book will reflect a strong Christian bias. This was the influence of my learning when I was very young. My background, especially as a non-practicing Christian in later life, should not in any way detract from the overall message that God has provided through me, his servant.

Concluding Remarks

A Message for the Soul of Man is God's way of refreshing our knowledge about God, the world, and ourselves. It is a way of taking stock of where we, personally, are now in relation to the world and its development over many thousands of years.

Each of us is called to examine ourselves (our soul), to determine our purpose in life and to influence our children to do the same as they grow up. You can be sure that the history of mankind is not over. There is much more to come!

The future calls for man to find a way to live in peace and harmony and develop our God-given talents for greater achievements to come.

Man, after all, was made in the likeness of God and, with the full development of man's abilities and intellect, he can master challenges far beyond his present ability. Revisiting the history of man can give you a very good idea of how far man can progress—and *has* progressed.

This is especially true if war, pestilence, environmental damage, crime, addictions, and other human frailties have been eradicated or overcome.

It all starts with each soul.

A Prayer

May God bless each of us with the ability to know Him, understand His message for our soul, realize our soul's value and purpose in living in our mortal body, and come to know our purpose in life while serving God's overall purpose for all mankind. In so doing, we seek to know, love, and serve God within our spiritual path, knowing the love of God and our ultimate destiny is eternity with God. Amen.

Author's Questions

Is it naive to expect that individuals, after reading this book, will be moved to change their lives in such a way as to acknowledge the continuing presence of God in their lives, be moved to change their human ways to resist the evils of this world, and to seek to fulfill a meaningful purpose for their life however small it may seem?

Individually, can we make our life on earth really worthwhile?

With the knowledge that *A Message for the Soul of Man* brings along with the revelation of God's purpose for man, why did God want this knowledge released now? What does the future hold for man and his soul? My instincts tell me that the future for man on earth is going to be fabulous!

As I think about God's energy keeping the body alive along with the presence of the soul, I wonder if a person can sense the absence of God's life-supplying energy (life force) when touching a dead body. Can you sense the sheer emptiness?

Finally, establishing that God has always existed prior to the introduction of different religious beliefs, is it possible that we can again introduce God into our courts and schoolrooms as an acknowledgment of God's existence even before our individual spiritual beliefs? This would certainly facilitate the acceptance of God and the soul of man as a universal truth.

The Parable of the Talents
— Matthew 25:14–30

Again, it will be like a man going on a journey, who called his servants and entrusted his property to them. To one he gave five talents of money, to another two talents, and to another one talent, each according to his ability. Then he went on his journey. The man who had received the five talents went at once and put his money to work and gained five more. So also, the one with the two talents gained two more. But the man who had received the one talent went off, dug a hole in the ground and hid his master's money.

After a long time the master of those servants returned and settled accounts with them. The man who had received the five talents brought the other five. "Master," he said, "you entrusted me with five talents. See, I have gained five more."

His master replied, "Well done, good and faithful servant! You have been faithful with a few things; I will put you in charge of many things. Come and share your master's happiness!"

The man with the two talents also came. "Master," he said, "you entrusted me with two talents; see—I have gained two more."

His master replied, "Well done, good and faithful servant! You have been faithful with a few things; I will put you in charge of many things. Come and share your master's happiness!"

Then the man who had received the one talent came. "Master," he said, "I knew that you are a hard man, harvesting where you have not sown and gathering where you have not scattered seed. So I was afraid and went out and hid your talent in the ground. See, here is what belongs to you."

His master replied, "You wicked, lazy servant! So you knew that I harvest where I have not sown and gather where I have not scattered seed? Well then, you should have put my money on deposit with the bankers, so that when I returned I would have received it back with interest. Take the talent from him and give it to the one who has the ten talents. For everyone who has will be given more and he will have abundance. Whoever does not have, even what he has will be taken from him. And throw that worthless servant outside, into the darkness, where there will be weeping and gnashing of teeth."

Some Discussion and Notes about "Talents"

Do not neglect the gift that is in you. 1Timothy 4:14 says, "God never gives a person a task without also providing him with what's necessary to perform the responsibility."

W. W. Dawley, referring to this truth, says, "God gave Moses a rod, David a sling, Samson the jawbone of a donkey, Shamgar an ox goad, Esther the beauty of person, Deborah the talent for poetry, Dorcas a needle, and Apollo an eloquent tongue—and to each the ability to use that gift. In so doing, every one of them did most effective works for the Lord."

Our heavenly Father has given at least one spiritual gift to each of us as believers, and He provides all we need to carry out our individual responsibilities (1 Corinthians. 12:6–7). We are all essential in the body of Christ.

Acknowledging these truths is not only a source of comfort and encouragement, but it is also a sobering reality, for it places before us an important obligation. God's gifts to us must not be squandered! They must be fully used, because someday "each of us shall give account of himself to God" (Romans 14:12).

Richard De Haan asks, "What has the Lord given you? Are you using your spiritual gift for His glory and the blessing of others? Don't waste your gift! Use it!"

Bierema says, "Lord God, I humbly ask of You; the strength to do Your will; I give to You my talents now; Your purpose to fulfill."

God's call to a task includes His strength to complete it. (Strength = ability, gift, talent?)

Further Discussion about Talents

When you're reading a mystery, aside from enjoying the story, what are you trying to do? When we read the parables of Jesus, questions often arise and demand that we look for the clues that can answer our questions. In Matthew 25:14–18, Jesus talks about "talents."

- We know that talents were money, in this case, large amounts of money.
- What do talents refer to in the world outside this story? There have been several different guesses that we've looked at: talents are "talents" (abilities), rewards, spiritual gifts, money. This demands that we look at the clues in the story to try to come to a conclusion.
- There are at least four clues to consider. The talent is something that belongs to God and not to human beings. "For the kingdom of heaven is like a man traveling to a far country, who called his own servants and delivered his goods to them." (Matthew 25:14). The talents are distributed "to each according to his ability." (Matthew 25:15). This seems to say that the "talents" are distributed on the basis of our natural gifts. The talents, therefore, cannot be our natural gifts. They are related to them, but they are not the same thing. These talents are something the Lord gives us so that they can be invested. This isn't stated directly, but it is implied in the story. They are something that can be risked or invested. The investment of the talents is made on behalf of the absent owner and not

the servant. The risk is taken by the servant; the benefit will belong to the Lord.

- What, then, are the talents? They are opportunities that God gives us to use on His behalf. They are opportunities to utilize our natural abilities for the sake of Christ. That is, the talents equal the opportunities that we have.

Questions

What other interpretation can you place on this parable? Try Luke 19:11–26. Are they similar parables? Why are there two similar parables? The two stories teach different lessons. Jesus used similar stories to teach different lessons. Each story should be studied in its context for what it teaches.

The Parable of the Minas teaches that men and women who have the same gifts entrusted to them may use them in very different ways and will be rewarded according to their diligence.

The Parable of the Talents teaches that two people with dissimilar gifts may use them with equal diligence and they will receive the same reward based on their dependability.

Do the two parables teach a person to lead a holy life or to succeed in this world with the gifts that they have been given? In other words, are all gifts spiritual? Both?

Making Your Life Worthwhile!

God's influence has been felt by many people over hundreds of years. If you question whether God exists or if God is present in your life and has a purpose for you—consider the following quotations from important people from history.

St. Francis of Assisi (1181–1226)
Catholic priest and founder of the Franciscan Monks

> Keep a clear eye toward life's end. Do not forget your purpose and destiny as God's creature. What you are in his sight is what you are and nothing more. Remember that when you leave this earth, you can take with you nothing you have received—fading symbols of honor, trappings of power—but only what you have given: a full heart, enriched by honest service, love, sacrifice and courage.

William Jennings Bryan (1860–1925)

> I have observed the power of the watermelon seed. It has the power of drawing from the ground and through itself 200,000 times its weight. When you can tell me how it takes this material and out of it colors an outside surface beyond the imitation of art, and then forms inside of it a white rind and within that again a red heart, thickly inlaid with black seeds, each one of which

in turn is capable of drawing through itself 200,000 times its weight—when you can explain to me the mystery of a watermelon, you can ask me to explain the mystery of God.

Florence Nightingale (1820–1910)
God's Work

My mind is absorbed with the sufferings of man. Since I was twenty-four, there never has been any vagueness in my plans or ideas as to what God's work was for me.

William Shakespeare (1564–1616)
Lantern to My Feet

God shall be my hope, my stay, my guide, and lantern to my feet.

Carl G. Jung (1875–1961)
Before My Birth

From the beginning I had a sense of destiny, as though my life was assigned to me by fate and had to be fulfilled. This gave me an interior security, and though I could never prove it to myself, it proved itself to me. I did not have this certainty, it had me. Nobody could rob me of the conviction that it was enjoined upon me to do what God wanted. That gave me the strength to go on my own way. Often I had the feeling that in all decisive matters I was no longer among men, but was alone with God. And when I was "there," where I was no longer alone, I was outside time; I belonged to the centuries; and He who then gave answer was He who had always been, who had been before my birth. He who always is was there. These talks with the "Other" were my profoundest experiences: on the one hand, a bloody struggle, on the other, supreme ecstasy."

You have a place in God's plan. It would be exciting to find out what it is!

God's Two Purposes for You

The message in this book states that God has two purposes for mankind. Your purpose for living is found within God's dual purpose for the soul of man. From birth, as your body and mind develop, you have the opportunity not only to discover what your abilities are, but you also have your early years to test them out. In this manner, you find your vocation in life. A great deal of happiness and satisfaction can come from the successful application of your God-given abilities to the challenges faced by mankind in all fields of human endeavor.

The first purpose for the soul was, through the use of God's gifts, to advance mankind. This continues at a breathtaking pace today, *ipsa loquitur* (the thing speaks for itself i.e., read the history of mankind). Man has been given domain over all the earth. Man has the responsibility to help the world achieve the ability to utilize all of the resources of this world while finding the best method of bringing about peace on earth and goodwill to all men. That message, usually heard at Christmas, is no mistake.

God truly wants each individual soul to use all of their God-given abilities, including intelligence, to become the best person they can—in the process *becoming an asset or a liability* to themselves, their families, their community, country, and world.

God's second purpose for the soul, taught through the Bible, was for man to learn the importance of his own soul and its ultimate eternal destiny and to actively seek to know, love, and serve God in order to be assured of the soul's place in heaven. God, through *A Message for the Soul of Man*, reiterates the importance He places on each soul—your soul!

Pursuing God's First Purpose

Fulfilling God's first purpose benefits everyone who works and contributes to improving his or her own lives and the lives of others. They become an asset rather than a liability in the world. Without knowing it, such a person is doing the work that God set out for them and utilizing their God-given abilities and talents. They will know a sense of fulfillment and satisfaction.

However, each soul, in their worldly journey, will come upon crossroads where choices have to be made. These crossroads occur quite regularly and are usually found at puberty (goal setting), leaving adolescence for adulthood (vocation), mid-life (adjustment), and near or at retirement (application of wisdom). Each crossroad calls for the exercise of choice as to which path the soul will take. The decisions can bring about one or more of the following situations.

Who Benefits from Following God's Dual Purpose for the Soul?

- *Addicts and/or addicts in recovery* (finding a sense of worth and redirection of life)
- *Adolescents and young adults* (a period of discovery of self and decision about goals and vocation)
- *Followers of non-mainstream religions* (recognizing that they have a soul—salvation)
- *People who are despondent* (finding a sense of self-worth as they are unique and valuable as the creation of a loving God)
- *People who do not know God* (a longing—there is an intrinsic need within oneself to find God)
- *People who are really concerned about the salvation of their soul* (Understanding God's message)
- *Seekers of worldly and spiritual fulfillment* (realizing that they have worth and are valuable)
- *Sinners* (learning that they have a soul, which can know redemption through turning to God)
- *Suicide bombers* (understanding their soul is not going to heaven when they thwart God's will to give life to every person on earth (soul and body).

- *Young children* (provide for them the dream of being part of God's plan for the evolution of man in the future. The discovery of their gifts, talents, and abilities can be exciting and play a major role in God's plan for humanity. This is the important role of parents and teachers!)

Before one ever finds God on a personal level, one can know the feeling of fulfillment in serving to help the world become a better place to live, thus meeting God's desire for man to control all of the earth's resources for the betterment of mankind.

Pursuing God's Second Purpose

There comes a point in your earthly existence where you come face-to-face with the death of your body. The experience is unique to you, but can be traumatic and upsetting. The realization that your life (soul) on earth is temporary and the great unknown looms in front of you can be very upsetting. We must face it. It is all part of God's plan!

You are a soul! Your soul is eternal. Your mortal time on earth was given you to determine the final destination of your soul in eternity. Simply, it is either heaven or hell.

God wants your soul to be with him for eternity. If you realize that *you* are a soul; that your body is only temporary; that you have had the opportunity to seek God and seek His loving grace for your soul, then you may have saved your soul and assured yourself of being in heaven for eternity.

You Do Not Know the Day and the Hour that Your Body Will Pass

While both of God's purposes for the soul are very important, you can fall short or fail in the first but, you must not fail in the second!

I pray that *A Message for the Soul of Man* will help you make your life worthwhile and that your soul will know eternal peace and happiness with God in heaven.

Advocating a New Direction for Mankind

An Understanding of What We Know and Believe

Before indicating a new direction for mankind, I would respectfully ask that the following points be acknowledged and accepted:

- Each person has a soul and that soul was created by God and is eternal and endowed with God-given attributes and gifts that will be/are manifested through the body in which it ultimately dwells.
- God exists and is omnipotent and the creator of all things. We freely admit to God's presence in this world and specifically with every person who exists on this planet.
- God created souls and placed them in human bodies for the purpose of giving each the opportunity and choice to know, love, and serve Him and assure themselves (their souls) of the everlasting life of their soul, residing with Him in heaven.
- God, in His great love for every soul, demonstrated that love by sending His Son, Jesus Christ, to become man and teach mankind how to live in order to know God, the Father, and understand the importance of knowing, loving and serving God, thus, becoming sanctified and worthy of salvation.
- The Bible is made up of two parts, the Old Testament—a record of God's teaching and interaction with man, and the New Testament—a record of the birth, life and death of Jesus and the ensuing birth of Christianity—all of which were

placed before mankind as a clear direction from God on how all souls can be saved from eternal damnation.

- The God of Christianity is the same God of the Jews and Muslims. The difference in belief comes from the choice made by each group to accept or reject Jesus Christ as Savior rather than as a prophet, wise man, or teacher.
- The primary purpose of Christianity is to save souls, including our own and practicing the teachings of God conveyed through His Son so that, after death of the body, our souls will reside with God in heaven forever.

A New Understanding

All members of the human race should:

- Emphasize the importance of each and every soul as God's creation and the great love God has for each.
- Recognize that every person on this planet has a soul regardless of gender, race, color, creed, or geography and to that end we are all equal and unique as God's creations.
- Recognize that every soul created by God was given gifts and attributes by God to serve two purposes as human beings.
- The *first* of these purposes was, through the use of God's gifts to the soul, to advance mankind on this earth, which continues at a breathtaking pace today. ;
- The *second* purpose, taught through the Bible and by Jesus, was for mankind to learn the importance of his own soul and its ultimate salvation and actively seek to know love and serve God in order to be assured of the soul's salvation.
- Recognize and believe that God has a plan for our souls individually and collectively, which is beyond the comprehension of man in many ways.
- Acknowledge that each Abrahamic religion is based on a belief in an all-powerful God and the desire that each soul be with God throughout eternity. The successful realization of that goal rests on the belief system each practices—whether right or wrong.

A New Direction

Every person should:

- Emphasize, extol, and promote the value of each soul as the creation of God and the object of His love, emphasizing His desire to have each soul rejoin Him in heaven for eternity—the salvation of souls.
- Reach out to all people on earth with a message of love for all of God's creations with a view to creating mutual understanding of how we all worship one God while respecting each other's path to the salvation of the soul and individual relationship with God.
- Emphasize God's purpose for all mankind in developing man with the ultimate goal of peaceful co-existence on earth while recognizing the importance of every soul and the purpose of each to contribute to the overall well-being of man.
- Recognize that the ultimate success (eternal happiness) for every soul is learning about God and serving Him and helping others come to understand their own uniqueness and their soul's relationship with God while at the same time serving all of mankind.

To serve man is to serve God! Before and after conversion!

We should all focus our thinking:

- On the soul (us)
- On God (our Creator)
- On our twofold purpose on earth (reason for living)
- On Jesus (for Christians, Savior and teacher)
- On eternity for the soul (heaven, with God)

PART 8

The Moment of Truth

Separation of Soul from Body

Sometime in the future, you will have an experience something like this.

You may be sleeping, driving your car, standing on top of a ladder, close to a bomb blast, on patrol in a foreign country, jogging, in a boat in a sudden violent storm, or one of many other ordinary human activities.

You notice that, while you are conscious of your surroundings, something has changed. You wonder what is so different. First, you don't feel any pain—for that matter, you don't seem to be part of the activity that is occurring around you. You don't feel cold or heat or even a breeze on your face.

Secondly, you realize that *you are not part of anything* that is occurring around you. At that moment, you have a sinking feeling—you realize that *you* are no longer a part of your body.

Experiencing Your Soul Leaving Your Body

You are dead! Your body is dead. You have come to the end of your mortal life. You have just experienced what millions have before you—and millions will after!

Death—the Moment of Truth

Throughout *A Message for the Soul of Man*, you have learned about the importance of your soul and your purpose for living. I hope that you have also learned about your ultimate goal for your soul and what you must do to reach it.

Sooner or later, all of our wondering and searching comes to an end with death! We die! Our body dies! The moment of truth has arrived!

Death of a Daughter

A couple of years ago, one of my daughters died suddenly in her sleep at the young age of forty-eight. The cause of her death was a complete mystery. It was so unexpected—and very difficult for the family to deal with. It still is. Later, we found out that she had died of acute pneumonia. We have no idea why she was taken from us so young.

Her death was a reminder to me about why this book was written and why *A Message for the Soul of Man* was even more important for everyone. If everything that has been written here is accurate, where should my daughter's soul be?

Death (Of the Body) Really Isn't the End of Your Existence

Obviously, my daughter's *soul continued into eternity*, but where in eternity we don't know. That will have been decided by her belief and how she lived her life. While we are on earth, we can consciously influence the eternal destiny of our soul. It is within the realm of possibility that the knowledge she (her soul) learned in life allowed her soul to seek God's forgiveness in death.

Death Is a Constant—and Many Times Sudden

Every day, we are reminded about how many people die in the world—many suddenly through war, suicide bombings, accidents, illnesses such as swine flu, the ravages of AIDS or overdosing on drugs or alcohol. Death is a constant in life and sometimes it's too close as it was within my family. Death often comes without any warning—as in my daughter's case—and it can catch us unprepared.

Your Death

At the moment of your body's death, you will know whether or not everything we have discussed in this book is, in fact, true. Unfortunately, you have to die to find out!

Biblical Reminders

"Man is destined to die once, and after that to face judgment." —Hebrews 9:27

How should you live your life?

A piece of scripture might help.

Ephesians 4:17–29

> So I tell you this, and insist on it in the Lord, that you must no longer live as the Gentiles do, in the futility of their thinking. They are darkened in their understanding and separated from the life of God because of the ignorance that is in them due to the hardening of their hearts. Having lost all sensitivity, they have given themselves over to sensuality so as to indulge in every kind of impurity, with a continual lust for more.
>
> You, however, did not come to know Christ that way. Surely you heard of him and were taught in him in accordance with the truth that is in Jesus. You were taught, with regard to your former way of life, to put off your old self, which is being corrupted by its deceitful desires; to be made new in the attitude of your minds; and to put on the new self, created to be like God in true righteousness and holiness.
>
> Therefore each of you must put off falsehood and speak truthfully to his neighbor, for we are all members of one body. In your anger do not sin: Do not let the sun go down while you are still angry, and do not give the

devil a foothold. He who has been stealing must steal no longer, but must work, doing something useful with his own hands, that he may have something to share with those in need.

Do not let any unwholesome talk come out of your mouths, but only what is helpful for building others up according to their needs, that it may benefit those who listen.

Your Soul's Destiny Is Yours to Decide

After reading this book and its message, you have a choice to make. My prayer for you is that you will be enlightened and, therefore, equipped to make the right choices in life—that your life will reflect the love of God in all you do. May God be with you—and you with God!

The Realities of Your Life
on Earth as a Soul

A Message for the Soul of Man was given to me for a reason. I believe that reason was to bring it (the message) to the attention of all the peoples of the world. God knows how I was to accomplish this in a world teeming in information flow and so many distractions. Having brought forth this book, I can truly say it is now in the hands of God.

I recommend *A Message for the Soul of Man* to all mankind with the hope that each person who reads it will live their life on earth with the knowledge of all the realities of life that have been brought forth by this book. Let me review these realities and trust that you agree with each one:

- **First Reality**—The conscious you is a soul! (Eternal—your soul lives forever)
- **Second Reality**—You have a mortal body you must look after—water, food, air, and all necessities
- **Third Reality**—God exists and He created everything, including your soul
- **Fourth Reality**—God has a purpose for everything He created, including man's instinct to procreate
- **Fifth Reality**—God gave you (your soul) certain gifts and unique talents, including time, free will, and the power of choice
- **Sixth Reality**—God wants you (your soul) to return to Him in Heaven. It is called Salvation. Satan will try to stop you through temptation to sin

- **Seventh Reality**—Learn to appreciate the gifts and talents that God gave you while you seek out your vocation as a young person
- **Eighth Reality**—You are to seek ways and means to advance mankind as part of loving your neighbor
- **Ninth Reality**—Seek God, get to know Him, understand Him, and love Him. Know that God is present in your life. Reading the Bible (God's word) is recommended
- **Tenth Reality**—Your body dies, leaving your soul unattached and subject to judgment
- **Eleventh Reality**—Know that you (your soul) continues to exist. You come to recognize that your soul has no gender, no marital or parental status, no skin color, and you are not confined to one language. Communication is accomplished through your mental processes.
- **Twelfth Reality**—Your freed soul belongs to no religion—it is not necessary—and you are in heaven with God. (Or are you?)

You are now equipped to live your life on earth. You (meaning your soul) have abilities and skills that can be nurtured and used to help you in your daily life and even help others with their lives.

You know that you have a purpose in life. God has given you the time and place to embark on a quest of self-discovery, which will culminate in establishing the destiny of your soul through all eternity.

For those who continue in life, as part of the continuing evolution of man on earth, you will experience many wondrous things through the power of God. It has already started.

I hope that *A Message for the Soul of Man* will assist you on your journey in the life prepared for you by Almighty God. In your lifetime, you may be called on by God to serve in a very unique and wonderful way. If God calls on you, I hope you will be ready.

May God bless you.

Closing Thoughts

This book has taken eighteen years to be gathered, assembled, and published.

Because of the magnitude of the work—referring to the content and the very nature of the principle subjects—God, man, soul, creation, the Bible, and the history of man, I feel that it could take a lifetime to fully comprehend all the ingredients.

This book is a serious work because it tries to convince every reader that they have an immortal soul that will leave the body and be subject to the judgment of God on the soul's future existence.

Of greater importance to me is that *A Message for the Soul of Man* is a message directly from God to me. At the time, I didn't really believe it, but as time went by I saw more and more evidence of how God influences people to do His bidding. I am no exception. I just play a different role.

What You Do with the Message Depends on You

I am convinced that everything in this book is true and presented to you so that each and every reader will be convinced of God's existence, presence, and influence. It is my hope that each reader will also fully realize that he or she *is a soul* and it is to each soul that God's message is conveyed in this book. In other words, this book was written for you! What you do with the message is entirely up to you. Will how you live be changed? Again, that's up to you.

I acknowledge God's great love for all of mankind. He desires that our souls return to Him. That is why, after reading this book, you will find that you will probably want to read it again—and maybe again. At least, that is what has happened to me. God works within us for His good purpose.

I never found out why God wanted His message made public now, but I am sure that the history of mankind from this year on will truly be magnificent as man continues to grow and flourish with the gifts, talents, and attributes that God bestows on all souls.

After reading *A Message for the Soul of Man*, you may want to pass this book to others to read. I encourage you to do this.

God bless you and may your life on earth be enriched by having read *A Message for the Soul of Man*.

A special note:

Now turn to the very beginning of this book and re-read the quotations of interest. Note that they don't mention the soul. Now you know the reason for this book and why God sent His message.

If you now have a clear understanding that *you have a soul,* the message has succeeded!

PART 9

Scripture Verses Index and more

Biblical Verses Index

Table of Biblical Verses arranged by Chapter (Alphabetical)

Book Section/Scripture Verses	Book	Chapter	Verse(s)
A New Revelation - Soul - Formative Years	Proverbs	16	9
Back to the Future	Genesis	1	27
	Genesis	17	1-8
	Matthew	22	36-39
	Matthew	28	18-20
	Psalm	8	3-9
	Romans	10	9-10
Defeating Satan	1 John	1	9
	1 John	2	24
	1 Peter	1	15-16
	1 Peter	1	3-9
	1 Thessalonians	4	3
	1 Thessalonians	5	23
	2 Corinthians	11	14
	2 Corinthians	4	4
	2 Corinthians	6	16
	Colossians	1	21-23
	Ephesians	6	11, 13
	Ezekiel	28	12-18
	Hebrews	10	26-31
	Hebrews	6	4-6
	James	4	7
	John	8	44
	John	15	4

	Matthew	22	37
	Matthew	4	1-11
	Revelation	12	9, 12
	Revelation	2	10
	Revelation	12	7-9
	Romans	7	15-19
	Romans	3	23
	Romans	6	23
Devotion On Music	Ephesians	5	19
Experiencing God	Acts	8	3
	Acts	9	13-15
	Acts	9	17-18
	Acts	9	1-7
	Colossians	3	15-17
	Matthew	28	18-20
I Am - Part 1	1 Corinthians	6	19
	2 Peter	2	19
	2 Timothy	3	2-7
	Ecclesiastes	3	11
	Ephesians	5	15-20
	Galatians	5	22-24
	Genesis	1	27-30
	Genesis	2	7
	Hebrews	2	5-8
	Romans	1	18-32
I Am - Part 2	1 Kings	3	5
	1 Kings	3	11-14
	2 Peter	1	20-21
	Exodus	3	5-10

	Exodus	3	13-15
	Exodus	20	1-7
	Genesis	1	27-30
	Genesis	2	15-17
	Genesis	4	9-12
	Genesis	6	11-21
	Genesis	9	1
	Genesis	12	7
	Genesis	12	1-3
	Genesis	13	14-17
	Genesis	22	15-18
	Genesis	22	2
	Genesis	22	10-12
	Genesis	28	12-15
	Hebrews	1	1-3
	John	1	14
	John	6	35-40
	John	8	58
	John	11	25-26
	Joshua	1	1-11
	Joshua	13	1
	Matthew	3	16-17
	Revelation	1	8
	Revelation	21	6-8
I Appointed You	Jeremiah	1	5
	Psalm	139	13-16
Implications of God's Message	Mark	12	30-31
	Matthew	16	26

Knowing, Loving and Serving God	2 Timothy	3	1-4
	Galatians	6	7-10
	John	12	26
	Luke	10	27
	Psalm	100	1-5
	Romans	8	28
Love and Your Soul	1 Corinthians	2	9
	1 Corinthians	4	4-13
	1 Corinthians	13	13
	1 Corinthians	13	4-7
	1 John	4	10
	1 John	4	7-12
	2 Corinthians	13	14
	Deuteronomy	6	4-9
	Hebrews	2	5-8
	John	3	16-17
	John	13	34-35
	John	15	9-13
	Mark	12	31
	Matthew	5	45
	Matthew	22	34-40
	Matthew	22	37-39
	Psalm	139	13-16
Man Revealed	1 Corinthians	12	4-7
	Jeremiah	1	5
	Mark	10	27
	Philippians	2	13
	Proverbs	16	9
	Psalm	139	13-16

My Journey into Spirituality	Matthew	4	10
	Matthew	10	38
On Being Alone	1 Peter	5	6-7
	1 Timothy	5	5
	Ecclesiastes	4	11
	Genesis	2	18
	John	16	32
	Lamentations	1	16
	Luke	5	16
	Matthew	11	28-30
	Matthew	26	36-39
	Nahum	1	7
	Psalm	25	16-17
	Psalm	34	15-22
	Psalm	55	22
	Psalm	69	20
	Psalm	139	1-12
	Psalm	142	4
Our Journey Through Life	2 Samuel	14	14
	2 Timothy	4	6
	Ecclesiastes	2	18-23
	Ecclesiastes	2	1-11
	Ecclesiastes	2	25
	Ecclesiastes	3	18-22
	Ecclesiastes	3	1
	Ecclesiastes	3	17
	Ecclesiastes	3	11-14

	Ecclesiastes	5	8-17
	Ecclesiastes	5	18-19
	Matthew	6	33
Parable of Talents	1 Corinthians	12	14-27
	1 Corinthians	12	6-7
	1 Timothy	4	14
	Luke	19	11-26
	Matthew	25	14-18
	Matthew	25	14-30
	Romans	14	12
Peace	1 Thessalonians	5	23
	2 Thessalonians	3	16
	Acts	10	36
	Galatians	5	22-23
	Job	22	21
	Philippians	4	6-7
	Psalm	4	8
	Psalm	34	14
	Romans	5	1
	Romans	15	33
Relationships and the Soul of Man	John	15	9-17
	Luke	10	27
	Luke	11	9
	Matthew	11	28-30
Salvation - Then and Now	1 John	1	9
	Acts	4	12

	Ephesians	1	13
	Hebrews	9	27-28
	Matthew	12	30
	Matthew	16	26
	Psalm	35	
	Romans	1	16
	Romans	10	9-10
	Romans	10	10
Review of Man's Biblical Beginnings	Genesis	1	26-30
	Genesis	2	7
	Genesis	2	4,7,15-23
Soul - Sermon 1	1 Peter	1	8-9
	1 Thessalonians	5	23
	Genesis	2	7
	Hebrews	9	27-28
	Luke	1	77
	Matthew	16	26-27
	Matthew	22	37-39
	Romans	6	23
	Romans	10	9-10
	Romans	13	11
Soul - Sermon 2	1 Thessalonians	5	23
	Ecclesiastes	12	7
	Exodus	20	
	Hebrews	4	12
	Isaiah	65	17
	Job	27	8

	Luke	23	45
The Moment of Truth	Ephesians	4	17-29
	Hebrews	9	27
The Message for the Soul of Man	Deuteronomy	6	5
	Exodus	20	1-17
	Genesis	6	3
	Luke	10	27
	Luke	23	46
	Mark	12	30
	Matthew	22	37-40
	Romans	8	5-8
Time & Eternity	1 Corinthians	15	50
	Genesis	1	1-5
	Hebrews	9	27
	John	3	16
	John	6	38-40
	John	11	25-26
	John	14	1-3
	Luke	1	30-33
	Luke	10	25-27
	Matthew	6	19-20
	Matthew	10	28
	Matthew	25	46
	Proverbs	12	28
	Revelation	21	6
	Romans	2	6-7
Understanding	Ephesians	5	15-20

	Nehemiah	8	2-12
	Proverbs	2	1-22
	Psalm	119	33-40
We are in God's World	Acts	17	24-28
	Psalm	145	18
What is Life	Ecclesiastes	3	1-7
	Ecclesiastes	3	1-15
	Ezekiel	18	4-32
	John	14	1-17
	Matthew	5	29-30
	Proverbs	6	16-19
	Psalm	51	1-6
	Romans	6	23
Who Are You Really When Alone	1 Chronicles	28	9
	1 Thessalonians	4	6-7
	Exodus	20	15
	Hebrews	4	12-13
	Psalm	139	1-4
You Are Never Alone	2 Kings	19	32-35
	Acts	12	5-10
	Colossians	1	16
	Daniel	3	10-12;19-28
	Daniel	6	22
	Genesis	28	11-13
	Genesis	32	2-28

	Hebrews	1	14
	Hebrews	2	1-8
	Hebrews	12	22
	John	1	51
	Joshua	5	13-15
	Luke	1	11-20
	Luke	22	43-44
	Matthew	1	20-21
	Matthew	13	40-43
	Matthew	18	10
	Matthew	24	30-31
	Numbers	22	26-35
	Revelation	5	11

Special Quotations of Interest

Go now, write it on a tablet for them, inscribe it on a scroll, that for the days to come it may be an everlasting witness. – Bible, Isaiah 30.8

The spirit of man is the candle of the Lord. -- Bible, 'Proverbs' 20:27.

It is the spirit that gives life, the flesh is of no avail. -- Bible, 'John' 6:63, RSV.

The soul alone raises us to nobility. -- Seneca, 'Epistles'

The human soul develops up to the time of death. -- Hippocrates, 'Aphorisms'

For every living soul belongs to me, the father as well as the son—both alike belong to me. The soul who sins is the one who will die.-- Bible, 'Ezekiel' 18:4.

What shall it profit a man, if he shall gain the whole world, and lose his own soul? -- Bible, 'Mark' 8:36

The soul is the mirror of an indestructible universe. -- G. W. Leibniz, 'The Monadology'

The kingdom of God is within you. -- Bible, 'Luke' 17:21.

God is with thee in all that thou doest. -- Bible, 'Genesis' 21:22.

Wisdom of the Ancient Near East contains the statement "Then shall the dust return to the earth as it was: and the spirit shall return unto God who gave it" Ecclesiastes 12:7

Suggested Reading

I would suggest the following books for additional reading in conjunction with **"A Message for the Soul of Man."** These books enrich the total concept of God, Soul and Man on the journey through life on this earth, in pursuit of God's and man's purpose. Your favorite Bible should be, of course, first in additional reading.

You – God's Brand-New Idea by Max Lucado; J Countryman, Div. of Thomas Nelson, Inc. Nashville, Tenn.

The Purpose Driven Life by Rick Warren; Zondervan, Grand Rapids, Michigan

The Attributes of God, Volumes 1 and 2 by A.W. Tozar; Wingspread Publishers, Camp Hill, Pennsylvania

The Greatest Miracle in the World by Og Mandino; Bantam Books, Div. of Doubleday Dell Publishing Group, Inc.

The Outline of History, Volumes 1 and 2 by H. G. Wells; Doubleday & Company, Inc.

Glimpses of God through the Ages by Esther Carls Dodgen; Hendrickson Publishers, Peabody, MA

A Rustle of Angels by Marilynn Carlson Webber and William D Webber; Zondervan, Grand Rapids, Michigan

Angels, God's Secret Agents by Billy Graham; Word Publishing, Nashville

Fearfully & Wonderfully Made by Dr. Paul Brand & Philip Yancey; Zondervan, Grand Rapids, Michigan

The Inventions That Changed The World – Published by Readers Digest, Pleasantville, New York, USA

Practice of the Presence of God – Brother Lawrence – Public Domain electronic Internet

Publications by National Geographic Society
Incredible Voyage, Exploring the Human Body
Body, the Complete Human
Inventions and Discoverers, Changing our World

References

All scripture quotations, unless otherwise indicated, are taken from the Holy Bible, New International Version®, NIV®. Copyright ©1973, 1978, 1984 by Biblica, Inc.™ Used by permission of Zondervan. All rights reserved worldwide. www.zondervan.com

'**Fearfully & Wonderfully Made**' by Dr. Paul Brand & Philip Yancey published by Zondervan, Grand Rapids, Michigan
Permission requested of Zondervan June 13, 2010

'**On Wings of Eternity**' by Jeff Deffinbaugh; Bible.org contributor

'**Growing Old with God**', Article June 2003. David Roper, Our Daily Bread, Copyright 2002 by RBC Ministries, Grand Rapids, MI. Reprinted by permission. All rights reserved.

'**The Four Calls**', Article. Henry Bosch, Our Daily Bread, Copyright 1967 by RBC Ministries, Grand Rapids, MI. Reprinted by permission. All rights reserved.

'**The Roots of Invention**' by Gordon Rattray Taylor, article from the book 'The Inventions That Changed The World' – Published by Readers Digest Association, Pleasantville, New York, USA

Powers Ministry

There are several components to the Powers Ministry.

Consider the **following points**
1. Salvation Army Doctrine 2 & 11
    2. We believe that there is only one God, who is infinitely perfect, the Creator, Preserver, and Governor of all things, and who is the only proper object of religious worship. *(What does that mean?)*
    11. We believe in the immortality of the soul; in the resurrection of the body; in the general judgment at the end of the world; in the eternal happiness of the righteous; and the endless punishment of the wicked. *(Does each person really understand the significance of this belief?)*

2. The Bible - God's word. The whole Bible was designed to educate each one of us to understand that special relationship that God has with all His creation including each soul.

3. God's Plan for Mankind. His plan for mankind is manifested in the very nature of God, His teachings through His word (The Bible - in particular, the Old Testament) and the teaching of His son, Jesus Christ (found in the New Testament) and finally in the history of man on earth.

4. Purpose of Ministry - to *save and preserve souls* by reaching out explaining to each
    a) The nature of God (absolutely essential to understand - *(know God)*

b) God's plan and how it is unfolding *(it is active and dynamic and always has been)*

c) Understanding the individual soul- from creation to final destination *(know thyself)*

d) Explaining how each soul is an integral part of God's plan, *(your purpose)* and

e) Finally, understanding what God is doing and what He wants *(of man - of us?)*

This Ministry is best directed to those who pose the question "What is my purpose for living?" These are people who can be Christians, seekers or sinners and want to know about life and what it is all about. Many will have personally suffered greatly up to their present time in life.

5. Conditions presently existing for this Ministry: Like many times throughout the history of mankind, the world is considered a place of iniquity, sin and wickedness. Our world to-day is beset with the excesses of drugs, substance abuse, addictions, pornography, immorality, violence and crime, greed - all kinds of acts of a sinful nature. (Some could say the devil is enjoying great success).

At the same time, we have possibly one of the most intelligent civilizations of all time. We live in an age of tremendous information growth, constant change with new technologies and techniques appearing almost daily. Never in mankind's history has man been subject to such a hectic pace of life.

God has chosen this time to send a new message - a message appealing to man's intellect - "A Message for the Soul of Man."

Speaking of the mind, think about this. God wants man to be equipped to meet the challenges inherent in exploring every frontier that exists in God's universe be it interstellar space, the conquering of disease, the exploration and the protection of our habitat, the creation of harmony among all men, the development of the mind of man to accommodate higher intellectual feats.

The future can be as exciting as any we have ever experienced. God loves every soul.

LaVergne, TN USA
10 September 2010
196504LV00005B/1/P